"Panoramic and intimate at once, Nunan disarms and charms his way to uncovering rich reservoirs of stories and voices."
— Benjamin Law, author of *The Family Law* and *Gaysia*

"Stranger than fiction, these are riveting stories about the hidden world of those who make Hong Kong their home, place of work, playground, or battleground, told with great candour."
— Alice Pung, author of *Unpolished Gem, Her Father's Daughter* and *Growing up Asian in Australia*

OTHER VOICES, OTHER EYES

EXPATRIATE LIVES IN HONG KONG

David Nunan

BLACKSMITH BOOKS

For Jenny and Bec
Third culture kids and expats for life

Other Voices, Other Eyes

ISBN 978-988-77927-7-2

Published by Blacksmith Books
Unit 26, 19/F, Block B, Wah Lok Industrial Centre,
37-41 Shan Mei Street, Fo Tan, Hong Kong
Tel: (+852) 2877 7899
www.blacksmithbooks.com

Selected works by David Nunan:
When Rupert Murdoch Came to Tea: A Memoir
Roadshow: A Personal Odyssey
What is This Thing Called Language?
Introducing Discourse Analysis
The Experience of Language Learning
Our Discovery Island
ATLAS
Go For It

Contents

You're an expatriate. You've lost touch with the soil. You get precious. Fake European standards have ruined you. You drink yourself to death. You become obsessed with sex. You spend all your time talking, not working. You are an expatriate, see? You hang around cafés.

(Ernest Hemingway)

I.

To begin at the beginning

Every journalist who is not too stupid or too full of himself to notice what is going on knows that what he does is morally indefensible. He is a kind of confidence man, preying on people's vanity, ignorance or loneliness, gaining their trust and betraying them without remorse. Like the credulous widow who wakes up one day to find the charming young man and all her savings gone, so the consenting subject of a piece of nonfiction writing learns – when the article or book appears – his hard lesson. Journalists justify their treachery in various ways according to their temperaments. The more pompous talk about freedom of speech and "the public right to know"; the least talented talk about Art; the seemliest murmur about earning a living.

(Janet Malcolm)

I am sitting in the Eastern Magistrates' Court in Hong Kong on an unseasonably hot and sticky day in early June. I have met people who will happily spend a day in the law courts. They take a cut lunch and gain temporary relief from their own troubles by losing themselves in the travails of others. I am not one of these people. I'm here to lend moral support to a friend who drank far too much one night and, uncharacteristically, decided to drive home. (He later said he had to drive because he was too drunk to walk). Instead of driving home, he drove into a wall and fell asleep. When roused by the police, which took considerable effort, and asked what he was doing, he replied, "Drunken driving." He was promptly arrested and charged.

It is while I am sitting through the thirty-three cases preceding my friend's that I'm struck by the richness and diversity of Hong Kong's expatriate population, seven of whom are today to have their fate determined by the magistrate, an imperious Indian woman with impeccable English. They include an emaciated Bulgarian girl caught shoplifting a packet of chocolate biscuits from a PARKnSHOP store to fuel her bulimia; an aquiline Englishman with a young Chinese wife who is head of a large financial firm, and who faces the same charge as my friend; a Nepalese dishwasher accused of rape; a French artist on a domestic violence charge; an Australian university exchange student who was apprehended while trying to score crystal meth; a terrified and bewildered Indonesian domestic helper arrested for overstaying her work visa; and, of course, my hapless friend.

For some time, the notion of writing about expat life has had my fingers twitching, but the urge was not translated into action until this day in court. I watch three-dimensional, two-minute tragedies playing out in real time: the hysterics of the exchange student receiving a fine and two hundred hours of community service; the impassivity of the diminutive Mainland waiter receiving a six-month sentence for impulsively pocketing and selling a mobile phone left behind by a customer. The Eastern Magistrates' Court is a microcosmic subculture of Hong Kong and its people. Each of the accused who stands before the magistrate with shoulders hunched and head bowed has a story to tell. At home that night, I reconstruct from memory, and the handwritten notes I've made (recording devices of any kind are strictly forbidden) of their stories. Because the accused have the right to be tried in their first language, I've heard the stories rehearsed in English, Mandarin, Cantonese, Nepalese, French and Bulgarian, then rendered and rehashed into English for the magistrate and Cantonese for the court officials. (No Indonesian translator was provided for the domestic helper, which is a story in itself). It's a bewilderingly polylingual experience. But as I work on my notes, something jells: there are Hong Kong expat stories that deserve to be told.

What I tentatively called *The Expat Project* began with a simple question: "What is the post-colonial expatriate experience?" While the question might seem deceptively simple, answering it was anything but. I couldn't even get my informants to agree on a working definition of this thing called an 'expat', and leafing through several dictionaries added little clarity. An expatriate was someone living in a country other than the place in which they were born. In the web of this definition were captured the Mainland waiter and the Indonesian over-stayer. The status as expats of Somali asylum seekers and sundry other racial groups was flatly denied by other expats as well as by local Chinese. When asked, most of my informants were more adept at saying what expats were not than what they were. I put the definitional difficulty to one side, and pressed on with documenting expat lives.

This book is based on many hours of conversations recorded in bars, homes, schools, shopping malls, restaurants and workplaces. Some were recorded at ferry piers, some on beaches and some during the course of hikes along one or more of the trails that meander across Hong Kong's islands. When, for one reason or another, recording the conversations proved impossible, or, as happened on occasion, the informant refused to be committed to tape, I made extensive notes. I also drew on journal entries and, yes, even that notoriously unreliable instrument – my memory.

For readers who have experienced expatriate life, I hope the lives and stories captured in these pages provide a spark, if not a shock, of recognition. For others, I trust they provide insights into peoples, customs and cultures in contact. Although located in Hong Kong, the most dynamic, dramatic and diverse city in the Asia-Pacific region, the narratives illuminate issues that are universal: from the tensions inherent in interracial contact, to the rich possibilities offered by such contact.

II.

EXPATRIATE STORIES

The lives and stories that we hear and study are given to us under a promise, that promise being that we protect those who have shared with us. And in return, this sharing will allow us to write life documents that speak to the human dignity, the suffering, the hopes, the dreams, the lives gained and the lives lost by the people we study. … if we foster the illusion that we understand when we do not or that we have found meaningful, coherent lives where none exist, then we engage in a cultural practice that is just as repressive as the most repressive of political regimes. (Norman Denzin)

*When you interview someone and incorporate the data into a story you are performing an act of betrayal. The interviewee wants you to represent **their** story, but your responsibility is to tell **the** story.* (Helen Garner)

Writers are the custodians of memory. (William Zinzer)

Every so often, in the course of an interview, a story would emerge, unfold and push aside my carefully thought out questions and the issues I wanted to address. However, I had no option but to let the story run its course. In some cases, the story revolved around some critical incident in an informant's life that they desperately needed to get off their chest. More often than not, the stories popped up unexpectedly, as much a surprise to my interlocutor as to me. In some cases, people I barely knew would share with me intimate details of their life and allowed me to ask questions that in most other contexts might well have earned me a slap in the face or a forearm jab to the solar plexus. The chapters in this section of the book are devoted to these narratives that took over and ran away with the interview. In contrast, in Section III, I draw together issues that emerged across conversations from multiple informants with a frequency that couldn't be ignored: politics, language, identity, racism – assemblages of themes that you might expect in an exploration of cultures in contact.

I.

A HAPPY HUNTING GROUND

The central assumption of the interpretive (auto)biographical method – that a life can be captured and represented in a text – is now open to question. A life is a social text, a fictional narrative production.

(Norman Denzin)

Cal wasn't remotely on my radar. I was in Sydney visiting relatives. Aside from that I planned to eat, drink and be merry in a city that was built for such purposes. However, for several days, I'd been immersed in transcribing an interview that should have taken far less time than it did. The interview had been recorded in difficult circumstances with an interviewee who insisted on answering questions that hadn't been asked, and ignoring questions that had.

The need to visit an eye specialist provided a brief respite from the tedium of transcribing, and the animosity I was feeling towards the interviewee. Following my visit to the specialist, I was making my way slowly up Macquarie Street, which had warped into an impressionist landscape thanks to the eye dilation drops, when I literally blundered into Cal. I muttered an apology and was about to step around him, when he took my arm and said, "It's me, Cal."

I haven't seen Cal since he retired and moved back to Australia, but recognize him by his voice and his distinctive cologne. We hadn't been particularly close friends in Hong Kong, but our relationship had been amiable enough. In Hong Kong, we had mutual friends, met at the occasional dinner party and bumped into each other at concerts and other events. He asks me if I have time for a coffee. I do, and in fact, had planned to find somewhere to sit until normal vision had been restored.

Cal steers me across Macquarie Street to a café set in a garden at the top end of Hyde Park. Over coffee, we exchange news. Cal has been back in Australia for a little over two years. He had married a Malaysian woman shortly before returning to Australia, and they live in a beachside suburb not far from one of his daughters from a previous marriage. He does some part-time consulting work, but has plenty of time on his hands, and is getting restless. There are several work opportunities back in Asia, but his wife has settled easily into life in Sydney and has her own circle of friends.

"It's a very quiet life here," he says. "Funny that Sydneysiders think of the place as buzzing with life. After Hong Kong, it's a bit like a country town."

"I get the feeling that you miss Hong Kong."

He laughs. "Oh, yes, Hong Kong was a very happy hunting ground, that's for sure."

I've become captivated by the metaphors my informants use to describe Hong Kong. The graveyard of relationships. Disneyland for adults. The 'can do' capital of the world. One Chinese informant described it as a transit stop. "Everyone who comes here is on their way to somewhere else," he said. "That goes for both Chinese and expats. Some move on as originally intended. Some move on but then return. Others never leave."

The happy hunting ground is a new one. Intrigued, I ask Cal if he would share with me the story of his time in Hong Kong. He readily agrees, and we meet for lunch two days later in a small, relatively quiet Italian restaurant in East Sydney.

*

Cal had a problem, and it was one of his own making. By failing to resist the temptations placed in his path by Lee, he broke his own rule of never allowing the number of lovers at any one time to exceed the number of days in the working week. Cal was well organized and fastidious in arranging his day-to-day affairs, and I use this phrase in its literal sense. He had one lover for each day of the week – no more, no less. On the weekend, he allowed himself up to three assignations on a Saturday. On Sunday, like the good Lord above, he rested. This compartmentalization was for Cal's convenience. Knowing exactly who was 'scheduled' for which day prevented confusion and the risk of double booking. This was not to say that he saw each of his five weekday lovers every week. Even Cal's stamina, legendary among his friends, would have wilted if confronted with such a punishing regime.

Cal made an interesting discovery about himself about a year after arriving in Hong Kong. He had been married twice before moving to Hong Kong. The first marriage quickly came and went, but the second lasted for many years, some of which were happy ones. He had three children as well as a stable home life. At some point however, the relationship between Cal and his wife ran out of steam – not at all unusual in this day and age, or, indeed, in any age. What was somewhat out of the ordinary was Cal's decision to make a lifestyle shift by moving to Hong Kong. Although, like most members of his generation (late forties) and class (solidly middle) he had travelled extensively, he had never lived abroad. The first thing that caught his eye when he saw the job advertisement was the salary. When he did the maths, he thought that his calculator was malfunctioning, but no, the salary was correct: three times his current salary and a tax rate that was laughable. He applied, was flown to Hong Kong for an interview, was offered and accepted the position, and within a month had relocated.

"I had no idea what I was letting myself in for. I really had never been to Asia. First impressions? I arrived on a Friday, and so on Saturday morning I went out, just to explore the neighbourhood. I saw immediately what a dazzling city it was – quite different from any other place I'd ever visited. I was instantly captivated. I came across a wet market. At the time, I didn't know that's what they were called – and there were two old gents in shorts and bloodstained singlets hacking at the carcass of a pig on the floor of a fresh-meat stall. Then I stopped off in a bar for a drink, and I overheard a couple of foreigners talking. One said, 'If you can't get it in Hong Kong, it probably doesn't exist.' The other replied, 'If you can't get it in Hong Kong, you'll find it in Bangkok.' I liked the density of the place. I liked the public transport. I liked the shopping and what was available. The quality of life was excellent, providing you had a good job. And I liked the people.

"When I got back to the apartment, I was rushing for the elevator and a woman courteously held the door for me. When I got into the elevator, I looked at her and said, 'I know you.' And she said, 'I know you too.' Years before, I'd lived in Melbourne and we belonged to the same book club. It was the most extraordinary coincidence. Here I am on my first day in Hong Kong, and I run into Nancy. She and her family lived directly above me. At the time, I thought it was remarkable, but I soon learned that these things happen all the time in Hong Kong."

Cal's first lifestyle decision was to 'go native'. Originally, he'd come on a three-year contract, and was determined to spend his social hours getting to know the locals. The last thing he wanted was to be trapped into an expatriate lifestyle with the kinds of people he had left his home town to escape. "I met a bloke who said to me, 'You want to be careful, Cal. Time passes very quickly here.' He'd also come out for three years. Now, thirty years later, he was retiring and going back to the UK. I didn't last that long, but eleven years was a reasonable stretch, I reckon."

He didn't speak Cantonese to any great extent, although he took lessons in the first few months after his arrival, and claimed to have reached a rudimentary conversational standard, which may not have meant much at all. He had the familiar experience of discovering that everyone he met had much better English than he had Cantonese, so they inevitably ended up speaking English. "They knew that I didn't do very well in Cantonese. I couldn't hear some of the tones, and they felt more comfortable speaking in English. The only other foreign language I'd learned was French, which I studied in high school, and the extraordinary thing was that when I was trying to say something in Cantonese and was lost for a word, a French word would pop into my head – words I hadn't thought of for forty years. Then I got into a relationship with someone whose English was good, who spoke a number of languages actually, and so I pretty much gave up on Cantonese."

Despite his lack of competence in Cantonese, he didn't have any difficulty in meeting locals. A gregarious nature, and a refusal to allow rebuffs to deter him, helped enormously. He met people in shopping malls, restaurants and supermarkets. "I accumulated a range of friendships just through chatting to people. I'd be standing next to someone in the supermarket, and I'd start a conversation. You know, 'I'm going to buy this vegetable. What's the best way to cook it?' That kind of thing."

As Cal had told me when we bumped into each other two days before, Hong Kong turned out to be a very happy hunting ground. At the risk of damaging any reputation he might have had for modesty, he described himself as a fit and, to Eastern eyes, reasonably attractive Western male. This was not exactly the description I'd have used, but Cal assured me that he was in 'enormous demand', and was constantly being approached by female co-workers, approaches he generally politely declined because they invariably became messy. In the beginning, he wasn't inclined to do one-night stands, although that would change with time. He described himself as quite conservative, preferring longer-term relationships. He established several of these, and allocated different days of the week to each of them.

His first long-term relationship came about when he noticed a section in the *South China Morning Post* entitled 'meeting point'. This was just prior to the advent of the craze for online dating. The newspaper contained dozens of advertisements: women wanting to meet men; men wanting to meet women; men wanting to meet men; women wanting to meet women. In the woman wanting to meet a man section, there was an advertisement that, according to Cal, described him perfectly – someone who was highly intelligent, with a higher degree, and an interest in intellectual pursuits.

She advertised in the *South China Morning Post* because she wanted to meet a Western man. They all want Western men, according to Cal. That was hardly surprising, given that they were advertising in the Western press. "When I read that advertisement," said Cal, "it seemed that I fitted the bill perfectly."

And so he replied, and they arranged to meet at the Cultural Centre on Kowloon side. She described the car she'd be driving, which turned out to be a Mercedes the size of a small ocean liner. When Cal went to the passenger's side to get in, she said, "No, I want you to drive."

First impressions were highly favourable. He thought she was extremely attractive, so that was a good start. She took him to one of her clubs on Kowloon side for dinner. She was very clever, and also happened to be very wealthy. Her English was excellent, and he later discovered she was fluent in a string of other languages. She spoke French and Italian because she was in the fashion business. She also spoke Mandarin and Japanese, and was a native speaker of Cantonese. Many men would have been intimidated by a woman with such an impressive list of accomplishments, but Cal wasn't the type to be intimidated by anyone.

As he hadn't been in a new relationship for a very long time he was a little rusty. To get over the initial awkwardness, and to find out a bit about her, he devised what he described as a 'humorous little game'. He pretended he had a set of cue cards in his hand, and was interviewing her. "I kept looking at my hand, and asking questions: 'So, where do you work? Are you married? Do you have children?' She thought it was very funny. I discovered that she had her own fashion house and owned a string of about forty shops all over Hong Kong. She was divorced and had two children, a five-year-old and a thirteen-year-old. She herself was in her early forties."

The evening went well, and they agreed to meet again. On the second occasion, he took her back to his apartment "for a cup of tea", as she later laughingly reminded him, and things progressed naturally from there. It was the start of a long-term, part-time relationship. When she was in Hong Kong, she came to fill his Wednesday slot, which suited both of them, although they also occasionally met on the weekend. She would either come to his apartment, or send the chauffeur and Mercedes over to pick him up. She travelled extensively. One week it would be to Paris to meet buyers, and then it would be to Milan or Tokyo for fashion weeks. On several occasions she arranged for Cal to accompany her and paid for everything. She was very clever, had an MBA in how to succeed in almost everything, and, on top of that, was doing a doctorate in business administration.

That relationship continued for most of the time that Cal was in Hong Kong. It plateaued after a while, which suited him. As she was unmarried, he took great care not to get too involved, which took some doing because it became clear that she was looking for a deeper level of commitment than he was. It became tricky, as they walked through Central, evading the hand that sought out his. He did his best to ensure the subjects of subsequent liaisons were married.

Cal began to fill in the other slots in his week. After the businesswoman, the next to be added was a strikingly beautiful nurse who was head of trauma nursing at one of the local hospitals. She was another woman who was fortunate enough to fit Cal's requirements: in addition to her beauty, she was a talented and independent-minded Hong Kong woman with a great sense of humour. She also had a Ph.D., which Cal saw as a bonus. As he was the most intelligent person he knew, he was not bothered by intelligence in others. Cal also admitted that he had a fetish for full lips, and this woman, let's call her Sandra, had lips like pillows. She was married, with one child, lived on Kowloon side, and filled his Saturday morning slot. Her excuse to her husband was that she was doing a course at the university, which was true, and led him to believe that the course lasted all day, when in fact the lectures were confined to the afternoon. Cal would rearrange the furniture prior to her arrival, and then rearrange it again after her departure. I never got to the bottom of the furniture rearranging, but by now he had several 'shifts' on Saturday, and seemed to think it important to have a different interior configuration for each person: perhaps to remind himself whom he happened to be sleeping with at any given point in the day.

Cal and Sandra met at a 7-Eleven. "When I saw those lips coming towards me, I thought, 'I've really got to meet this woman.' In fact, I didn't have to do much at all. It was instant, mutual attraction. There were lightning flashes all over the supermarket. No, that was a very easy one to detect. It was very exciting and was to last for ten years – longer than some of my marriages. She was never going to leave her husband, I established that early on. She really got off on the excitement and the risk. Like the other married women I met, she was bored out of her brains with her husband. She wanted to climb all over me. Later, when she couldn't use the university course as an excuse because she'd graduated, I'd go and pick her up from work and bring her over to the apartment and we'd bang our brains out and then I'd drive her home. It was like that for some years. And she loved it. And I liked it. I thought it was great. You know, 'Oh, who's on tonight?' sort of thing. 'Oh, it's Thursday. Oh, OK, it's Nina tonight.' And on top of it, all the time I was having a wild affair with the Filipina maid who lived on the floor below. I'd go down to her when her employer was at work or away. I generally discouraged her from coming up to my apartment."

The remarkable self-discovery that Cal made occurred in the early hours of Saturday morning. He'd enjoyed a leisurely few hours with Venus, his Friday night date, at her apartment. Venus claimed to live in Mid-levels although in reality the apartment was situated squarely in Sai Ying Pun. Venus was newly and resolutely single, and therefore somewhat more available than Cal would have liked.

Having consumed the second of the bottles of Sancerre brought along by him to lubricate the evening's fun, Cal was feeling slightly tipsy as he took his leave and made his way along Caine Road. Rather than proceeding down Ladder Street, the route he usually took back to his apartment, he turned down a narrow street almost opposite Venus's apartment and entered the tangle of alleyways constituting lower Sai Ying Pun.

Later, he told himself it was the faint sound of music rather than the desire for a nightcap that prompted him to push on the heavy metal door that led into a bar in a street to the west of the Man Mo Temple. There was no signage announcing the bar, and during the day he would have passed it without noticing that it was anything other than a metal door. The space inside surprised him. A long bar ran along one side of the narrow space with low tables along the other wall. At the far end, glass doors opened on to a garden featuring a small fountain. Couples occupied the tables, drinking and holding hands as couples do. Cal felt that he had stepped into a parallel world. All of the individuals in the room, two bartenders and eight drinkers, were male. A year into his tenure in Hong Kong, Cal had never seen anything like it.

His first instinct was to withdraw, his second was to hoist himself onto one of the bar stools. One of the bartenders, a slim, young Asian man, hardly more than a boy, placed a coaster in front of him, and smiled.

"You're new here," he said. "Welcome. What can I get for you?"

"Campari, please," said Cal, surprising himself with his choice. He rarely drank Campari. In fact, he couldn't remember the last time that he had drunk it.

"Racks?"

Cal scratched his head. "Um, racks? Sorry?"

The man-boy scooped up a tumbler of ice. "Would you like it on the racks?" His accent was almost American, but not quite.

"Oh, rocks, oh. Sure." The perfumed bitterness of the drink was just what he needed at that time of night. So he had another one. And then another. He wobbled slightly on the bar stool. The man-boy, who introduced himself as Lee, was talking to him. He seemed to like Cal, which was no surprise to Cal. Everybody liked him: everybody, that was, except his ex-wives, but that was to be expected.

A considerable time later – it must have been close to dawn – he woke and was surprised to find the man-boy, Lee, beside him in his bed. Thoughts came back to him in a slow sequence. The man-boy encouraged him to do things he had never done before. One thought in particular stayed with him. He turned it over slowly in his mind. "This is good. I can do this and I want to do this. Actually, this is a part of me: a part of who I am." Fancy getting to this late stage in life before making such a remarkable discovery! The man-boy stirred, turned, then reached out and touched him. Forgetting his hangover, Cal gave himself over to a rediscovery of the sensations of the night.

"It came as a huge surprise to me to discover that I was attractive to men, and that I was very versatile when it came to relationships and sex," he says. "I guess that I must have always been bisexual, but before I moved to Hong Kong, I'd never had a relationship with a male. Even when I got here, I sort of blocked it out for a while. At the time, homosexuality was illegal, so you have a choice. Behind this door is a beautiful woman, and behind this door is a man you'll go to prison for. One thing that happened during my Hong Kong years was the emergence of the gay scene. When I first arrived, it was invisible, but these days, they're very much out there.

"When it comes to relationships and sex, I'm ambidextrous. Back in the 1940s, in his research on males, the sex researcher Alfred Kinsey discovered that heterosexuality and homosexuality wasn't a bifurcation, but a continuum, and he developed a seven-point scale from zero to six. Zero was exclusively hetero, one was mainly hetero but with some encounters with the same sex, two was mainly hetero, but quite a lot of encounters with males. Three was equal, and I'm equal. I'm turned on by everyone.

"In my eleven years in Hong Kong, I had relationships with forty women and about two hundred men, so I was pretty busy. The main difference was that women wanted longer-term relationships, while men were happy with anything. Men were sluts and women were, well, women were women. Men wanted sex. Women wanted a relationship. So the ratio of five to one I suppose kind of reflected that. The women were a more restricted group. In the case of the men, there was a high turnover, although there were two that I saw on a long-term basis, so I guess I would have classified them as husbands. The relationships were reasonably long-term and I was quite happy with them. So, if I were asked how many long-term relationships I'd been in, I'd have to say three wives and two husbands."

Cal presents himself as a modest person. The combination of a modest persona and iron-clad confidence is unusual and goes a long way in explaining his self-proclaimed success in establishing relationships, however fleeting these might turn out to be.

One night he is having dinner with Mark, a former colleague, and Mark's friend Sam, who is visiting from Vancouver. Mark and Sam, both Canadians, met when they were working in Tokyo. In addition to a common nationality, both had met and married Japanese women. Both eventually moved on from Japan, Mark to Hong Kong, and Sam back to Canada, where he works as an investigative journalist. Cal feels the 'investigative' adornment to Sam's occupation is unnecessary – what, after all, are journalists supposed to do if not investigate?

Sam is currently on the Hong Kong leg of a tour around Asian cities collecting data for an article he is writing on cross-cultural relationships, a subject he feels that he is well-qualified to write about, given his own marital status. He interrogates Cal on his experience and is fascinated to learn of Cal's late discovery of his bisexuality. How does one go about the business of making contact with a male partner? By this time they are well into their second bottle of wine, and Cal admits that he is an expert at picking up people. "That's one thing I absolutely know how to do," he says, in his modest way, "When we've finished dinner, I'll show you how to do it."

After dinner, he takes them to a nearby gay bar. Neither Mark nor Sam has ever been to a gay bar, although Cal has a suspicion that Sam's interest might be more than purely professional. Cal guides them to a table and they order drinks. Then Cal gives his demonstration.

"This guy was walking towards our table, which was at the beginning of a walkway, and I did my thing. I made eye contact, and used a facial expression to signal interest. My friends couldn't see it, but I could. And the guy walked past the table and down the walkway, and then he turned and made a hand gesture indicating that I should meet him at the bar. So, I followed him to the bar, and arranged to meet him on the weekend. Then I went back to the table and said 'That's how you do it.' And I explained to them exactly how I'd done it."

Cal then took his friends to another bar, where they were comfortable until Cal made eye contact with another guy, who joined them at their table and began, in Cal's words, rubbing him all over.

"So, yeah, I can do that. I absolutely know how to do that. It's a case of doing or not doing, and when you're in a relationship you don't do it. If you're happy with your partner or your wife, you just switch it off. But when you're single and you live by yourself, which described my situation in Hong Kong, it's only natural to throw the switch to 'available'. So I did."

*

"Tell me more about this metaphor you use of Hong Kong as a happy hunting ground."

"When I came to Hong Kong, I had my romantic and emotional life in reverse. Most people get their sexual adventures and experiments out of the way when they're young, before they settle down, but in Australia, I'd married young and had children and been very stable and predictable. It wasn't until I came to Hong Kong in my early 50s that I broke out and had the experiences that most people have in their early years. Before I came to Hong Kong, I'd heard about this ready availability of people of whatever persuasion for whatever reason, but I didn't really believe it until I came here and experienced it for myself. In terms of my heterosexual partners, it seemed to run completely contrary to the stereotype of the Chinese married woman as being submissive and compliant. In reality, they're very different. They're smart, they're tough, but at the same time, they have very good hearts."

"Would you say you were atypical? I mean, did you get a sense of what the locals you got into relationships with thought about you as an expat?"

"What do locals think of expats? 'Stupid gweilo' is a pretty common expression. 'Here comes someone I can rip off.' But in my case, the reaction seemed to be, 'Here's someone that I can't understand. Here's someone who's really exotic and I'd like to climb all over him.' It was a mixed bag of things. There's a pretty widespread perception that expats are arrogant, and one thing that worked in my favour was the fact that I'm not. I was always courteous and deferential, and they were just astonished by that. The reaction I got *always* was one of astonishment and pleasure. That's my character. I'm like that no matter where I am. It's just that in Hong Kong it struck people as exceptional. On the other side of the coin, a common reaction of expats is that locals are unfriendly, that they're unknowable, that, in fact, we exist in parallel universes. I would never say that. They're not unfriendly. Another reaction is that once you make friends with a local, they're friends for life. Well, some were friends for life, some were available when I wanted them to be, some were very nice but committed to another relationship, I was highly tolerant of people's circumstances. 'If I can have lunch with you, that's fine. If I can go to bed with you, that's fine. If I can see you three nights a month, that's fine. If I can go away with you on holidays, that's fine.' That sort of thing. It was horses for courses. This place is full of unique characters. Most of the people I met, I don't think I'd have met in any other place – only in Hong Kong."

"So, you'd say that Hong Kong is unique."

"Very much so."

"How would you compare it to Australia? I mean, do the 'adventures' you've described go on here?"

"Sure, but not to the same extent. I may have been attractive to people before I went to Hong Kong, but I didn't respond. I only had one affair in all my married years, and it was when my marriage was coming to an end. It was an affair with a woman who was much younger than me. My wife had arranged for her mad sister to move in with us and I couldn't tolerate that after about nine months, so I had a wild affair. No, back then, it was more a case of not responding to signals that people put out."

"And now that you've returned to Australia?"

"I've been back two years now. By the time I left Hong Kong, I was ready to return to a stable life. A year or so before I came back, I got into a relationship with a Malaysian Chinese woman who worked in financial services. We got on really well, and ended up getting married, and I sponsored her to move to Australia. I'm quite content."

"So, no more wild adventures."

"No. As I told you before, Sydneysiders think that it's a wild, happening place, but compared to Hong Kong, it's pretty sedate. I just don't think you could get away with the kind of lifestyle I led in Hong Kong – certainly not to the same extent. I've had one or two gay flings here, but that's the extent of it. Actually, one of the guys I'd had a long-term relationship with in Hong Kong followed me to Sydney. I was surprised at that. If my marriage hadn't worked out, I would probably have settled for him as a husband, but so far my marriage is fine."

2.

JUST ANOTHER WAN CHAI SUNDAY

For many people, tourists especially, Wan Chai is a vital part of the 'real' Hong Kong, a colourful mélange of densely packed streets, intriguing back alleys, traditional crafts and vanishing trades. Wan Chai, meaning 'small bay' in Cantonese, began in pre-British times as a small Chinese settlement grouped around the present Tai Wong Temple on Queen's Road East. Also known as Ha Wan (Lower Circuit) both names have long since become redundant as there is no longer a bay or a circuit there any more. (Jason Wordie)

Most older Hong Kong neighbourhoods are a jumbled mess, none more so than Wan Chai. Here you find the old cheek-by-jowl with the new; a clutter of ramshackle commercial buildings that are an embarrassment to the neighbouring glass towers in Admiralty and Central. Here can be found government offices – most notably Revenue and Immigration Towers – decaying residential tenements, a park and sports ground, lane-ways that appear to have rickets, and outdoor markets to remind you that Wan Chai was once exotic. A gleaming convention and hotel complex, recently minted residential blocks, and restaurants announcing their modernity ('modern' bistro, 'Mod Oz' munchies, 'modern British cuisine'), just in case you didn't get it: a reminder that for a couple of decades Wan Chai has been making a not particularly successful attempt at reinvention. And then, of course, there are the bars. By day, it heaves with office workers. At lunch time, under no circumstances should you get yourself trapped between the workers and their destinations – the dim sum and noodle bars. By night the crowd is of a different complexion: tourists, junkies, prostitutes, pushers, and pullers. Back in the day when Western fleets made regular visits, this is where the crews came to be fleeced.

You name it. If you can't see it, buy it or steal it in Wan Chai, it probably doesn't exist. Certain Hong Kong neighbourhoods have an underbelly. At night, Wan Chai is all underbelly. Expats go to Wan Chai for sex, drugs and rock and roll. On Sundays, Filipina, Thai and Indonesian maids, evicted for the day by their employers, wearing too few clothes and too much make-up, head to Wan Chai to meet up with their friends. If an expat takes a fancy to one, she will get free drinks and a meal. If they hit it off, she can look forward to augmenting her regular income in a short-stay hotel with her temporary gweilo companion. If things really work out, the arrangement might become longer-term.

A Wan Chai favourite watering hole for expats of a certain stripe was the Old China Hand. If you had a weakness for dreadful British-style pub food from the 1970s such as bangers and mash, if you didn't mind the random cockroach turning up in your pint of Tetley's, and if you were relaxed about toilets that could rarely be trusted to flush, then you would have no complaints with the Old China Hand. To the dismay of the old, and not-so-old China hands who drank there, this self-proclaimed 'legendary' pub closed its doors in 2015. Whether this was done by the health department or the rising rents is unclear.

While the Old China Hand was a favourite meeting place between domestic helpers and expats, these encounters did not always end happily. A case in point were the two young Indonesian maids who, on separate occasions, met a British banker called Jutting. Charmed by this University of Cambridge graduate, they agreed to go back to his apartment, just around the corner, for a bit of fun. Unfortunately for them, Jutting's idea of fun was to slit their throats and mutilate them in other ways before returning to the pub to continue his drinking. The murders took place just a few months before the Old China Hand was forced to close its doors for the last time. If the pest inspectors or the avaricious landlord had been on the ball, those two poor souls might have escaped their unspeakable fate.

*

At dusk, on a warm evening just after the double murders had taken place, and not long before the enforced closure of the pub, I happen to be making my way down Lockhart Road. Pushing past the knot of drinkers who spill onto the pavement to smoke and obstruct passers-by, I bump into Barney, a tennis coach at one of the exclusive clubs on the Island. (Exclusive, not because there's anything refined or high-brow about them – rather the reverse, in fact – but because their membership fees exclude mere mortals like me.) Barney isn't an Old China Hand type, so I'm surprised to see him. He tells me that he's waiting for his girlfriend Sally, an Indonesian domestic helper and one of several women whom he has been dating on and off for years. Like many Indonesian helpers, she doesn't let religion stand in the way of her social life, describing herself, when queried, as 'Muslim lite'. Sally, who is in Causeway Bay shopping with a friend, was supposed to meet him at 6.30. It's now after 7.00, and she hasn't shown up: no surprise there. Sally has a number of virtues but, like most helpers, punctuality isn't one of them, particularly on the one day in the week she can claim as her own.

Barney offers to buy me a beer. I accept on condition that it comes in a bottle – no glass, no cockroach, thanks. As the sky darkens, the crowd continues to swell. It's getting rowdy now. The bar pumps the music up, forcing the drinkers to shout to be heard. The music is turned up even louder. It's a competition that nobody wins. Two young men holding bottles of Tsingtao are arguing loudly in what sounds like Russian. One pushes the other, who stumbles and falls to the ground near a couple of girls who are sitting on the curb smoking cigarettes. The bottle flies out of his hand and lands on the pavement, spilling its contents. The girls, both blond and very young, look around in surprise at the sudden outburst of aggression. Despite the amount of alcohol that is consumed in watering holes such as the Old China Hand, the drinkers are generally benign, and physical violence is rare. Expats come to Hong Kong to make money, not war. One of the aspects of Hong Kong that expat parents comment favourably upon is the safety of the place. Their fifteen-year-old daughter may come home with a drug habit, but the chances are that she'll come home.

It happens quickly. The Russian who is still on his feet swings a boot at his companion. Fortunately for the friend, it's only a glancing blow, but it makes a dull thump. Some of the other drinkers look around, but seeing that it's only a couple of inebriated Russians, get on with their drinking. The girls scramble out of the way. The Russian on the ground reaches for the bottle that he dropped, grasps it by the neck, smashes the base on the pavement, and climbs slowly to his feet. When his friend comes at him, he raises the bottle. Seeing what's about to happen, one of the girls instinctively steps forward to intervene. The jagged end of the bottle rakes across her face. She screams, and raises a hand to her face, which spurts blood. When her friend tries to help, she's also slashed, not across the face but across her forearm. She holds up the arm and looks at it with a puzzled expression, as though it belongs to someone else.

Two police officers appear – too late to be of much use, as is often the case. Sobered up by the sight of the men in uniform, the Russian drops his bottle and rushes off down Lockhart Road. His companion disappears in the opposite direction. The police scratch their heads, then one takes statements from the girls while the other calls for an ambulance to transport them to nearby Ruttonjee Hospital. They then attempt to take statements from bystanders, none of whom appear to be interested.

While all of this is going on, Barney receives a text from Sally to inform him that she won't be able to make it to the Old China Hand. "Oh, well," he says. "Just another Wan Chai Sunday."

3.

THE GRAVEYARD OF RELATIONSHIPS

She imagined everything she had never imagined before, and she gave herself to all that was most base and most pure.   (Paulo Coelho)

Marti, an American acquaintance of his, knows all sorts of things, and she's not at all shy about sharing her knowledge. The less forgiving refer to her as a font of irrelevant information. Despite her habit of oversharing, he's always liked her: she's personable and pleasant and has a winning smile. Being a know-it-all is a minor character flaw. The source of her information and insights into the human condition is the ubiquitous 'they'. A precious nugget of knowledge is invariably prefaced by; "They say that…"

Marti moved to Hong Kong several months before him, by which time she knew everything about the place that was worth knowing. Shortly after he arrived, she invited him over to Sunday brunch at her apartment in Chai Wan at the eastern end of Hong Kong Island so that she could share the wisdom she had accumulated.

Her apartment block was situated on the waterfront opposite the old Kai Tak airport which was shortly to close. It was a sparkling day. In the air, there was a hint of the summer to come. After a swim in the harbourside pool, they sat on her balcony drinking champagne and watching planes making the tricky steep, banking manoeuvre required to avoid taking out an apartment block or ploughing into the hill that was inconveniently situated at the end of the runway.

"You know what they say about Hong Kong?" she said.

He confessed that he had no idea what 'they' had to say about his new home, but figured that he was about to find out.

"They say that it's the graveyard of relationships."

He wasn't sure why she was telling him this, nor how he was supposed to respond, so he simply smiled and nodded and held out his glass for a refill.

Remembering her past lovers, some of whom he had met and some he had not, he asked, "And how about you? How do you deal with the graveyard problem?"

"I have a simple solution," she said. Later, when the champagne had run its course, she guided him to her bedroom and gestured to the plastic pleasure toys neatly arrayed by the head of the bed.

4.

ONE FOR THE ROAD

Just when the caterpillar thought the world was over, she became a butterfly. (Barbara Haines Howett)

She was feeling the strain before they left Yung Shue Wan Main Street. They had left the Central Ferry Pier late, all because of Howard, who had been detained at his office, despite the fact that it was a Saturday. They could hardly leave without him because it was his company that owned the junk. They could see it bobbing some way off on the water with a flotilla of other junks, bob, bob, bobbing. Existentially futile captures it perfectly: she must remember that for her diary. Every now and then, one of the wooden vessels peels away from the flotilla and lurches drunkenly towards their pier. Once it has been secured, a group of passengers detach themselves from the waiting throng, scramble aboard, and secure a seat, either at the front of the junk, in the larger rear deck, or on the roof. It was a complete mystery to her how the junk and the boarding party managed to pair up: just like a mother goose and her imprinted chicks, she thought. Meanwhile, they wait, wait, waited.

Ryan wouldn't hear of it when she voiced the thought that she might stay in the flat out of the heat. His response was predictable. "Howard went to a lot of trouble to get the junk. It's very competitive, particularly on the weekend. This is supposed to be a welcome-to-Hong-Kong treat for you." She refrained from pointing out that it was less than a week since she'd arrived from New York, and was still jet-lagged. Add to that a hangover and lack of sleep thanks to the welcome-to-Hong-Kong office party he'd arranged for her the night before. "You can't call yourself an expat until you've done a weekend junk trip – it's a rite of passage." She had no intention of ever referring to herself as an 'expat', but didn't want to start a fight, not at this embryonic stage of their new life together, so she kept her mouth shut.

When Howard eventually turned up with his wife and daughters, he was suitably effusive in his apologies. Ryan made the introductions, but she failed to catch the wife or children's names. Ordinary and unmemorable names, like the people themselves. While the introductions were taking place, another couple joined them as well as a family consisting of parents and two children. She had noticed them loitering on the pier, but as Howard was the common link, had no idea that they were part of the same junk party. The young German couple was on a short-term visit to Hong Kong. The husband was doing some sort of consulting work for Howard's firm. The family was Australian: the parents large and overweight, and the children heading in the same direction. They were sloppily dressed and had harsh, nasal accents that she found unpleasant.

Howard, who had removed his jacket and tie, strode to the end of the pier and began flailing his arms in the air. One of the junks immediately detached itself and ploughed through the choppy water towards the pier. Getting aboard was tricky, and the Fat Family's son almost ended up in the water, which would have been no great loss to humanity, she thought. She imagined that the father, Bruce, or Dave, or whatever he was called, would be one of those financial advisers whom she'd been warned about, and the wife would list her occupation as 'domestic duties'.

Once on board, she sat at the rear of the junk, a little apart from the others. When they had cleared the choppy waters of the inner harbour and could move about, Howard opened a large ice chest and handed out cans of beer. She noted, with faint disapproval, that Ryan accepted one, although, like her, he was normally a moderate drinker. When she declined a beer, Howard offered her a wine, but she gave a grim little smile and said she'd be perfectly happy with a glass of water.

The original plan had been to arrive at Yung Shue Wan at noon, and walk the spine of Lamma Island, stopping at the strip of seafood restaurants at Sok Kwu Wan on the other side of the island, before heading back to Central. However, it was well after one o'clock by the time they disembarked and Howard had instructed the boat boys where to meet them on the other side of the island.

Yung Shue Wan Main Street was jammed with locals and expatriates. Expats, drinks in hand, spilled out of the bars. They were oblivious to her, and blocked her progress. Howard and his wife strode steadily and resolutely ahead. She had to admire the way they navigated their way through the crowds without obstructing those coming the other way. It was a peculiarly Hong Kong gift, and one that she, a New Yorker, was yet to acquire. Howard's two daughters skipped about, seemingly unconcerned about the heat; the older one, balanced precariously between childhood and puberty, was undeniably pretty; the younger one overweight and flushed, not yet conscious of the gifts that nature had denied her.

Through the Main Street crowd and onto the path that led ominously upward, the pace picked up. She knew they were later than had been planned, but was it necessary to attack this outing as though it were a military campaign? In contrast to Howard's girls, the offspring of the Australian couple, ugly, sandy-haired and freckled like their parents, began to whimper in the most irritating manner. She wanted to slap them. They weren't the only ones who were suffering. The girl was particularly annoying, hanging off her stolid mother like an unwanted carry-bag. Before arriving at the ferry pier, she had decided on her persona for the day – calm, collected, ever so slightly aloof, ever so slightly Upper East Side. (Although she had been born a Midwesterner, she had erased this inconvenient truth and could totally do Upper East Side). Now, however, confronted by stifling heat, crowds and strong smells of unfamiliar foods, she felt her features rearranging themselves into a childish sulk. She saw intimations of her pre-pubescent self in the brat hanging off its mother's arm, which made her dislike the child even more.

Why hadn't she been warned that the track was so rough? Her shoes, so carefully chosen to show her calves to advantage, were utterly unsuitable for this outing. Ryan should have known. Resentfully, she let herself fall behind, and affected a slight limp. God it was hot. New York could get hot and sticky in midsummer, but this was of a different kind. With every soggy breath, you felt that you were drawing in not oxygen but unadulterated heat. Why, if they'd had to come at all, couldn't it have been in the fall? When would they stop for a break? She could see wet patches spreading across the back of Howard's white shirt. It was a mystery that he hadn't thought to bring a change of clothing. There was momentary satisfaction when the sole of his left shoe parted company with the upper. Now they would have to stop. Now surely they would have to turn back. But then she remembered: the junk, their lifeline to civilization (or what passed for civilization in this part of the world) had been sent to the other side of the island. There could be no turning back. Howard stooped and reunited sole and upper with a handkerchief. How practical and unflappable he was, how nauseatingly British.

The upward progress was slowed by a gaggle of elderly Chinese. Although she had been in Hong Kong less than a week, she had come to find the sing-song squawk of the local dialect extremely irritating. Coming from New York, that most cosmopolitan of cities, she was of course familiar with a wide range of languages, including Chinese, but here it was unrelenting. At this moment, however, she was grateful for the respite provided by the group ahead of them, and temporarily forgave them their brutish tongue. She caught up with Ryan, relieved him of the water bottle, and drained it. "That's all we have," said Ryan reprovingly. She shrugged and handed back the empty bottle. It wasn't her fault that he'd miscalculated the amount of water they would need for the walk.

At last they neared the top of the ridge, where the trail forked. "Please stop," she said to herself. "This is unbearable." Howard, impervious to telepathy, turned left and pressed on relentlessly up the trail that became ever steeper. Even his frolicking daughters began to flag. "How much further, Daddy?" the dumpy one asked. "We'll soon be at the top, Sweetie," he said. "It'll be all downhill from there."

She pictured herself sitting in the cool, dim recess of their flat, blinds drawn, the reassuring hum of the air-conditioning system, a novel upturned on her lap, Schubert's string quintet on the CD player (rejection by the New York School of Music hadn't diminished her passion for chamber music). She would compose an ironically dismissive account of her initiation into expatriate culture through her first junk trip and hiking expedition. Her friends had been most amused by the account of her adventure in the wet market.

"Shit! Fuck!" Startled, she looked up ahead. Howard was standing at the summit of their climb, confronting a pagoda-looking structure that marked the end of the trail. "Sorry, folks," he said. "We took the wrong turn." How pleasing it was to observe the quiver in his stiff upper British lip, to hear the murmured admonitions of his wife for his use of 'language' in front of the children. It was enough to make her temporarily forget her own distress.

They beat a retreat. While the going was easier now they were heading downhill, the heat grew more intense. They hadn't proceeded far along the correct path when they came across a gathering of hikers, including the old Chinese people whom they had passed before taking the wrong turning. All eyes were on something happening just off the trail. Howard's girls and the two Australian brats pushed their way through the assembly to see what the attraction was. One of the girls gave a squeal – the fat one, she assumed for no good reason. What she saw simultaneously sickened and fascinated her. A large python had caught, strangled, and was in the process of ingesting a feral cat. It looked a very painful process. The snake didn't seem to be enjoying it much, and it can't have been at all pleasant for the cat. The unlikely incident confirmed in her own mind the fact that despite its veneer of sophistication, Hong Kong was uncivilized.

When Ryan's company made it clear that his career path would be facilitated by a tour of duty abroad, he had been offered the choice of the Singapore or Hong Kong office. Although she'd never been to Singapore or Hong Kong, she wasn't keen on either place. When you lived at the centre of the known universe, what was the point of living anywhere else? However, Ryan was a sensible type who put his career above all else, and he persuaded her that it wouldn't be the end of the world to spend a couple of years in the lap of expatriate luxury. So she did her research, and settled on Singapore, which looked cleaner and more manageable than Hong Kong. Ryan flew out on a reconnaissance flight, and returned declaring Singapore to be the dullest place he had ever visited. "You'd die of boredom there within a week," he said. So, Hong Kong it was. Perhaps she should have visited Singapore and formed her own opinion.

Sickened by the snake incident, and the fact that only the spectators seemed to be getting any pleasure out of the meal, she pushed through the crowd, and set off along the trail by herself. For the first time, she found herself ahead of the junk party. Was she imagining things, or was it really cooler here on the ridge with a breeze coming off the ocean? Maybe it had to do with the fact that, for a short time at least, she was able to progress at her own pace. She paused and took in the view. It was one of those rare days when the pollution had been rolled back to China and the view was spectacular. Other islands were dotted about the ocean. The vegetation bordering the trail had a clean, earthy smell. Although it differed from the scents of her childhood in the Midwest, there was something familiar, something pleasing about it. For the first time since her relocation from New York, she was possessed by a lightening of the spirit: you wouldn't call it happiness, but it wasn't far off.

The only blight was the trash strewn along the trail: cigarette packets, drink cans, bits of paper: another indication of the unevolved state of the place. Determined not to let the trash at her feet change her mood, she kept her eyes set firmly on the horizon and the trail ahead.

The rest of the party, having watched the cat finally disappear into the snake, caught up with her. Ryan fell into step beside her, and she surprised herself, as well as him, by allowing him to take her hand.

When she had learned that their walk would terminate at a seafood place, she had assumed that they would be eating in something that was recognizably a restaurant. Instead, she found herself in a large open space bounded on one side by a rustic waterfront, and on the other by fish tanks containing all manner of alarming sea creatures. Although it was approaching three o'clock, the place overflowed with parties of diners. Some groups were exclusively locals, some exclusively expats (*gweilos*, she'd been told was the endearing Chinese term for foreigners), and some groups were mixed. Everyone seemed to be in a happy frame of mind.

They were seated at a circular table by the water, which had an oily consistency and oozed and sucked around the pylons supporting the restaurant. It also supported dozens of polystyrene boxes and other bits of floating rubbish, and had a toxic smell. She steered Ryan to two chairs facing away from the water. There was nothing that could be done about the horrible smell of rotting fish, but at least they wouldn't have to look at the unappealing water. It was a momentary setback to find herself sitting next to the Australians, but there was nothing to be done about that either. She anticipated the questions that would already have their lips twitching: "How long have you been here?" and "What do you do?", questions that had bombarded her at the party the previous evening. In response to the query about what she did, she had made the mistake of saying that she didn't do anything – she'd only just set foot in the place, for heaven's sake. The reply had people nonplussed, and she was discarded as a person of no interest. It wasn't that they were rude, they just couldn't think of anything to say to someone who had no visible means of filling in their time. She wouldn't make that mistake again. She refused to be humiliated or patronized by the Antipodeans.

Determined to keep the conversation steered firmly away from herself, she got in first, and asked the Australians what they did. She hadn't been in Hong Kong long enough to learn not to be taken aback by anything that people said or did. It therefore came as quite a surprise – you could almost say a shock – to learn that the lumpen Australians were not what she had assumed them to be. He was a cardio-vascular surgeon, one of the best in Hong Kong she was later to learn. His wife had her own real estate business, letting luxury apartments to expatriate executives.

The food was another surprise. They had barely settled into their seats when beer, wine, water and soft drinks appeared at the table. The plates of food, which Howard must have pre-ordered, appeared not long afterwards. Although the restaurant was primitive, the tables set with faded gingham cloths and plastic dishware, the food was remarkably good: salt and pepper squid, baby lobsters steamed with ginger, a large fish poached in broth. The dishes kept coming. At first she eyed the plates with suspicion. Little care or attention had been paid to the presentation of the food, but she was hungry after the long walk, and so she allowed herself a lobster tail, and a small piece of fish. It turned out to be unusually tasty. Her mood continued to improve to the point where, the second time Howard pressed a glass of wine on her, she accepted. After her third glass, she found herself chatting animatedly to the Antipodeans. They really were very nice. Even their children were forgivable. And they never once asked her how long she'd been in Hong Kong or what she did. There was a distinct possibility that she would allow them to become her friends.

On their way back to the junk, she regretted having consumed the fourth glass of wine. She thought that all they had to do was to walk the fifty metres to the ferry pier set in the middle of the stretch of seafood restaurants. Her buoyant spirits sagged when she discovered that the junk was waiting for them in another bay, a twenty-minute walk from Sok Kwu Wan village. This required them to retrace their steps towards Yung Shue Wan before branching off on a side track which took them through market gardens and another village before surmounting a small hill, and descending onto a pretty beach which was marred by a hideous power station with several tall chimney stacks, each of which belched smoke into the sky. The rest of the party had armed themselves with cans of Tsingtao for the return walk and were feeling no pain, but recalling her own pain from the morning walk, she stuck with water.

As they descended to the beach, the young German couple accompanied her. The male (Hans? Franz?) was an architect. His partner didn't volunteer an occupation and given her own sensitivity on the subject, she had no intention of asking. Being German, they would be less easily deflected than the Australians. The walk was bearable: shorter and on a trail that had been paved. The sun was on its way toward the horizon, so it was also cooler. On the beach, they noticed two junks about two hundred metres offshore. Howard tried calling the boat boys only to discover that their phones were switched off. How tiresome, she thought. Small setbacks constantly threatened to derail her positive mood. Howard attempted to attract the attention of the boat boys by leaping up and down on the beach, flailing his arms in the air and shouting. When this failed to work, he began to remove his shirt and pants. Thankfully, the children had wandered off down the beach and were spared the sight of his puffy, white flesh, and his utter ridiculousness, standing in nothing but his boxer shorts with the water lapping about his ankles. She was not so spared. She had a sense of foreboding, remembering the amount of alcohol that he'd consumed throughout the afternoon. She herself had no taste for swimming and had been traumatized when Ryan had once taken her kayaking. Howard's wife voiced her own concern, but he turned his back, waded into the water and struck out toward one of the junks. He swam very slowly, and for a time it seemed as though he was making no progress whatsoever, but gradually, the bobbing head grew closer to its target.

The men turned their attention to demolishing the plastic bag of beers, but she and the wife kept their eyes on the bobbing head. The pretty pre-pubescent daughter returned from the far end of the beach. "What's Daddy doing?" she asked. "He's fetching the junk," said her mother. The German architect scanned the water, which had taken on an ominous, oily sheen as the sun descended.

"There is only one problem," said the German.

"What? What problem?" asked the wife.

"He's swimming toward the wrong boat."

The others laughed at Howard's foolish mistake, but the wife saw nothing to laugh about. "He must be getting tired," she said. "He doesn't get a lot of exercise." Realizing its mistake, the head changed direction, and began creeping toward its intended target, about fifty metres away. The light was fading rapidly now, and it was becoming increasingly difficult to follow the progress of the head, which at one point disappeared beneath the water momentarily before reappearing. Her anxiety increased. The junk was their lifeline to civilization, while Howard was their lifeline to the junk. The second time the head disappeared, it didn't reemerge. "I can't see Daddy," said the pretty daughter in a small voice. The fat one, who had joined her sister, began to cry. The wife put her arms around the girls and stared at the spot where Howard's head had last been seen, as though she could make it reappear by force of will. At this point, all that remained of his existence was a small pile of crumpled clothing on the beach: a soiled white dress shirt, grey suit pants, a pair of grey socks – one with a hole in it – and a pair of shoes, one of which was very close to the end of its natural life. That pathetic pile of clothes and the broken shoe might be the last things his daughters would have to remind them of who and what he was.

While she was concerned for Howard's safety, she was also irritated. The utter foolishness of his alcohol-fuelled action looked likely to ruin the day for everyone. She put her foot down when Ryan suggested that he might swim out and see if he could do anything. What could he possibly do? The Australian doctor, who presumably knew more about the tenuousness of life than the rest of them, agreed with her. The Germans had been standing apart, continuing to scan the water. Then the architect said, "There he is," pointing towards the junk. Each with his or her own interrupted interior narrative watched in silence as the bulky form pulled itself onto the boarding platform at the rear of the boat.

When they clambered aboard the junk, Howard was sitting at the large common table on the rear deck with a beach towel wrapped carelessly around his ample waist. He had a beer in his hand and was looking smug. She was puzzled at the look until she realized that he had no idea of the consternation he had caused. Why shouldn't he glow with self-satisfaction? He had reunited them with the junk and had thereby saved the day. And he had done it with old-fashioned masculinity: no need for technology whatsoever. Disappointingly, all his wife had to say was, "Oh, Howard!"

As they headed away from Lamma, she took herself and glass of wine to the front of the junk and settled on the padded bench. The breeze had lifted and was blowing cool off the water. They became part of a flotilla heading home. Heading home. Had she really allowed herself to entertain those words? Ahead, Hong Kong Island was a blaze of lights, running from Aberdeen all the way up to The Peak. Yes, she decided, she could manage Hong Kong. The first order of business was to get a job. She would work on that tomorrow. It couldn't be too difficult, not with her talents and Ryan's contacts. Buoyed at the notion, she held out her glass as dishevelled Howard, reunited with his work clothes, lurched past with a wine bottle.

"One for the road?" he asked.

"One for the road," she replied.

*

I bump into her at the bank where she is closing an account. In a few days, she is returning forever to New York, the place where she belongs. In less than a year, her steely resolve has dissolved. Ryan will stay on for six months, and then join her at Christmas. "Will he?" I wonder.

A freelance editor friend of mine, who has looked over the manuscript for me, pauses at this story. "What's it got to do with Hong Kong?" she asks. "Everything," I reply.

5.

How the war was won

The only thing more unthinkable than leaving was staying; the only thing more impossible than staying was leaving. I didn't want to destroy anything or anybody. I just wanted to slip quietly out the back door, without causing any fuss or consequences, and then not stop running until I reached Greenland. (Elizabeth Gilbert)

I first encounter Esther in a small backstreet restaurant west of Hong Kong's Central district. The restaurant, a Spanish tapas bar, is run by a father and son team from Katmandu. Actually, the restaurant largely runs itself while the father and son stage small family wars in full view of the diners. When a truce is called, father and son form a temporary alliance and turn on the Filipino chef, a hot-tempered type whose continued employment is down to his killer croquettes and sizzling garlic prawns. In the midst of the mayhem, comfortingly retro dishes emerge from the kitchen from time to time.

On this afternoon, I'm there to settle an outstanding bill from the previous evening. How the restaurant manages to stay in business is one of many small mysteries. At the end of a meal, a request for the bill by a regular diner will be met with a wave of the hand and the injunction to 'pay later', where 'later' could mean anything from tomorrow through to the beginning of the next century.

I notice Esther at once, as I'm meant to do. She's strategically seated opposite two male dining companions, an arrangement that suits all three. One of the men, Toby, also a regular at the restaurant, waves me over and invites me to join them. He introduces me to Esther and the other member of the group, a younger Chinese man called Mike. The three are colleagues at a nearby college, and are lunching together to celebrate Mike's recent promotion and Esther's recent divorce.

Esther is an attractive Indian woman in her early 40s, petite, with sharp features, large soulful eyes and mid-length hair that falls carefully about her face. She is dressed in a style more suited to someone in their 20s: spray-on jeans that end mid-calf are designed to show her figure to advantage, and the platform shoes to provide the height that nature has denied.

Esther likes to talk. My arrival barely punctuates her animated denunciation of the creep formerly and recently known as her husband. She has mastered the art of the mood switch, from anger and contempt to sadness, before landing on a kind of wistful self-pity. "I only married him to stop him pestering me, and then I had a heck of a job getting out of it," she says. "One thing is for sure, I'll definitely never get married again. This is it for me." She brings the performance to an end by delicately popping a piece of bread roll into her mouth and, as if noting my existence for the first time, turns to me and asks, "So what do you do?"

Esther was brought up in a traditional, middle-class family of academics in Delhi. Growing up in a very sheltered environment, her life, and those of her siblings, revolved around classes and study. "Thirteen hours a day," she tells me. There were major restrictions on how often they were allowed out and where they went: there were certainly no members of the opposite sex in the picture.

It was an unspoken assumption that she would follow her parents into academia. When she had finished her bachelor's degree, under pressure from her father, she embarked on a Master of Science degree, but the drudgery of long hours in a laboratory looking down a microscope at wiggling creatures in a petri dish drove her to search for opportunities outside of the academy. A newspaper advertisement for Cathay Pacific flight attendants seemed a reasonable, if not perfect solution: an opportunity to see the world, and independence from her family. It also had the not-unexpected consequence of thoroughly pissing off her father. Through her breathtaking act of defiance, she had flushed her academic future down the toilet: and, she was reminded, settled on an occupation only marginally better than prostitution. The fact that she would be earning more than her father only made things worse. He said to her, "This is not a profession. You're going down the drain. You'll make nothing of yourself. You'll just be a worm in a dirty drain." Apparently, this Indian term of abuse is particularly insulting, but it did nothing to change her mind.

When she learns of my project, she volunteers herself as an informant. "I could tell you things," she says conspiratorially. I resist reminding her that this is the whole point, and we agree on a time and place.

At the interview, she airily waves away my list of questions. This is her interview, not mine, and she'll decide the agenda, thank you very much. I've learned that if informants want to get something off their chest, they have to be allowed to do so. In Esther's case, it was her husband – their meeting, marriage, messy breakup, and the tug of war over their son. This was her story, and she would tell it her way, from the night she impulsively and dramatically walked out of the marriage leaving her small son behind, to the heroic way that she snatched him back.

*

The minute she heard herself say the words, she knew she had made a massive mistake. She was so angry that she compounded the blunder by repeating them. The following morning, she remembered those words, and the look on his face: fear alternating with triumph. Earlier in the evening, when she had destroyed his precious musical instrument and computer, and then laughed in his face and gloated, saying, "What will you do? What can you do?" he had been downcast, defeated. But with the threat, she had delivered a powerful weapon into his hands, and he knew it.

However, a week later, as she lay in bed listening to the early morning noises from the street below, and the old man upstairs clearing his throat and spitting the product into a basin, she had an unaccountable sense of happiness. Then it came to her with a rush: this was the day that she was going to get him back. She was excited, but also nervous. She would only get one shot at spiriting him away from under their noses. If she failed, he would disappear, and there was every chance she'd never see him again. She wouldn't even put it past them to take him back to India. Twice she had called. On both occasions, her father-in-law had answered the phone. She begged to see him, but the request was refused. He wouldn't even let her speak to the boy. She asked to speak to her husband, but that, too, was refused. The poisoning would already have begun. "Your mummy is a wicked woman. She has run away and left you. She doesn't want to see you any more." He wouldn't believe them to begin with, but would be totally bewildered by her sudden absence. They would slowly but inevitably brainwash him, so she had to be quick and decisive. When they argued and he clung to her, Vikram called him a 'mummy's boy'. And so he was. Vikram imagined it to be a term of abuse, but it was just the opposite – a term of endearment. But the fact remained: it had been a mistake to threaten to kill the boy.

The irony was that she hadn't particularly wanted a child. She wasn't sure that Vikram wanted one either, but his parents did, and being a dutiful Indian son, he always did as he was told. Invariably, regardless of the time or wherever in the world they happened to be, at the end of an argument he would sneak into an adjoining room to call his father for counsel: and she would listen at the door and despise him.

When she resigned from the airline and they moved to Canada, he had put it to her that it was the perfect time to have a child. She thought, "Why not?" There was nothing much to do in Vancouver, and so she got pregnant. Like many of the life-changing decisions she made, this one happened on the spur of the moment. Not that she ever regretted having the boy; in fact, he quickly became the most important thing in her life. However, it did make life that much more complicated, particularly with Vikram's restlessness and constant moving: from Vancouver to San Francisco, and then to London, before finally returning to Hong Kong. And when the marriage really started to crumble, she felt that she couldn't just walk out as she would have done had it only been the two of them. It took a major drama for that to happen.

Others would say it was a stroke of luck that the previous evening her friend Lucy had noticed Vikram at the Airport Express, checking in for a flight to Singapore. It was also luck, so they would say, that Lucy was one of the few friends to whom she had confided the story of their split. But Esther didn't believe in luck, she believed in fate. Her Hinduism had taught her about fate, which was a far more satisfying notion than luck. It had also taught her other important verities such as honesty, suffering and vegetarianism. (Although, in rare self-reflective moments, she had to admit that she was still working on patience and compassion for others. Self-restraint was another virtue that would have to wait for her next incarnation).

How foolish it was of Vikram to think that he could pass unnoticed through the Airport Express check-in counter, or, indeed, Chek Lap Kok airport itself. From all his years in Hong Kong, had he learned nothing of cheating and dissembling? Had he not taken a lesson from the misfortunes of his friends? You can reinvent yourself in Hong Kong, but if you make a false step, someone will see. In Esther's experience, it was usually the husband, overconfident and arrogant, who would let the mask slip. She had female friends who had been getting away for years with their double lives. She had not been averse to an occasional one-night stand herself. She remembered the first one. Vikram was away on one of his interminable "business" trips and she'd gone to a party with a girlfriend. She had a few drinks, and when a young, good-looking guy hit on her she thought: "What the heck? Why not?" The guy still called occasionally, but she never answered the phone. There were others, but she never took them seriously. Her commitment from the very beginning was low: there was never a lot of passion for her in sex. When she got involved in her work, when she listened to music, when she read a book, there was passion. When she sat and looked at the sea, there was passion. But when someone came along to whom she was vaguely attracted and they ended up in bed there was never any passion. She would act on the impulse that had resulted in marriage, motherhood, and now impending divorce, and would come to regret it: she regretted many things, but not the child – never the child.

She finally rolled out of bed, pulled a wrap around her shoulders, and made some tea. There were things she had to do, but there was no hurry as it was still early. She was meeting Lucy at twelve; they would have lunch together, and then go to the apartment. Her heart began to pound as she anticipated all of the things that could go wrong. Vikram might have returned early from his business trip. His parents, who would be baby-sitting the boy, might make a scene and try to prevent her from taking him. That was why she needed Lucy. "Breathe," she told herself. "Stay in the moment." It was an eternity to twelve o'clock. If she dwelt on all of the things that might go wrong, she'd go crazy.

She sat with her back to the window, the cup of tea wrapped in her hands. There wasn't much to look at inside the flat – bare walls and minimal furniture – but she preferred it to the crumbling concrete wall obscuring whatever view the window might once have had. Not that she wasn't grateful for the flat. On the night of the confrontation, after she had made her terrible threat and Vikram was on the phone to the police, she had grabbed her handbag and some books for teaching the following day and run from the apartment. She congratulated herself for remembering the books: even in a crisis, she had a practical bent. She went to a cheap hotel in Tsim Sha Tsui because she had very little money. So what if it was used by Mainland prostitutes, and that it was dirty and noisy? It was only a temporary refuge.

Bolting from him and from the apartment had been yet another impulsive act. It was only the following morning that the finality of the act, and the precariousness of her situation, dawned on her. She could never go back, and would never want to go back. After sleepwalking through her morning class, she sat for an hour in a coffee shop thinking about the mess she was in, and silently grieving for her abandoned son. She had to figure out a way of getting him out of the clutches of Vikram and his family, but before that she had to find somewhere to stay other than a hotel infested with prostitutes, their clients, and cockroaches. The poor little boy would be distraught at her disappearance. When she had called the apartment and Vikram's father had answered the phone, she tried to stay calm as he called her a wicked woman and all sorts of names. Of course, he wouldn't let her speak to her son. He said that Vikram had gone to the police station, and that they were going to have her arrested and committed to the psychiatric hospital.

It was then that she had called Lucy, the only friend she'd retained from her days at Cathay Pacific. The others she had shed, one by one, as they had come to bore her, or had otherwise outlived their usefulness. Lucy loathed Vikram, and had been urging her to leave him for some time. She accused Esther of lacking the courage to leave, but Esther, who had an overdramatic view of her life, said that it took more courage to stay and try to make the relationship work. She wasn't sure whether or not she was imagining it, but she thought she detected a note of satisfaction in Lucy's voice. But Lucy had a short-term solution to her accommodation problem. Her sister was in Europe for a month, and her flat was available. She could move in immediately, which is what she did. The flat was in a shabby street near Jordan MTR station. It would not have been Esther's first choice, but it was infinitely superior to the brothel in Tsim Sha Tsui.

She and Lucy then set about plotting ways of getting Anu back. Kidnapping from his pre-school was a possibility, but was highly risky. Armed with a police report detailing the threat she had made, the family would have alerted the pre-school, and it was unlikely that she'd have made it through the front door. Then, yesterday afternoon, a week after she had fled from the flat, the wheel turned, and fate delivered a means of being reunited with her son. And it would play out in a few short hours.

Lucy, of course, had wanted to know the intimate details of the events leading up to her flight from the apartment, and Esther, who saw herself as the centrepiece of the drama, was happy to oblige. One or two embellishments may have crept into the story as she rehearsed it to herself, but it was accurate enough. She had to admit, even to herself, the heroic nature of what she had done. She knew, or thought she knew, what friends and colleagues thought of her: that she was loud, that she was given to self-dramatization, that the centre of attention was the only place to be. These were virtues, not flaws of character. Most of her colleagues led mundane lives: drab in some cases, you could say, if you were honest. Not only did she crave excitement, she demanded it. If the day lacked drama, she invented it.

"It happened unexpectedly, late one afternoon. I just snapped. He'd been out all day, and came creeping into the apartment. I'd just put Anu to bed, and was preparing my classes for the next day. Unlike some of the other instructors at the college, I take my work very seriously, and put a lot into preparing my classes.

"Vikram and I are opposites in many ways. I'm very loud, very 'out there'. What you see is what you get. Vikram is quite different. He keeps things inside, and then he goes and does things behind my back. If there was ever some issue I wanted to talk about or some disagreement between us, he'd find a way not to talk about it. He'd walk out or say; 'I have a meeting', or he'd close the door. There was a lot of stonewalling. So, on this fine day, when he came in and said he'd been at a meeting, instead of just letting it go, I started yelling, asking; 'What kind of meeting? I know it wasn't a meeting. You were with that woman, blah, blah, blah. Because my friend saw you, and you've been lying to me, I know.' He didn't say anything, just turned away, so then I said to him, 'Show me your phone. I know you call her, OK?' And he started lying, saying; 'Oh no, I don't have my phone with me, I left it in the café where we had the meeting.' I said, 'You're lying to me again. All I have to do is call your number, and your phone will start ringing. It's in your pocket. I can see it. Liar!'

"I didn't like to get into those kinds of arguments because they're very petty, but that day I made a scene. I brought up about money I'd given him. I said, 'Give me my money back – all the money that is in the joint account. You said you put it in stocks or bonds or whatever. I want my money back.' I'd brought up the issue of the money a few weeks before, and he had broken out in a cold sweat, and I found it weird considering that we were in a lift at the time. I thought something was not right about it, and it kept bothering me. He said, 'No, that money was used for the mortgage.' I said, 'No, you told me it was in stocks and bonds.' He said, 'No, it was used for the mortgage. Most of it was used when we had the house.' And I said, 'So, now you've sold it. So where's the profit from that?' Then I started bringing up all of the other things: I counted off his affairs on the fingers of my hand.

"At that point, he did what he always does, just turned around and walked out the door. I knew he was going back to meet the woman. To tell the truth, that wasn't the thing I was most concerned about. His cheating on me was not a huge thing, let's put it that way, because I was never in the relationship as it is, so I just thought; 'Do what you want.'

"It was cheating on all levels that I couldn't bear. It was many things combined, you know. Cheating about money, the fact that he was not there for Anu, and the fact that he was not working. And I thought to myself, 'He has no use-value.' I mean, go cheat, but be with your son. Do something useful. I was getting very annoyed. And then there was the woman that he was meeting and putting before his family. They started meeting on the pretext of music. They always find some excuse. And then he bought her an Indian instrument called a tanpura. He had it made specially in India, a handcrafted string instrument. Very beautiful. And she plays this instrument. So that night he went out because he didn't want to talk to me, and like a crazy maniac I went into his study where he kept the tanpura and cut every string systematically. It was very hard. They're very strong, you know. Then I spotted his computer and I smashed it too. It was actually hard to break. After I broke it I felt better.

"I went back to the living room, and waited for him to come back. When he did, I said to him, 'You've been challenging me, so now I'm challenging you. What would you do, right? What would you do? What *can* you do? Go and see. Go and look at what I did in your room.' I was nasty. He went and looked, and when he came back I could see that he was really upset, but he didn't say anything, so I said, 'You want us out of your life? Right? Maybe I should just kill myself and kill my son, and then you'd be free to do whatever you want. You don't want to have anything to do with us, right? You'd be free. Yes, that's what I'm going to do, I'm going to set you free.'

"That was really the last nail in the coffin of our relationship. It was a big mistake to talk about killing myself and my son – which I never really meant. The first thing he did was to call his parents, as he always does, and asked them to come around. Then he called the police and reported that I had made a death threat against his son. *His* son, the one he had no time for. While he was on the phone, I grabbed my things and ran. I had no idea where I was going, but there was only one word running through my head: *Escape*! I thought, I'll find a cheap hotel and spend the night. I thought, I'll let him sweat all night, and then he'll be begging me to come back. And I will come back, but only to collect my son."

In the end, it turns out to be easier than she had expected. As is often the case, none of the anticipated disasters eventuate. "Just be natural," she says to Lucy, as they ride up in the lift, even though her own heart is thumping. If Vikram had had the brains to change the lock on the front door, that would have posed a major obstacle, because his parents could simply have refused to admit her, but the key turns easily in the lock. Taken by surprise, the parents are glued, as though by some force of nature, to the dining table where they are having lunch.

"Hello," she says, pasting on her brightest smile. "This is my friend Lucy. I think you've met her." Without waiting for them to deny this, she says, "We're just going out for a walk." At the sound of her voice, Anu comes rushing into the room and flings himself on her, crying out, "Mumma, Mumma, Mumma." It is all she can do not to burst into tears.

But she keeps the smile pasted on her face, and says, "You're coming for a walk with Mumma. Let's get you a jacket and a couple of things." She hustles him back into his room, and hurriedly stuffs some clothing, a couple of books and a toy or two into a carry bag and then returns to the living room. "All right," she says to Lucy, "Let's go. We don't want to be out too late." And with that they are gone.

When Vikram returned from his trip to Singapore to discover that she had taken the boy, he went back to the Tsim Sha Tsui police station and made a formal charge that she had kidnapped the boy and was going to kill him. They had no idea where she was, but the police called her on her mobile phone and asked her to come to the station, which she did. She took Anu with her. The police asked a few questions, and checked on Anu, and released her. Then they called Vikram and said; "There's nothing to your complaint. The child clearly loves the mother. He wants to be with the mother. This is just a domestic dispute, there's nothing to it."

Vikram was very angry with the police, but when it became clear that they weren't going to do anything, he started on a campaign of harassment. She had to take her son to the college where she taught because she had no other option. He would sit quietly outside her classroom with his books while she taught. Vikram called the principal and tried to make trouble. When that didn't work, he made the police call the college and find out what she was doing to her son. He did everything he could to damage her reputation. It was all very embarrassing, but neither the college nor the police did anything. The police just dismissed it as a domestic dispute.

*

"That first time we met, in the Spanish restaurant, you said that you only married Vikram to stop him pestering you? Were you serious?"

"More or less. When I first moved to Hong Kong, I mainly hung out with other Cathay people, especially the Indian girls. But after about a year, I started getting bored, and so I started seeking other friendships. That's when I met Vikram. One evening, I was taking it easy, listening to

Indian classical music, which I'm very interested in, and preparing a meal for myself. My flatmate, who is also interested in Indian music and sings very well, had a visitor, an Indian guy who was a few years older than me. 'This is Vikram,' my flatmate said. 'He knows a lot about Indian music.' He stayed for a meal and discussed Indian classical music. He was very surprised that I knew as much if not more than he did. A few days later he called me up and invited me to a concert. Because I was bored with the Cathay girls, and wanted to get into a more intellectual circle with like-minded people, I accepted. We went out a few times, but there was never any romantic intention on my part. My attitude towards him was, 'Oh, he's harmless.' I thought through him I could meet interesting non-Cathay people."

"So, you were using him?"

"Well, we all use each other, right? You use me, I use you."

"So, you didn't have a boyfriend at the time?"

"I'd never had a boyfriend, never had a relationship. The other Cathay girls were all dating, even the conservative Chinese ones. Some had been dating since high school. For a long time Vikram and I were just casual friends. We'd go to a café or some music event. He always called me up. It was never the other way around."

"When did things change?"

"One day, about eight months after we first met, he took me to a friend's place. His friend's partner was there as well, and he opened a bottle of champagne, which I thought was a little bit strange, because Vikram didn't drink, and I only drank now and then. We were chatting about this and that, and then, out of the blue, the friend said, 'So you're dating each other.' And I immediately said, 'No, no, no, don't be ridiculous, we're just friends.' But then Vikram said, 'Oh, I want to marry you. Come on, you have to admit that you want to marry me. Come on, admit it…' I treated it as a big joke. I laughed and said, 'Stop being silly.' But the couple who were there persisted in talking about how we were dating each other. At that point, I started to get annoyed and said, 'No, there's no such intention, no such intention at all.' Then it went further, when Vikram said, 'No, my plan is to marry you. We're going to get engaged. Say yes, say yes, say yes.' So it started as a joke – well, I had thought it was a joke – but then it became more serious on his part. At that point, I got very annoyed, and said, 'Just stop this nonsense, we're not going to talk about this now. We'll talk about it later.' And I changed the subject and refused to discuss it any more. I could see that Vikram wasn't very happy."

"So, the whole evening and the marriage proposal were part of a plan?"

"Well, if the plan had been to annoy me and embarrass him in front of his friends, it worked out pretty well. That night, we left his friends' place quite late. It must have been around midnight or one o'clock. It was certainly much later than I had intended to be out. I had a flight the next day and was anxious to get home. It was a winter's night and very cold. At the time, I was living in Prince Edward. Vikram was walking me to the train, but before we got to the station, he asked me to sit on a bench. I just wanted to get out of the cold and get home, but I agreed to sit with him. So we both sat down, and he held my hand and he said 'I won't let you go home until you say 'yes', because I'm in love with you.' And he started talking about how he had been in love with me all along, and listing all the reasons why we were perfect for each other. I felt nothing for him at all: all I felt was cold, tired and very annoyed, so to get rid of him, I said, 'OK, yeah, if that's what you want.' At the same time, I was thinking to myself, 'It's never going to happen.' I was more concerned about my flight than I was about this proposal of marriage. I had a long flight coming up that afternoon, and it was already about five in the morning by the time he left me. I was very focused on the fact that if I didn't get enough sleep I wouldn't be able to do my job properly. Saying yes to the marriage proposal wasn't a very smart thing to do, but I make a lot of impulsive decisions. It's very silly, I know, but that's the way I am."

"But, obviously, you did get married."

"At some point we started dating. At one point I broke it off and he got his father to come over from India to 'talk sense' into me. He's very dependent emotionally on his father. We talked, and after that it was understood that we were back together again. Some time later, we took a trip to India, and he said, 'We've been dating, and in India you can't be that casual, so why don't you call your dad and let him know.' I was extremely nervous about that, because I knew how he'd react. I kept making stupid excuses, like; 'No, no, he'll be asleep. He won't pick up the phone.' Finally, I couldn't put it off any longer, so I called my dad, and he was very unhappy, as I knew he would be. After that, we returned to Hong Kong and got engaged. A year later we got married. I felt that the relationship and the marriage were wrong from the start, and that I'd walked into something that was never going to work. I make decisions like this all the time, even now. When it came to his constantly going on about getting married, I thought, well, a husband is a husband, and finally, at the end of the day, they're all the same, so why not?"

"Were you ever happy?"

"No, my relationship with Vikram was practically zero from the start. As I already said, within the very first year I realized just what a mistake I'd made. I was still with Cathay then, and I used to come back from flights, and on the bus back from the airport, I used to cry a lot. I knew it was not the right thing and that I'd taken a wrong direction in my life."

"What about him?"

"He didn't seem like a player, and, in fact, he wasn't at that time. He was my first boyfriend and I was his first girlfriend. However, over time, things changed. He started having other relationships. These were the dot-com days. He and his colleagues sold the company they had started to Tom.com, and he made a lot of money. After that, he changed. He became more arrogant. That's what money does to you. That's the way it is in Hong Kong. People come here and find themselves making more money than they ever dreamed of, and it changes them."

At the end of our conversation about her marriage, Esther apologizes, saying, "I've probably been talking about the wrong things." I reassure her that in conversations such as this, there's no such thing as the 'wrong' issues. The issues that the informants choose to talk about are the ones that are important to them. And in the case of this interview, there was no way she was going to talk about anything else.

6.

No place like home

Maybe you had to leave in order to really miss a place; maybe you had to travel to figure out how beloved your starting point was.

(Jodi Picoult)

Dear Dad,

I hope that all is well on the home front. Sorry I haven't been in touch for a week or two, but I've been on the road again, and Internet connections are a bit "iffy" in some of these places. You really don't know how lucky we are in all sorts of ways at home until you travel.

I trust that Mum's doing better and that you managed to get some satisfaction with the chaps who are working on the central heating. Marg says they're predicting a cold winter this year. Here, what they laughably call winter lasts about six weeks, and if the temperature drops below fifty the rich fly off to Thailand, and the old people die off like flies.

It's ironic that in my last email, I answered your question about racism in Hong Kong. You didn't believe me when I said that as far as I could see, it doesn't exist. Well, guess what? Only yesterday, I experienced racism, and it happened to me. It came as such a shock. We're going to give up Hong Kong soon enough (and I won't get you started on that subject!), but right now it does still belong to us.

You remember I told you that I'd moved out of my place in Mid-Levels because the greedy landlord put the rent up to such an extent – over fifty percent, if you can believe it – and that I moved out to a place called Ap

Lei Chau? It's a tiny flat – well, nothing unusual about that, this being Hong Kong and all. Anyway, the only real downside is that I can't walk to work. That was the real advantage of my other place: out of bed, into the shower, and down the hill I'd march along with all of the other wage slaves. The only feasible way for me to get to work these days is to catch a bus. Luckily, these are plentiful, and cheap. It's surprising really, when everything else in Hong Kong is so expensive.

Yesterday, I queued up for the bus like everyone else. He has a real aversion to queuing, does your average Hongkonger. It's one of a number of things we never managed to teach them, and now, sadly, it's too late. What they haven't learned by now, they'll never learn. You appreciate that the buses can get pretty jam-packed, especially during rush hour. You think the London transport systems can get crowded? It's nothing really compared to Hong Kong. I have to say, it takes a bit of getting used to, having your personal space invaded constantly. I've learned certain tricks, like when someone stands too close behind me – shop assistants are notorious for doing this – I just step back suddenly. You step on their toes a few times, and they soon get the message.

So, anyway, there I am yesterday, queuing up for the bus, and I get on the bus, and I'm lucky enough to get a seat. It just happened to be empty, so down I sit, and blow me down if the Chinese bloke sitting next to me doesn't get up and move away. I don't know whether I smelled or not, but there I was on a crowded bus, a spare seat next to me, and no one will sit down next to me. They'd rather stand up all the way from Ap Lei Chau to Central than to sit next to me. I have to tell you Dad, you won't mind me saying this, but you've got a few racist tendencies yourself, you know you have. In fact you're proud of it. Well, I have to tell you, that for the first time, I was on the other side of it, and it's not a nice feeling. There I was, on the bus to work, minding my own business, the only white face on the bus, and no one wanted to sit next to me. It gave me something to think about, I have to say. Why should I be discriminated against, just because I'm white? It would never happen back home, and it made me realize that as they say, there's no place like home. Some of the people I work with have 'gone native': long-term expat types. They don't seem to realize that the sun has set on the Empire. Get in, make your money, and get out, that's what I say. They're polite enough, the locals, but when it comes down to it, you have to face the fact: they really don't want us here.

Anyway, give Mum a big hug and all my love. Give her all my news. I know that she won't remember any of it, but you never know. Marg says that one day she'll remember all sorts of things and then the next day she doesn't know who anybody is. It's just such a bugger that it's come to this.

Love,
Desmond

7.

A NEAR DEATH BY DROWNING

And that's when I know it's over. As soon as you start thinking about the beginning, it's the end. (Junot Diaz)

Jack is a writer. Over the years, he's done all sorts of writing, although these days he plies his trade as a freelance journalist. He writes feature articles on issues in the Asian region that are of interest to the Western media. Given the obsession in the West with all things Asian, this means that he can write about almost anything and get it published. In addition to investigative articles on issues such as Indonesian forest fires, and human trafficking, he writes colour articles for airline magazines and trade journals ('puff' pieces, as they're called). This work doesn't bring in much in the way of income, which is of little concern to Jack. In a former life in the United States, he made an offbeat but lucrative living as a ghostwriter. Ghosting vanity memoirs for obscure CEOs and public figures could net him $500,000 a year. Crafting an autobiography for major public figures or those with a certain notoriety boosted that figure considerably. He knew a lot about the book trade, and had a tolerant, if somewhat condescending, attitude towards those of us who took a more romantic view. To him, selling books was not much different from selling soap. During a brief lull in the memoir trade, he augmented his income by getting books by authors who would otherwise have sunk without trace onto the *New York Times* bestseller list. The method, as he described it, had a certain plausibility. "You don't have to write *Harry Potter* to get rich in the book trade," he once said.

Jack appeared in Hong Kong on his way back to the US from an assignment in Cambodia where he wrote an enigmatic piece called *In Search of Pol Pot's Ghost*. He stayed on longer than he expected – not uncommon in this part of the world. Someone, it could have been Charlie or Max, brought him along to the Tuesday Club. It was Charlie who insisted the group have a name. He suggested 'The Parched Throat Society', but the rest of us laughed that one down as being embarrassingly Californian.

Jack liked what he saw in us, and we liked what we saw in him. He also fitted the Club profile, although to dignify it with the label 'club' was to imply a status that it didn't have and didn't deserve. It consisted of a loose affiliation of men of a certain age who were divorced, separated, or had never married. We had carved out moderately successful careers, lived alone most of the time, and were told that we drank more than was good for us. I'm not sure how the drinking rumour got started. We might have been habitual drinkers, but we weren't alcoholics: well, that was the story we told ourselves. "An alcoholic," said Max, "is someone who drinks more than I do."

Now and then, when the spirit moved one of us, an email would circulate suggesting that the Tuesday Club convene the following week. There may have been a reason for Tuesday, but I've forgotten it, if I ever knew. We tended to meet at the Foreign Correspondents' Club, where most of us were members, or one of the other gweilo hangouts around Soho. In Australian parlance, the food at the FCC was "pretty ordinary", but you could get a decent bottle of wine at a reasonable price, and you could have a conversation without having to shout at each other across the table – not that our conversations were anything to write home about.

Like most social groups, the Tuesday Club had a set of unwritten rules. These were never spelled out. In fact, they had never even been explicitly discussed. They entailed a set of cultural assumptions that a potential member either got or didn't get. If he was boring, boastful or failed to settle his account on time, nothing was said. He was simply removed from the email list. Jack got it and fitted in from the start. He attended most of the Tuesday lunches, although he would disappear on assignment from time to time. At one point, he mentioned that he was working on a piece on the latest North Korean famine. Shortly after that, he disappeared permanently, or so we thought, and we wondered whether he'd made one trip too many to Pyongyang.

He turned up again about a year later, passing through Hong Kong on his way to Mindanao to collect data on the Muslim separatist movement in the southern Philippines. He contacted Charlie, and a meeting of the Tuesday Club was convened. At the end of the lunch, I asked him if he had an hour to spare to be interviewed. He did, so we found a quiet corner separate from the main bar and dining area.

Interviews are unpredictable. Some begin seriously and end as burlesque. Some are seen by the interviewee as an invitation to confess, or as an opportunity for cut-rate psychoanalysis. Some are over almost before they have begun, while others outlive the battery life of my recorder. It's remarkable how often insightful gems are dropped as soon as the recorder is turned off. Some informants are determined to be anything but informative: others are resolutely obtuse. Now and then, an otherwise pedestrian interview is ignited by a single question.

I begin the interview by asking Jack why he chooses to work in parts of the world where being kidnapped, killed, or having his fingernails removed without anaesthetic were distinct possibilities.

"Some journalists can get by with Wikipedia and imagination," he says. "But I lack imagination. Maybe I also have a death wish. Who knows?"

He seems disinclined to say much about his work in regional conflict zones. The interview comes to life when I ask him why he decided to leave Hong Kong.

"I had a brief but very intense relationship that didn't work out, and figured it was time to move on," he says.

"Tell me about it."

"It all started with a near death by drowning."

*

He wasn't looking for a relationship. In fact it was the last thing on his mind. He had only recently wriggled out of one that was becoming tediously serious. Hong Kong has an oversupply of available individuals of both genders and all sexual persuasions. A bit of flirting goes on, and most of the time nothing happens. But occasionally there's a spark, usually when the both of you have had one or two drinks too many and the stars are aligned.

Last time, for Jack, he was picked up by a bored tai-tai whose spouse was out of town. This time, the spark was the brief and entirely accidental sight of the woman in question standing naked in his shower, water cascading over her dark, cropped hair and streaming down her back, her skin burnt almost black by the sun except for the triangle of flesh that had been protected by the bikini: it was only a second or two, but the startling whiteness of her buttocks was enough: that was the spark.

It was one of those random events that people of faith like to ascribe to fate. He had set himself the task of making progress on the cage people of Mongkok article, but the words withered at his fingertips. On an impulse he decided to swim off his hangover. Summer hadn't quite arrived, and the water was a bearable twenty-seven degrees. It was mid-morning in the middle of the week, and he had the pool to himself apart from a small, round Chinese gentleman standing in the next lane, admiring the container ships on the harbour and patting the surface of the water with the palms of his hands. "Chinese water torture," he thought as he completed a tumble turn. Gentle exercise was one thing, but the hand-patting was ridiculous.

Jack completed a dozen extremely slow laps and paused at the shallow end to catch his breath. The mild exercise was beginning to work, and the throbbing in his temples had almost stopped. The rotund man in the next lane stopped torturing the water, and pointed to the far end of the pool. "I think she's drowning down there," he said in impeccable English.

He seemed mildly excited at the possibility of death. "She just jumped in and never came up."

At the far end, a diminutive female pool attendant was kneeling by a starting block and peering into the water. Jack pushed off from the wall and sprinted the length of the pool, reaching his destination with a last gasp. The figure, hair floating upwards, was waving her limbs to and fro, but wasn't getting anywhere. He hooked one arm over the rope that separated the lanes and dragged her to the surface with the other. As soon as her head broke the surface, she started gulping for air and coughing up water and sputum. The young pool attendant tried to grab her and almost fell in herself.

An older, male lifeguard sauntered across from the office. Jack almost lost his hold on the woman. He managed to get his forearm between her thighs – not particularly delicate, but definitely effective – and hauled her towards the lifeguard who grabbed hold of her wrists. Between them, they got her out of the pool and onto the tiles where she collapsed and continued expectorating gobs of water and saliva. Jack climbed out of the pool and half-carried, half-dragged her off the hot tiles and onto a reclining deck chair, positioning her on her side with her legs drawn up, as this was the only way to get all of the water out of her lungs.

With potential tragedy averted, he perched on the edge of the chair, resting his hand on the curve of her hip to ensure that she stayed on her side, or so he told himself. She paid no attention to him, and was silent between the bouts of violent coughing. He wasn't sure that she was even aware of his existence, although he was very much aware of hers. Her limbs were long and slim. She was almost skinny but not quite, and he had noticed how solid she was when he hauled her onto the deck chair. She obviously worked out and had the look of a natural swimmer, although her brief adventure in the pool didn't support that notion.

Two things about her appearance struck him as unusual. The first was that she was deeply tanned – almost black. Most Chinese women see whiteness as a virtue, and will go to extreme lengths to deny their flesh the pleasure of the sun. Lying in the sun was also losing favour with

Caucasians who realized that being unfashionably white was preferable to being fashionably dead. The second noticeable aspect was that she was wearing a tiny, crocheted purple bikini that only just covered those parts of her body that decency demanded be concealed. He decided that she was in her mid to late thirties, although it was difficult to tell with Asian women.

Eventually she stopped coughing, opened her eyes, and gave him a long, slightly unfocused look. Then her eyes, large, and an unusual grey-violet colour, turned to the hand resting on her hip. "I'm sorry for the trouble," she said, her voice husky from prolonged coughing. Under interrogation she revealed that her name was Jade. He noticed that she had a tiny jade Buddha attached to her left wrist with a red thread, and guessed that jade had a particular significance for her: significant enough to select it as her English name.

She had another coughing fit, and was doubled up in distress. He grabbed a towel and wiped saliva off her chin. While this was going on, the Chinese non-swimmer emerged from the pool and waddled by looking vaguely disappointed that the unexpected drama had ended so tamely. She finished coughing, caught her breath and gave him a disarming smile. She had an extraordinarily wide mouth, and when she smiled she had the look of a happy duck. Her eyes were set too far apart with pupils that were slightly out of alignment: an unusual face, odd, you could almost say, but one that worked. He decided that she must be Eurasian.

When she says, "I'm fine now. You can go back to your swimming," he shakes his head. "I'm done with my swim." He suggests that she should go to the hospital, but this is immediately rejected. She's fine, she repeats, she's tough, she never gets sick, and she's managed to rid her lungs of all the water. This last assertion turns out to be overly optimistic as she immediately has another bout of coughing and regurgitation. He says that at the very least she should have an X-ray. If there's any water left in her lungs, she could end up with pulmonary oedema. No, she would not go to hospital, she would go home and rest. Determined to execute her plan, she stands up, wobbles, and sinks back onto the deck chair. He lets her rest for a minute, then takes her by the arm and helps her to her feet. There's a hospital with an accident and emergency department not five minutes away. He'll drive her. She pulls free, and manages to stay on her feet. There will be no hospital trip. Which bit of 'no' did he not understand?

Although she seemed to have recovered, he couldn't let her walk away. He was surprised at how the landscape of his day had changed, but even more surprised at how the state of his mind had changed. Impulsively, he suggested a compromise. He lived close by. Why didn't she come back with him, take a shower, have something to eat, and then, if she felt all right, he would escort her back to her home. Reluctantly, she agreed to the first part of the proposition, but drew the line at the idea of being escorted home. She repeated the mantra. She was sorry for troubling him. She would be all right. She was tough. She never got sick. The Mexican standoff ended with a short car trip.

"Do you want something to eat?" he asks. She shakes her head, says she's cold. Odd, he thinks, with summer just around the corner and the warm density of the air. She would like a hot shower, if that's not too much trouble, and then she'll get out of his way. He shows her to the bathroom, fetches a towel from the linen closet in the hall, gives it a sniff, and returns to the bathroom. The tiny purple bikini is balled up on the floor. She hasn't bothered to pull the shower curtain, and a small flood is already creeping across the tiles towards the hallway. She stands with her face to the wall, one hand raised to her face, the water from the rain-shower cascading over her head and shoulders, curling between her thighs and then to the floor. He had planned to drop the towel on the hand basin and take his leave, but is frozen by the amazing whiteness of her buttocks. He stands there like a cretin, towel in hand, transfixed. The spell is broken when she says, "The water won't run hot." "Give the tap a good hard twist," he says, embarrassed as a schoolboy. He drops the towel on the hand basin, and beats a retreat to the little alcove that he dignifies as his study, there to stare at the blank computer screen and struggle with his imagination. The afternoon sun is yet to push its way through the pollution and onto the tiny square of balcony, but even now the morning hangover seems a century ago.

He pulls himself together, thinks food, and is pouring the contents of a can of tomato soup into his one-and-only saucepan when he hears her gagging. He finds her curled up on the sofa, an elongated dying bird in panties and bra, clutching the damp towel for comfort. Her teeth are chattering and she's burning up. Her eyes flutter open at the touch of his hand. "So cold," she says. "I need to lie down."

In the bedroom, they lie together under a cotton cover. He strokes her hair and discovers her body with the tips of his fingers. The afternoon is making progress, and his writing deadline looms. In the kitchen something diabolical is happening to the soup. He leaves the bedroom long enough to pitch the one-and-only saucepan into the sink, scorching his fingers and cursing in the process. Long enough for her to throw up again into the pillow. Schoolkids are horsing about in the street below. Is it that time already? In other circumstances he'd have followed the instinct to crawl back under the cover and hold her, but the imperative now is to get her to the hospital. This time, she raises no objection as he retrieves the simple shift from her bag, helps her into it, and manhandles her downstairs and into a taxi.

Night has descended, and he has worked his way through the best part of a bottle of wine when his phone begins to vibrate. She's calling on a landline because mobile phones are frowned upon, or so she says. She wants to thank him. She has double pneumonia and would have been in serious trouble had he not bullied her into hospital. She promises to call him back. In the few short hours he's known her, he's developed a suspicion that the only predictable thing about her is her unpredictability. It's distinctly possible that this is the last he will ever hear from her.

Three days pass. Breaking a promise he made to himself, he calls the hospital. She's an itch that can't be scratched away. He learns that she has checked out, and no, they can't pass on her contact information. He is left with a disturbing sense of loss. He knows how to track people down, it's one of the tools of his trade. But he needs more than a first name –

assuming that 'Jade' is genuine – and in any case it's clear that she doesn't want to be tracked down. As the days pass, his expectations shrink. Irritated at his own weak-mindedness, he sets her aside and focuses on the piece that has him stuck – the cage people of Mongkok. And then she calls.

The Captain's Bar on the ground floor of the Mandarin Oriental Hotel is easy to locate and reassuringly dim, even on the brightest and most pollution-free of days. She is dressed in the same simple, light-grey shift, with a mauve scarf draped over her shoulder. His memory has failed to archive her offbeat beauty. He had booked a table in the Japanese restaurant in the Landmark building across the street, but his feet propel them both back to the doorman and into a taxi. The automatic pilot of his heart has taken over. It happens with a speed and inevitability that takes both of them by surprise. She voices no objection and he wonders whether this is what she was expecting. Dare he hope? He's certainly not going to run the risk of asking her.

It would be an exaggeration to say that she was a firecracker in the bed department, but she is willing enough. She's almost apologetic in asking if she can get on top, as it's the only way that she can climax. But it must work for her, because for the next few weeks, she keeps coming back for more. After the second occasion, sprawled on the bed and smugly satisfied with his performance and her response, he attempts to extract from her details of her romantic history. He wants to know about the competition: the curse of the male ego, risking the ruination of a mutually-satisfying afternoon. Is she seeing someone else? No. Most of her answers are monosyllabic, except when he asks her how long it's been. About six months. On the rebound after the breakup of a long-term relationship, she had an affair with the nineteen-year-old son of her closest friend. Her friend knew about it and "approved", but she ended the relationship after a few months, realizing how foolish it was, and embarrassed at the thought of bumping into friends in Central with a lover less than half her age. The boy had cried at the sudden end to his first grown-up adventure. She compounded her cruelty with words that are meant to console but have the opposite effect: "You'll get over it." It's the first confidence she has shared with Jack, and he hopes that marks progress in their relationship.

During those short weeks he thought that the relationship was going somewhere, not that he necessarily wanted it to get too serious. In the beginning it had been a powerful physical attraction and, he admitted, a desire to conquer, if not possess. To his regret, in the end it turned out to be one of those relationships that came from nowhere and went nowhere. He was comfortable, and she never made the mistake of boring him. She surprised him with an unexpected sense of humour, and she liked to talk, but it was rarely ever personal. Underneath the laughter, there was a great deal that was left unsaid.

It ended as suddenly as it had begun. She came over late one Saturday afternoon. He promised himself, as he always did, that he wouldn't take her straight to the bedroom, and as usual he broke his promise. They stayed in bed as evening fell, listening to jazz, and making love. For the first time, she agreed to stay the night: another sign of progress. The following morning they were hungry. As usual, there was no food in the apartment, so he suggested that they go to Central for lunch. He had an article to finish before they could go out, and while he worked, she flicked through the Sunday paper. He had just finished the piece and was making corrections when she appeared in the study alcove. He sensed immediately a shift in her mood. She crouched on the floor, arms encircling her long legs and told him there was something she needed to say, but she was afraid that it would make him angry. He reassured her: nothing she had to say could make him angry. She said nothing for a minute or two, and was obviously having some sort of inner struggle. Then the words tumbled out: it couldn't go on – it had to stop here. The words numbed him. He certainly hadn't seen this coming. He asked her why, but she was resolute. It wasn't a cosmic question, it didn't require the application of industrial strength logic, but for reasons of her own, she wouldn't, or couldn't, say. And he knew it was over. You always knew.

He didn't want it to end with her walking out the door. His ego couldn't take it, not on a Sunday morning. He convinced her to come to lunch, and tried negotiating. He wasn't after the sun, the moon and the stars – an occasional meal, and maybe she could stay over now and then. Surely that wasn't asking too much – was it?

She was quiet for most of the meal. He was surprisingly hungry but she barely touched her food. Not for the first time, he tried to coax from her the details of her life. He knew nothing about her – not what she did, not even where she lived. Then, suddenly, she said, "You want to know about my life?" When he nodded, she said, "Do you want the shallow story? Or do you want the deep story?" The deep story, of course. It turned out to be one of those stories that was only remarkable if it happened to you.

She was the second child in a devout and deeply protective Christian family. When she was twenty-three she met a man at a church event who was several years older than she was. She fell in love, but resisted his attempts to trick his way into her bed. ("If you really love me, prove it by sleeping with me.") She told him that she wanted to wait until they were married, but, after some months, finally gave in when he said that in his own mind they were already married. "I felt he was my husband in spirit, so I gave in." When she got pregnant, he insisted on an abortion, even though it was against God's commandment, and she desperately wanted a child. "He arranged everything, but was too busy to come with me, so I had to go through it alone. He didn't even pay for it." Her parents disapproved of the relationship, so she moved out of the family home and into a small flat in Kowloon. He suggested that they buy a flat together. This made her happy because it showed his intentions towards her were good. The flat was in his name because his father provided the deposit and insisted on it. "I paid the mortgage. He always said he'd put the flat in our joint names, but he never did." He only stayed in the flat a couple of times a week, usually when he wanted sex. The rest of the time he stayed with his parents.

Over the years, she had seven abortions, and they followed the same pattern: he never accompanied her, and she always paid. On the seventh occasion, the gynaecologist warned her that if she went through with this one it was unlikely that she'd ever be able to have children. The gynaecologist turned out to be correct. The womb, apparently, can only take so much battering and scraping, and hers had had enough.

Shortly after the final termination, she spotted her boyfriend in a coffee shop with another woman. Later, when she confronted him, he admitted that he had been 'seeing her'. More than that; they were getting married. He said that he was not to blame, that it was God's will. "God's will for him. God's punishment for me. Why would God do this to me? He was my God too." When she said that, it was the closest that she had ever come to crying.

Because the Church had given up on her, she gave up on the Church, eventually embracing Buddhism. It got predictably nasty after that. She was ejected from the flat, which she'd effectively bought. She removed the furniture, which she'd also bought, and was sued by his parents. She counter-sued for possession of the flat. Then she had a breakdown, attempted suicide, and spent months in and out of hospital – which explained her fear of going to hospitals after the near death-by-drowning.

Although she hadn't eaten much of her meal, she said that it was time for her to go. He tried his 'friends with benefits' strategy once more, but she just smiled and shook her head. He asked her if it was a problem with the sex. (The male ego thing again.) Another shake of the head. He pursued the guessing game for a little longer, and eventually ran out of options. Finally, in frustration he said, "Well, if you're going to go, then go." And so she did. Picked up her bag and left. He caught up with her in the street and only just managed to stop himself from pleading with her. He tried to take her in his arms, but she backed off. "Call me," he said, to her retreating back, but she never did. That was the last time he ever saw her.

It took a while to get her out from under his skin. He was angry and felt humiliated. In the past, when it came to relationships, if there was any terminating to be done, he was almost invariably the terminator.

For the sake of his bruised ego, he later decided she had left, not out of concern that the relationship wouldn't work, but out of fear that it might. Past traumas had left a pathological aversion to attachment. He thought of the nineteen-year-old boy, and felt sorry for him. It was always harder on the young.

*

A couple of days after I had interviewed him, I got an email from Jack apologizing for the fact that he'd spent too much time on the story of Jade, and not on the questions I'd wanted to ask. I gave the same response to him as to other informants: It's their story, rather than my questions, that counts. From a flurry of email exchanges, it's clear that Jack is still smarting. His male pride has been badly dented, and he persists in his belief that Jade wriggled out of the relationship because of commitment phobia. If he tells himself often enough, he may just come to believe it. His ego couldn't cope with the more likely truth that she just wasn't interested.

There are always alternative explanations. He was her first expatriate relationship. She may have decided, having sniffed the air, that she didn't like the smell. She may have had deeper, darker stories than the one she had shared and was afraid of being unmasked. She may have decided to pick off the male species one-by-one as revenge for what had been done to her. Or it may simply have been the fact that she is one of the new breed of Hong Kong women: independent, confident, and happily single. She wasn't afraid of the relationship; it was simply excess to her requirements.

8.

The ruins of the day

All happy families resemble one another, each unhappy family is unhappy in its own way. (Leo Tolstoy)

Repulse Bay is a superior residential enclave in the Southern District of Hong Kong Island populated by superior people. It isn't necessary to live there to remind yourself that you're loaded, you'll already know that, but it's a convenient way of reminding others. Don't even think of purchasing a property there unless you're prepared to fork out USD5,000 per square foot for your chosen abode. In the 1990s I knew the manager of an Australian company that made massive amounts of money by digging up bits of Australia and shipping it to China to be turned into steel. He had an apartment overlooking the beach at Repulse Bay. It was a splendid apartment, and so it ought to have been, with an annual rental that was the equivalent of one entire shipload of Australian ore. I'm told that the beach, like the rest of Repulse Bay, is entirely artificial, the pristine sand having been shipped, so it's said, from elsewhere – Australia perhaps? The sand squeaks between the toes with an Aussie accent, but it doesn't seem quite white enough to be the real thing.

Surprisingly, there is controversy about the name. No-one can assert with any certainty how, when, or why it got its name. My favourite version is that in the 1800s it was used as a base by pirates who were eventually repulsed by the British navy. Whatever its origin, the irony of the name is almost certainly lost on those it attracts.

Repulse Bay is much favoured by expats who have chosen not to acknowledge that they have taken the drastic step of leaving their native soil. Once settled into a high-level, luxury flat, you need never leave the place. Your husband Max leaves early for his office in Central. Shortly afterwards, the school bus picks up your fifteen-year-old daughter, Melody. You then have the day to yourself. How delicious it is to have more space than you know what to do with: here alone with the invisible domestic helpers getting on with their invisible domestic helping. You emerge from your bedroom and take coffee and juice on the balcony. The view stretches from the beach to somewhere just short of eternity. Even the filthy Mainland air is held at bay by the comforting mountain range at your back. Silently, you congratulate yourself for your social conscience, which impels you to do good things for others from time to time and prevents you from too ostentatious a display of privilege and wealth.

You plan your day. Downstairs for a swim, then a tennis lesson with the resident coach who has the knack of enabling you to be a better player than secretly you know yourself to be. Then it will be hair and nails before lunch at The Verandah with Virginia and Heather. The Verandah is still reassuringly White, although it's less so than it used to be.

In the afternoon you collect one of the invisible helpers and head to the supermarket. Here, you can find most of the ingredients you need for the evening meal: Norwegian salmon, French duck breast, even the avocados are edible, just like you can get at home – and, goodness, just look at the size of the globe artichokes from Italy. The day glides by, your chores are done, and you haven't even had to cross the road. Back in the apartment, it's too early for a sundowner, but you have one anyway.

Your daughter Melody sees Repulse Bay in a different light. You barely notice as she returns from school and slips into her room. You are fully occupied instructing the helpers and their friend, on loan for the evening, on arrangements for your dinner party. For the third time in as many weeks you remind her that the corkscrew is unnecessary when opening the Veuve – you'll save the Krug for the guests. Pleased with your patience in the face of Filipina obduracy, you turn your attention to the menu.

Melody, emerging from her room, has a temporary outbreak of charm brought on by the arrival of the guests and then goes out. Homework with school friend Tilly, was it? Yet another rehearsal for the school drama night? Well, you've no time to bother now – your guests require your undivided attention. It's most vexatious that Max has been detained at the office on this of all evenings but, being the trooper you are, you refuse to let your annoyance show.

By the time you have refilled your guests' glasses (a task too delicate to be entrusted to the invisible ones in the kitchen), your daughter has crossed the road and is on the beach. Sandals in hand, she makes her way to the southern end. Dusk has turned to night, but she spots her friends in their usual spot. And, yes, Jamie is there as he promised he would be.

As your guests lick their lips at the sight of seared duck breast, done bleu, accompanied by slow-braised red cabbage and onion marmalade, your daughter is salivating over Jamie as he generously allows her to explore body parts to which she has only recently been introduced. The weed that Jamie's friend Beau has passed around is stronger than the usual stuff, and the Jim Beam and Coke is more spirit than soft drink. So much so that she has to cease salivating over Jamie's body to regurgitate the Jim Beam and Coke into the sand. Mercifully, she won't have any memory of this embarrassing incident, because shortly after throwing up, she passes out.

Unfortunately, you are not similarly saved. Jamie and his friends make an anonymous call to the police and then abandon Melody prior to their arrival. The police find the girl wandering along the beach in an advanced state of stupefaction and shake her address out of her. Then they deposit her on your doorstep, where she throws up again as your guests are leaving. Minutes later, your husband Max arrives home full of apologies and smelling of guilt.

Your evening has turned from success to disaster in minutes. Having deposited Melody on her bed to be dealt with tomorrow, you search for Max, deciding that the showdown with him won't wait.

9.

Cosi fan tutte

Here's all you have to know about men and women: women are crazy, men are stupid. And the main reason women are crazy is that men are stupid. (George Carlin)

The conversation with Lucia begins, as many do, with a bit of verbal sparring: her early life, the events that brought her to Hong Kong, trials, tribulations and frustrations. She is focused on her story. I wait patiently for *the* story. Not all conversations have one. Many of them meander from one trivial topic to the next before petering out. Sometimes my informants are being deliberately evasive. Yes, they have a story, but for any number of reasons – fear of exposure, shame, or lack of trust in my guarantees of confidentiality – they will not give it up. Often, they simply have nothing interesting to say, and the conversation collapses under its own boring weight. But then, Lucia gives it up. "All I wanted was what all women want," she says. An unseen hand reaches into the back of my memory and drags out the 'graveyard' metaphor.

Lucia is Italian – no surprises there. Originally from a small town outside of Genoa, she escaped to Rome once she had finished school. She was smart. She possessed striking features. Even in a city of stunning women, she stood out. She went to Rome with a desire to study art, but had no plan, and like numerous beautiful young Italian women with a vague dream but no strategy for achieving it, she ended up working for Alitalia, pushing food and drink trolleys up and down aircraft aisles.

When she joined Alitalia, she consoled herself with the thought that at least she'd get to see the world. What she got to see was the inside of airport terminals, shuttle buses and hotel rooms. More often than not, she woke up unsure of exactly where in the world she was. When, on visits home, her cousins envied her for her glamorous lifestyle she refrained from telling them what it was really like: living out of a suitcase, drunk and disruptive passengers, and the bruises you got from manhandling food and drink trolleys in turbulent skies.

"I was having the trip from hell," she says. "Then, two hours into the flight, I got asked to work the first class cabin, and there he was." He was attractive, English, and wealthy (an assumption she made from the cut of his clothes and the fact that he occupied seat 2A). His name was Charles, another indication of his station in life. Apart from that, there was nothing about him to dislike, so she accepted his invitation to dinner as they were on the final approach into Hong Kong. Two days later, having missed the onward flight to Manila, she woke up with a hangover you could photograph. Three years later, she woke up to the fact that she had two adorable children and a husband she despised.

Lucia smokes thin, filtered cigarettes. She says they're low in tar. The events of the last few years have aged her, but the remnants of her beauty linger on: the fine facial structure, the luminous eyes and full lips. She wears a perfectly tailored suit, but then she would: she's Italian, and for years she was married to the wealthy Englishman.

The smoking poses a problem. For the interviews, we need somewhere that's quiet, discreet, and allows smoking. Hong Kong is unrelentingly noisy but increasingly smoke-free. She suggests a café in Sheung Wan that has an outdoor terrace. It's in a cul-de-sac, and at mid-morning should be relatively quiet. And it is, until a pair of jackhammers set up a duet in an adjoining street.

I want to know more about the breakdown of her marriage, an event Lucia has touched upon a couple of times. What was it that had brought a sudden end to what on the surface appeared to be a stable, archetypical, expat family: a wealthy, executive husband, a beautiful wife, and two talented young sons.

She only smokes half of her cigarette before stubbing it out and lighting another. Her espresso sits untouched on the table. Then she starts to speak. Her syntax and choice of words are flawless. Only the Italian accent betrays the fact that she is not a native speaker of English.

*

Of course, it was a great shock. We were taking a shower, when he appeared in the bathroom. He seemed to have come from nowhere. Peter was soaping my back when his face went pale and he dropped the soap. I thought he was having a stroke or something. I pushed the hair back from my face, and turned to see what Peter was looking at, and there he was, just leaning against the – how do you say? – the doorjamb. Peter was saying something, but I had no idea what the words meant. All I could do was look at him. My heart was beating like crazy and I was thinking: "this isn't happening". But, of course, it was. I thought he would go berserk, but he didn't seem to be angry. He had this smug look on his face, like: "Oh, I've caught you at last." He certainly wasn't looking like an outraged husband. At that moment, Peter didn't have a clue who he was. He was just an intruder. Peter scrambled out of the bath towards him, slipped on the wet tiles and ended up sprawling on the floor. Before he could get to his feet, Charles gave me this smug look, there is no other way to say it, and turned and walked out of the apartment.

I met Peter on a flight back from Italy. My mother had been diagnosed with leukaemia a couple of years before, and I was flying back to see her every few months. Each time I saw her she was a little weaker. The transfusions that kept her going were becoming less and less effective, but they said there was nothing more they could do. She was much too old to have a bone marrow transplant, which was the only other option. At the end of this trip, when I said goodbye to my mother, I knew that it was the last time that I would see her. Thankfully, my brother had moved back to Genoa from Rome to look after her.

When I got to the airport, I started crying. This surprised me as much as it did the check-in clerk. She was very nice. She asked me what the matter was, and when I told her, she got me an upgrade. Charles would never pay for me to fly business class. The days when he would buy me expensive gifts had long gone. Now, his disposable income was for his mistresses. He flew up front all the time, of course, but he said I didn't need to because I didn't work. He didn't consider that raising children was work. Not when you had a live-in helper. If I wanted to fly business, I had to use my miles. I didn't really care one way or another, but on this flight, when I was feeling that the last remaining decent part of my life was crumbling away, it was nice to have some space, and to be offered a glass of champagne.

I can't remember how we got talking. Usually, I just put in earplugs, and read a magazine. No-one bothers me then. Sometimes I watch a movie. I pass the flight in my own little bubble.

I noticed him when we boarded. I'd been seated in the centre row of the section, and he was in the seat next to me. He was drinking champagne and sending text messages, along with just about everyone else in business class. I stowed my bag, was offered a glass of champagne, which I accepted, and opened my magazine. I turned the pages, my eyes sliding over the print and the glossy advertisements. I thought about my mother, and the aching love she had for my brother and me, and how, as soon as we could, had both run as far and as fast as we could away from that love. And now I was about to lose something I never knew I needed. I drank my champagne faster than was wise. It made me feel sad and sorry for myself. Truly, to understand the Italian family, you have to have been born into one.

As soon as my glass was empty, he leaned across, waved his own empty glass at me and asked me if I'd like a refill. Not being much of a drinker, I hesitated. Often when I'm flying, I don't drink at all – maybe a glass of wine or two with the meal service, that's about it. But I'd been thinking about my mother and this and that and, well, anyway, I smiled at him and nodded. He took my glass and handed it, along with his own, to a passing flight attendant and requested a refill. When the drinks came, he clinked my glass and said, "Cheers." At first, I thought he was British, but there was something about his accent that wasn't quite right.

So I was on my second drink, and we hadn't even taken off. There was some kind of delay – the usual thing – and the flight attendant kept topping up our glasses. I felt a bit uncomfortable. I had my magazine in my lap, but I thought it would be rude to read. But he made it easy. There were no stupid pick-up lines. It must have been obvious to him that I was in an emotional state and that I'd been crying, but he didn't ask me any personal questions. I can't really remember what we talked about now. It wasn't so much what he said, but how he said it, how he was. You can know some people for a lifetime and never get close, never feel that you will ever know what is in their head or their heart. I felt that way about my sister-in-law. But, before I'd finished my second glass of champagne, I felt very comfortable with Peter. After our third glass, and the wine we shared during the meal service, I felt that we could be friends. It was partly the alcohol, of course, but it was more than that.

I hadn't been looking forward to the flight at all, but it passed quickly. We talked through the meal service. Well, actually, he did most of the talking. That's the way most men are. But he wasn't like most men, who can turn any topic into a story about themselves. He didn't talk about himself. In fact, I later realized that I knew almost nothing about him. At some point after the meal service, he suggested that we watch a movie together. It wasn't one of the recent releases, but one that the airline had stored in its 'arthouse cinema' section. Afterwards, he asked a flight attendant to bring us coffee, brandy and water, and we talked about the film. He talked like a film critic, explaining things I hadn't even noticed, and about how and why the director had structured the story in a certain way and about the clever camera angles. I sometimes wonder how you can enjoy a film when all the time you're taking note of the cleverness of the director. When I was younger, I loved going to the movies, but in Hong Kong it can be a very frustrating and annoying experience. The locals talk non-stop, either to each other or on their mobile phone. So, anyway, because of Peter's company, I didn't spend the flight dwelling on my mother and getting more and more depressed.

Well, that's how it started. You want to know why it developed? I wanted what all women want. Appreciation. Respect. After the years of marriage, love might have been too much to expect, but not affection. I had earned the right to affection, but I didn't even get that. What I craved most was companionship. It had come to the point where I never felt so alone as when I was with Charles. I think for him, like most men, love is a means to get sex. For women, sex is a means to get love. At the end of the flight, Peter gave me his card, and asked me to give him a call. I thought about it once or twice, but I never did, because I knew where that would lead. Despite the difficulties between Charles and me, I wasn't interested in having an affair. Affairs were something that other people had. At that point, I was prepared to put up with my loneliness and my unhappy marriage for the sake of my children.

In the beginning, my relationship with Charles was wonderful. He had rescued me from a job that I had come to dislike. In Hong Kong I could start a new life – reinvent myself, like many expats do. It's a city for reinvention. No-one knew about my background and history, and no one cared.

Charles had a small apartment in a fashionable complex in Mid-Levels. Because he travelled a lot, he didn't need anything bigger, and it was certainly big enough for the both of us. But to begin with, there was something impersonal about it. It was more like a luxury hotel suite than an apartment. He gave me whatever money I needed, and soon gave me a second credit card, linked to his. I took on the job of giving the apartment a more human touch. The apartment complex had a shuttle bus service. I would sleep until mid-morning, then get ready and take the shuttle bus down to Central to have lunch and shop. He didn't seem to mind too much about the things that I bought, although one day I bought a piece of pottery. It was an expensive piece by a famous Thai potter from Chiang Mai. He was away on a trip at the time. When he came back from the trip and noticed the piece of pottery – well, it was quite large, so he could hardly ignore it – he was annoyed. It was clear that he didn't like it, and he wasn't impressed with the price I had paid. "What's it for?" he asked. "It isn't for anything," I said. It was the first time he had expressed displeasure at my spending. After that he started checking the Visa card statements and putting interrogation marks next to questionable items. He never said anything – he didn't have to.

It wasn't long before I grew bored with the lifestyle. I got to know people. That wasn't difficult in Hong Kong. But the relationships were just on the surface, you know? People would come and go. "Where are the Smiths or the Joneses?" "Oh, they went back to Canada last month." There was one person I got to know quite well, a Welsh woman, wife of a judge. They'd been here forever. Every week she would invite me to the Helena May to join her mahjong group. The Helena May is a funny, old-fashioned ladies' club – very colonial. But I liked it.

At first, Charles took me to receptions and dinners organized by his office, but that happened less and less frequently as time passed. That didn't bother me too much. These events were even more boring than wandering around the malls and food halls. Charles and his colleagues thought of themselves as the new masters of the universe, but once they were drunk, they became as idiotic as anyone else. I found the whole lifestyle of the expat community to be basically superficial.

In the beginning, the fact that I was existing on a tourist visa wasn't a problem. For the first year, we would go to Phuket or Cebu for the weekend, and my visa would be automatically renewed; and I went back to Italy twice to visit my mother. I was lucky that Charles was happy to give me the money to travel. The alternative would be to do what the backpackers have to do – take the tedious trip to Macau every three months. The main problem was the fact that I didn't have an ID card. Without a card there were many, many things you couldn't do. You couldn't open a bank account or go to the hospital. You couldn't get a driving licence – not that I wanted one. So after a year, I put it to Charles. Marriage was the only option. He was reluctant at first. At the time, I wasn't sure why, but then he reluctantly agreed. We had a civil ceremony, and the only witnesses were a couple of his friends. To be honest, the marriage ceremony in itself wasn't such a big deal. It was love that I wanted, not an expensive wedding.

As a father, Charles was largely absent. His attitude was one of distant affection. He acted more like an uncle than a father. Of course, he was what you'd call an older father, but there are hundreds of expat males in Hong Kong who enter into fatherhood in their 50s or even later. Virtually all of them are married to younger Asian women, and the family they start is often a second one. It's a bit of a cliché, isn't it?

When I was expecting our first child, we moved to a larger apartment and acquired a live-in domestic helper. I had the second child quickly after the first – there was only twelve months between them. And so Charles arranged for a second helper. This one was mainly responsible for the children. The two helpers had to share the same room, which was located off the kitchen. With the two of them, I had very little to do. Charles had been promoted and was away even more than he had been in the past. And when he was in Hong Kong, he would leave home early and come home late after the kids were asleep. My life had moved in a direction that was far away from what I had imagined.

And you know what? There was nothing unusual in this. I would see it happening all of the time. The expat family arrives here and their life is transformed. The first thing is that their salary is going to triple. Then there are all the additional bonuses of cars, luxury apartments, live-in domestic helpers and all that. These people, who would only be on an average salary in their own country, become rich. However, the money comes at a cost. The husband literally belongs to the company. His time, his life, everything is owned by the company. This goes for all employees – directors, managers, all of them. They're going to work their arses off, and they're not going to do forty hours a week like in Europe. Everyone here works a minimum of sixty hours a week. Here, sixty hours is nothing – really a minimum.

And so it was with us. After Charles was made a director, he'd come home exhausted. He became even more obsessed with making money and talked about retiring early to a place he had bought in France. But I couldn't see that happening. Frustrations began to grow, because there was no relationship, just work, work, work. I did the usual things to fill in time: played tennis, mahjong occasionally, book club once a month. Some of my women acquaintances joined a network that did charitable work. Personally, I never got involved in those networks. I just couldn't do it. I find them so artificial.

So you have all of that going on, and then you have all these pretty, young Asian girls who have a very, very different philosophy of relationships. And for a European male, it's unexpected. It's amazing! And it takes the expat men by surprise. These women have absolutely no sense of guilt or shame. Their attitude is: "He's rich, and that's what I am interested in." I've been out with these Asian girls and listened to their conversations. They compete with each other boasting about how much they sucked out of the guy each week. When I went to Pure Yoga I used to eavesdrop on them showing off. "Just look at my new Louis Vuitton." "Huh, that's nothing, last week he bought me a Hermes." They're basically prostituting themselves – giving the guy sex and doing it for the money.

I never thought that Charles would fall for it, so it came as a shock when I discovered that he was having an affair. He called me up one day and asked if I could come by his office to co-sign his tax return. He was doing some kind of income splitting to reduce his tax or something. I didn't understand it, and I didn't care. Anyway, I was in Central, so I went to his office. He was in a meeting, but his assistant said that he had left the form on his desk for me. I went to his office, signed the form, and then, I don't know what made me do it, but I opened the drawer of his desk. It was just one of those things you do on a whim. Inside was a packet of Viagra and some condoms. I should have just shut the drawer and left, but instead, I took them out and left them sitting on the tax return that I'd just signed.

He came home early that night and was in a cold rage. How dare I do that! What was I thinking? Anyone might have seen them. How dare I go through his drawers? etc. etc. He was trying to make out that I was the one who was in the wrong. I stayed calm. I just said, "Who is she?" He refused to answer, just stormed out of the apartment. Later, I found out that she was one of the middle managers in his office, not that it really mattered who it was. I don't know if she was the first, but she certainly wasn't the last.

I assumed he'd gone out to meet the woman, and that he wouldn't be back that night, so I went to bed. But at around two o'clock in the morning I heard the front door open and close. I lay awake, listening to his movements. He was stumbling about. He poured himself a scotch, even though it was clear that he'd been drinking. Then, after a while, he came into the bedroom. I pretended to be asleep, but he shook me hard and started grabbing at my breasts. It had been some time since we'd had sex, and now I knew why. It was also a long time since I'd got any pleasure out of it. He was only interested if he'd been drinking. And to be honest, he wasn't doing it for the sex, he was doing it for the power and control. If I was dry, which was most of the time, he'd spit on his hand and swipe me down there – truly disgusting. And he would have these fantasies and talk to me like I was a prostitute. That seemed to excite him.

On this of all nights I wasn't going to have any of that. I got out of bed and went to the guest room. He tried to follow me, but I locked myself in and he was too drunk to figure out how to open the door. He stumbled around some more, talking to himself, had some more scotch, and then there was silence.

The following day, I stayed in the room for most of the morning. The helper – we were down to one by this stage – had got the boys off to school. When I finally got up at around eleven o'clock, the helper told me that Charles had taken his travel pack, and that he wouldn't be back until the end of the week. That was a great relief because it gave me some time to breathe.

That day, I decided to give myself a treat. I went to the Four Seasons and had lunch at Lung King Heen. Like all Chinese restaurants, you're meant to share, and so when I was seated, the waiter asked me if I was expecting anyone else. I said no, I was dining alone. I ordered a bottle of vintage Krug and six of the most expensive items on the menu. The waiter tried to suggest that perhaps I had over-ordered, but I ignored him. It cost a fortune, but I didn't care. I had two glasses of champagne, took a small spoonful of food from each dish and left the rest. Then I went to the spa and had an afternoon of pure pampering. Afterwards, I was crossing the lobby, about to take a taxi home, when I heard someone call my name. I turned around, and it was Peter. Although I'd thought of him once or twice since our one and only meeting on the flight from Rome, I wasn't sure that I'd have recognized him if I bumped into him, but I did. Instantly. It was quite a coincidence, coming on that day of all days. Some of my friends don't believe in coincidences. Do you?

Peter seemed genuinely happy to see me. I was flattered that he remembered me. There was a slightly awkward moment when he took my hand and touched it to his lips. It seemed like an old-fashioned way of greeting, but we were hardly intimate enough to kiss or even hug, not in the lobby of the Four Seasons.

"I thought you might have called me," he said. "But I understand." I wasn't sure what it was that he understood. I told him that I had lost his card – a lie, but he accepted it. He produced another card, and gave it to me. Then he said, "I'm just rushing to meet a client, but I'd really love to catch up with you. Can we meet? How about lunch tomorrow?" When I hesitated, he said, "Or any time."

"No, tomorrow is fine," I heard myself saying.

"Wonderful," he said. "Let's meet at noon in the lobby of the Mandarin Oriental. I'll book somewhere decent."

That turned out to be something of an understatement. When I turned up, ten minutes late, he said, "I was afraid that you were going to stand me up." Then he guided me to the elevator, which we took to the top floor of the hotel, where their fancy French restaurant Pierre was located.

The food, the wine and the service were as you would expect, but it was the company that I treasured most. Peter was very easy and very natural to be with, just like he had been on the plane – a perfect gentleman. We talked about different things – the conversation just drifted from one thing to another. When I asked him what he did, he was rather vague – some kind of art dealer and collector, bringing European work to Asia, and Asian art to Europe. He also had a small art collection of his own. He mentioned a couple of modern German artists whom I'd never heard of. He dealt in emerging rather than the established artists whose work was overpriced.

The afternoon passed quickly. I appreciated that he didn't ask me personal questions, which might have been awkward. Later, I realized that he had revealed very little about himself. I didn't mind. In Hong Kong you get used to that. He was just very comfortable to be with, and didn't put a foot wrong. After the meal, we went down to the café above the lobby area for more coffee. Then I noticed the time and remembered I had an appointment at the school with my younger son's teacher. When I gathered my things and said I had to go, he looked disappointed. He asked if he could call me, but I said that would be difficult. I would call him. "Please don't keep me waiting too long this time," he said.

To be honest, I was in two minds about calling him. I was nervous, knowing where things could lead. "Nothing has happened," I told myself. "Nothing has to happen." Part of me wanted something to happen, but another part of me didn't. I loved my sons, and I was used to the comforts of a wealthy expat lifestyle. My brother came and visited once, and thought I was so lucky. We had the fancy apartment and the fancy cars and the live-in maid. I didn't have to work. He was envious, but there were aspects of my lifestyle that he had no idea about – the fact that the luxury apartment was a prison to me. I felt that I was suffocating.

I waited until the middle of the week before calling him. He was pleased to hear from me, and invited me to the opening of an exhibition at a gallery in Soho the following evening. It was risky. Hong Kong is a small place. Someone will see you. But I had a hunger for a social life, and companionship that went deeper than my luncheons and mahjong companions. "Nothing had to happen," I said to myself. But in my secret self, I knew the chances were good that something would.

And so I went to the exhibition. It was in one of those small galleries in Hollywood Road. You wonder how they manage to stay in business. Of course many of them don't. Peter was already there, a glass of wine in hand, chatting to a tall, skinny Englishman who kept sniffing and wiping his nose with the back of his hand and who turned out to be the manager of the gallery. A waiter came by with a tray holding glasses of wine. I took one, went up to Peter and was introduced to the manager, whose name I immediately forgot.

The artist was a young German guy who had come out for the exhibition opening. He looked to be no more than in his late 20s, with a sweet face, hair to his collar and wire rimmed glasses. Peter had already purchased two of his pieces for a client, a private banker who wanted them for his boardroom. I liked the paintings. They were abstracts done in a range of pastel tones. The artist came across to greet Peter and to thank him for his purchases. He was pleasant and very modest about his work, not that he had anything to be modest about. As we were chatting, a woman I vaguely knew came in to the gallery. She was the wife of one of Charles' colleagues. She recognized me and gave me one of those distant smiles that says, "You're not significant enough for me to remember your name, but I know who you are." Feeling uncomfortable, I moved away from Peter on the pretence of getting another glass of wine. Then, I did a circuit of the gallery, appearing to inspect the paintings. When the waiter passed me, I exchanged my empty glass for a full one, my third in a little under twenty minutes. It crossed my mind that when I was with Peter I drank more than I was accustomed to. Agreeing to Peter's invitation had been a mistake. The night before, it had seemed like a good idea, a bit of an adventure, an opportunity to meet new people. I would never have agreed to meet him if Charles had been in town. It occurred to me that I was frightened of Charles. It wasn't fear that he might hurt me physically. He held me captive with his mind, and of course he had total control over me financially.

When Peter came over to me, smiling, but with a faintly puzzled look on his face, I told him that I had to go. Disappointment was written all over his face. He wanted to know what was wrong, but I didn't know what to say. I was confused and had a feeling of things closing in, that my centre of gravity had shifted. I didn't finish my wine, but put the glass on a table next to some exhibition catalogues and left.

He caught up with me before I reached the end of the block, took me by the arm and steered me into a taxi. He gave the driver directions in fluent Cantonese, and we drove to an apartment block in Mid-Levels. The apartment was large and light. It had recently been renovated, and the smaller bedrooms had been opened up into the living area. He didn't waste any time, but took me into the main bedroom where, without any preliminaries, we had sex. I didn't object or resist. It happened so quickly, and there was a sense of inevitability about it. Afterwards, I remembered the mantra I'd repeated, "It doesn't have to happen." But of course, it did.

I had my first serious boyfriend when I was in my final year in high school. He was at university and came from a wealthy Genoese family. A couple of days a week, he would pick me up after school and take me to his small apartment for an hour or two. At the time, I thought I was in love, as you do. One afternoon, his father was waiting to pick me up. He said his son had been involved in an accident. He wasn't badly injured, but was in the hospital. The father said that he would drive me home, but instead, he drove me out into the countryside and raped me. At that time in my life, I was unable to say no, even though it felt wrong. With Peter, it wasn't rape, and it also felt right. I had no guilt, just a faint uneasiness. What surprised me was how starved I was for tenderness and affection and that's what I got from Peter.

I didn't think of it as an affair, which of course it was. The word 'affair' had a dirty sound to it. As I said, it was what other people had. Like the woman from the Helena May, who had become a good friend. She once told me she had had an affair that ended badly and that hurt her deeply. Her husband took her back, but things were never the same between them. "You can't put the toothpaste back in the tube," she said to me. The thing is, in Hong Kong it's very easy. My friend and the guy she was having the affair with both lived in Mid-Levels. He would call in on her after work and be home in time for dinner with his wife and kids – and the wife would never know. Sometimes they would meet up in his lunch break. Too easy, really. That would never happen to me. I would be careful. I would have my family and my lover.

I saw Peter every day for the rest of the week, and then when Charles came back from his trip, I saw him whenever I could – usually once a week. I wanted to see him more often, but that would have been careless. Once a week was easy. The kids were at school during the day, and Charles was either at work or on one of his business trips. Interestingly, after that night when we had the fight, he never attempted to touch me again. I assumed that he was getting what he wanted from the woman in his office.

I made it hard on myself by getting more involved with Peter than I ever intended to do. I'm not sure if I was really in love with him or in love with the idea of being in love. I wanted to spend nights with him, to lie in the dark and be held. One time, my husband was on a business trip and I went over for dinner. We had some wine, and afterwards we went to bed. I fell asleep and was woken up by my helper calling me on my mobile phone. It was two o'clock in the morning. The helper wanted to know where I was. My younger son had woken up vomiting. He had a fever and was calling for me. The helper would have known what was going on, they always do. But as my friends say, it doesn't matter what they think: they're not paid to think.

*

It was a careless mistake that brought about Lucia's downfall; one mistake, that is, in addition to the first and fundamental one of allowing hands other than her husband's to find their way under the skirt of her tailored suit. Once their relationship had developed, Peter had given her a key to his apartment. She had slipped this onto her key-ring along with the numerous other keys she kept, thinking that Charles was too self-absorbed to notice something so inconsequential. He not only noticed it, but managed to have it copied.

He pretended to be outraged because it gave him the high moral ground: never mind his own affairs. But she never forgot the 'gotcha' look in his eyes that night as Peter sprawled on the tiles and she held her arms across her breasts. Methodically, and mindful of the adage that revenge is a dish best served cold, he took everything from her. The boys were banished to Europe. Then she was banished from the apartment. Peter, aware that the fun was over, also disappeared. That hurt her most of all. And in the end, all she was left with was her tailored suits.

10.

TOILET SEAT RULE

There are two circumstances that lead to arrogance: one is when you're wrong and you can't face it; the other is when you're right and nobody else can face it. (Criss Jami)

She was the first-born of three sisters. "The good thing about growing up in a house dominated by women was that we could ignore the toilet seat rule."

"What rule is that?" he asked.

"The rule that the toilet seat must be raised when the toilet isn't in use," she replied. "In our house, the toilet seat was always down."

"But that's the rule. The toilet seat must always be down."

She shook her head. "You're wrong there. The seat must always be raised when the toilet isn't in use. You go into anyone's place and what do you find? The toilet seat is raised."

"Not in my place," he said. "The toilet seat is always down. Just like we were taught when we were kids."

"So, I've noticed," she said. "Which is why I mentioned it."

"Oh, I see, so you're giving me a lecture on etiquette? And I thought that you were just making one of your idle observations."

Later, as he sat in his favourite bar fulminating over a second gin and tonic (she never tolerated alcohol in her place), he wondered at how such a flaming row could have been sparked by something as trivial as the positioning of a toilet seat. These days, every idle comment on his part resulted in friction. She had been riled by his comment that if her rule were true, it was a sad reflection of the patriarchal nature of her culture where even the positioning of the toilet seat was dictated by the male anatomy. Then she had become inflamed by the remark that in his culture lowering the toilet seat was common sense. It's a matter of hygiene, he had said. Another racist reflection on her culture, she had replied. It was so typical, he thought, as he entertained the notion of a third gin and tonic. The illogicality of the female brain; impervious to such a simple scientific fact. Stubbornly and perversely unevolved. Add that to a culture where tradition trumped common sense and where did it get you? As the question was purely rhetorical, the need to provide an answer was unnecessary, which was just as well. Yes, he thought, on reflection, one for the road was an excellent idea.

11.

ONLY IN HONG KONG

What makes expat life so addictive is that every boring or mundane activity you experience at home is, when you move to a foreign country, suddenly transformed into an exciting adventure. When abroad, boredom, routine and 'normal' cease to exist. And all that's left is the thrill and challenge of uncertainty. (Reannon Muth)

Finding somewhere relatively quiet to record the interviews is becoming a problem. Noise follows me, and it isn't until a friend suggests the simple expedient of Skype that the problem is partially solved. (It only works with those trusted individuals with whom you have established a reasonably intimate face-to-face relationship.) Transcribing sound files against a backdrop of jackhammers (Hong Kong's 'national anthem') tearing into the relatively old to make way for the spanking new, the snarl of traffic, the clash of plates in a dim sum restaurant, or the laughter of drinkers, all present unwelcome interruptions to the interviews. I suggest we meet at four o'clock on a Wednesday afternoon at The Globe, a large, subterranean space on Graham Street and she agrees. The Globe is not normally a quiet place, but I figure that at this time of day, at this time of the week, it should be. There is a secluded 'library' area off the main bar area where I've recorded interviews in the past for other projects.

When I arrive, the library is occupied by a young couple who seem to be trying unsuccessfully to iron out the kinks in their relationship over a bottle of wine, so I retreat to the dining area at the rear of the bar. As

I had hoped, the place is quiet. Dee arrives and we begin the interview. Two minutes into the interview, the bar staff start setting the tables for the evening meal service. The bang and clatter of plates is going to have a serious impact on my ability to transcribe the interview.

"This isn't going to work," I say, switching off my recorder.

"Some other time," says Dee. "Would you like to have a drink?"

"Might as well. I'll get them."

When I return to the table with the beer, Dee says, "You know, I'm in the middle of this extraordinary situation," and she launches into a story that I just have to capture despite the noise. "I'm going to record this," I say, reaching for the recorder. It's uncanny how often the best stories emerge after the recorder has been turned off.

"OK," she says. "I didn't think you'd want this sort of stuff. So I'll tell you my story and you can record it, but you've got to change the names and everything, OK? When I tell people the story, their reaction is one of incredulity. But also putting me in a place that I don't think is really me. They have to define you." With that enigmatic statement, she begins.

*

My story started as a very banal incident, It was late and I was walking down Hollywood Road. I was a bit drunk – but that had never happened to me before – ha ha! I'm not quite sure what I was doing on Hollywood Road, it wasn't my most direct route home. I'd been drinking with work colleagues and it would have been more logical to head down the hill to Queen's Road and catch a tram home to Wan Chai. I guess that's what happens when you have one glass of champagne too many – logic goes out the window.

A band was playing in the bar and I knew two of the band members. I used to sing with them when they were with a different group. During a break in one of their sets, they came over for a chat and one of my workmates suggested that I sing something with the band. I wasn't all that keen because I hadn't sung for quite a while. The guys in the band were happy with the idea, so at the end of the night, during their last set, I got up and sang. Everyone says I'm an extrovert, so I guess that just goes to prove it. During the set, I noticed a crowd of very young people standing around the bar. They weren't exactly the types you'd typically see in this kind of bar, but then what's typical in Hong Kong?

Anyway, we had the inevitable 'one for the road', and then went our separate ways. By that time the bar had pretty-well emptied out. I found myself walking up Hollywood Road – no idea why. As I say, it wasn't my most direct way home. The young people from the bar were standing in the middle of the footpath blocking my way. Anywhere else, you'd be a bit cautious, but in Hong Kong you don't have to worry. Anyway, I stepped around them, thinking nothing of it, and was waiting to grab a cab, when this young guy came up and started chatting to me. Immediately, I was flattered, thinking, "Oh, why is this young guy talking to me?" He told me he'd been in the bar and seen me singing and thought I was terrific – which I wasn't, I can tell you. But of course, I was even more flattered by that. He asked me if I was a professional singer, and I said no, it was just a part-time interest of mine. He wanted to know what my day job was, so I told him that I worked for a graphic design firm in Wan Chai. He said that he'd just graduated from Hong Kong U in computer science and was interested in graphic design and could he have my card. Normally, I don't give my card to strangers, but he came across as just this really friendly young guy. Also, I was anxious to get home because I had a presentation to do at work the next day, so I thought, "Oh, I'll just give this young guy my card and get rid of him." People exchange cards in Hong Kong all the time, and you never hear anything more from most of them – it's just one of those rituals.

By young, I mean he was about the same age as my son. I knew nothing about him except that he was black, extremely good looking, and very sweet – although later I learned that he wasn't at all what he seemed to be. Actually, that's a considerable understatement. I knew nothing about him: not his nationality, not whether he lived in Hong Kong or was here as an exchange student.

I didn't expect to hear anything more from him, but a couple of days later, I started to get text messages from him. When I got the first message, I didn't even remember who he was, but when he mentioned my firm, I thought, "Oh, he's pretty keen to get a job." I'm not on the recruiting side, so there wasn't much I could do except to arrange an introduction. I couldn't really recommend him because I knew virtually nothing about him. Then he started asking personal questions. He asked me if I was married, and it was then that I cottoned on: he was hitting on me. I was having coffee with a friend when I got that message. I showed it to my friend, and she said, "You really want to be careful, Dee."

Then he wants to see me, and I said, "No way, I'm going off on holidays to Bali." And then he said, "Well, can I Skype you?" I said, "Nope. I'm going to be sitting on the beach drinking beer. I'm not going to be Skyping anyone." So that's what I did, went off to Bali, swam, drank, had a brief fling with a guy who sat down next to me on the beach and bought me beer. He was kind of fun. Played guitar with one of the hotel bands. As for the gorgeous black guy, I promptly forgot all about him.

After the holiday, I came back to Hong Kong refreshed and relaxed and got on with my life. And then, one day some weeks later, I'm sitting in this bar on the corner of Lockhart Road and Luard Road. I often stop off there for a drink on my way home from work because it has nice tall windows looking onto the trees on Luard Road.

So, on this afternoon, I'm sitting at the window on Lockhart Road because all of the tables on the Luard Road side are occupied. I'm looking out of the window at the office workers heading towards the MTR and trying to decide what to do with the rest of my life. Things at work aren't all that good – well, that's a euphemism for the fact that they're shit. I came to Hong Kong for a year, and that was twenty years ago – a familiar expat experience, I know. Maybe it's time to move on. I'm thinking Latin America. When I was a kid, I lived in Mexico City and Santiago, my Spanish is good, and I love the lifestyle. Recently, I'd re-established contact with a Brazilian-American friend I was at school with for a while. She manages a chain of language schools in Sao Paulo, and said she could get me a job. I knew nothing about language teaching, but she said that didn't matter – not many foreigners who teach English do. I don't speak Portuguese, but with my Spanish and French, I didn't think it would take me long to pick it up.

So all this is going through my mind, and then there he is, his gorgeous black face and those eyes of his inches away from mine. Leaning in through the window. His hair is longer, but nothing else about him has changed. "Hello you," he says to me. "Hello you, yourself," I reply. And that's when it really started.

His body was a little skinnier than I'd remembered, but apart from that, he was even more beautiful than I'd remembered – sexy, smooth, and very black. He joined me for a drink. One drink led to another, and one thing led to another. At the time, it seemed so natural, so inevitable.

So that was the beginning of the amazing experience with this guy, an experience that could only happen in Hong Kong. And what a roller-coaster of an experience it's been. It's either a divine plan by God, an atheistic lesson in how to look after yourself, or just a plain, bloody good story. There's no other way to describe it. We got pretty-much involved with each other from that point on.

At this time, he was riding high. He was working as a male model: extremely young, extremely good-looking, lots of friends, plenty of money. Not a problem in the world. For the life of me, I couldn't understand what he saw in me. Later, he took to describing me as an "angel from God". He's very much a Catholic and tends to think in that way. And I was an extremely lapsed Catholic, so that was one major point of difference between us. Then his story started to unfold, and what a story it was.

I told a couple of close friends about what was going on, and they were very skeptical. They believed that I'd absolutely been conned by the master of all con men. But, remarkably, it's one of those one-in-a-million stories which isn't a con story. To begin with, I never had any doubts about him or his story, even though I had no evidence that what he was telling me was true. Then things reached a point where I'd think, "Oh

I've been conned." Then, when I eventually saw the evidence, I knew that everything that he'd told me was true.

I think it's pretty safe to say that I've had an adventurous life. There's nothing particularly remarkable about that. This place is full of expats who have extraordinary stories to tell. When you're the daughter of a diplomat, you have an open invitation to adventure. You can embrace the adventure, or turn your back on it. I embraced it. The first years of my life were spent in Seoul. When people ask me about the various languages I speak, I say that my native language is English, but my first language is Korean. My parents have videos of my sister and me as toddlers speaking to them in Korean. I lived in Mexico City and Santiago, Chile where I learned Spanish, and in Rome where I learned Italian. I've been married, had kids, been divorced. Had my fair share of relationships. But none of my past experiences prepared me for the adventure with this guy. At times, I feel I'm being tossed about on the ocean in a small rudderless boat.

I'm an optimist. Despite some bad things that have happened, I like to look on the positive side. I've made some spectacularly bad decisions, but also some pretty good ones – sixty-forty, I'd say. My instincts tell me that my decision over the boy was a good one, although, despite what I said earlier, there were one or two times when I had my doubts. But there I was, well into middle-age, with this extremely young, extremely good-looking boy about whom, at this stage, I knew virtually nothing. He flattered me by calling me his guardian angel. It was good to be desired physically, and needed emotionally.

One Sunday, he took me to Mass and then to lunch at an expensive restaurant in Central. At that stage he still had money from his modelling work. He ordered a bottle of French champagne and way more food than was necessary: Peking duck and a whole pile of dim sum dishes such as steamed shrimp dumplings, pork buns, spicy Shanghai dumplings. He hardly ate a thing – just picked and poked here and there. I ate more than I should have, but by the time we were done, there was still plenty of food on the table.

So there we were – a gweipor past her prime and a gorgeous young black guy, but no-one batted an eyelid. This is the fashionable end of town and our fellow diners were far too important to notice us. At the end of the meal, he left a larger tip than necessary, just to show he could.

Then suddenly his luck ran out. The modelling work dried up and his friends disappeared. He was never much of an eater, but now he hardly ate at all. He lost weight, which he couldn't afford to do. He started letting me in to some of his secrets. It's been an unfolding story. I got to see little bits of it, and finally I got to know the whole story.

The first surprise was that he had a son by a former girlfriend. Then, he let me in on the big surprise. His father died in mysterious circumstances and left this huge, huge fortune. He came from a large family – mother, three sisters, and a whole lot of relatives. Anyway, on his twenty-fifth birthday, it turned out that all of his father's money had been left to him. He was the only son, so his father left him the inheritance. And he's the one charged with looking after his family. The problem is that the money can't be found. His father hid it in various bank accounts in different parts of the world, and he's been trying to track it down ever since. I met him and started my relationship with him just after he turned twenty-five, which shows just how wicked I am! That was over four years ago. I have to say that the last four years have been emotionally turbulent – my worst nightmare, my hell, my heaven. Everything!

Here he is with this massive inheritance, but until he can get hold of it, he's totally broke. So, I did something pretty extraordinary which nobody can believe, least of all my parents and my kids. I was telling one of my friends the story, and she said, "So he sucked money out of you," and I said, "Of course he did." My family and friends – well, the ones I told – said the guy was a conman. It was obvious. And to be honest, I have to say that there were times that I had my doubts.

It happened like this: I hadn't seen him for over a week, and then he called me one night and said he needed to see me. "Sure," I said, "come round." But he preferred to meet in a bar and suggested a place that is usually pretty quiet. This time there was no champagne. We drank Diet

Coke and lemon. He didn't say anything for about three minutes, just stared at the wall behind my head, and then he spoke. "I am in terrible trouble," he said. "I don't know what to do."

"What kind of trouble?"

He didn't answer the question directly, but said, "Do you think it would be possible to lend me some money?"

I guess I kind of knew this was coming. "All you have to do is ask," I said. I asked him how much he needed and he said "A hundred thousand dollars – Hong Kong dollars."

For many people in Hong Kong, that's nothing – peanuts. But for me it was a lot and I told him so.

"I know," he said.

I finished my Coke while I thought about it, and then I said, "All right, I'll arrange it tomorrow." Later, when a friend asked me why I did it, I said, "It's pretty simple, really. I did it because he asked me." He told me he'd pay me back and more when he got his inheritance, but to be honest, I wasn't thinking about that.

Then I got to know his mother and all his siblings, and they confirmed his story. Well, I guess they would, wouldn't they? I never got to meet his mother face-to-face. It was through phone calls and Skype. The irony is, that even though I was the one giving him money, his mother was very skeptical about me at first. His sisters too – they were all very skeptical. They thought I was a fortune hunter who was out to get his money, that I wanted to marry this young guy so that I could get my hands on the family fortune, even though none of them had a clue where the fortune was.

I don't know how his father amassed this fortune. Obviously, it wasn't legally acquired. And it's pretty clear that he was murdered. So that was another concern I had. If I got mixed up with the family, I could be putting myself at risk, not just financially, but physically as well.

I got to know more about the details of his life. Originally, the family had come from the Caribbean, but had moved to the States when he was a small boy. His father spent most of his time away on business. Although he adored his mother, she had no control over him. He ran wild and was constantly in trouble with the police. His older sister had married a Chinese man and moved to Hong Kong, and it was eventually decided that he should go and live with her. That was how he came to be in Hong Kong. He finished school here and then went to the University of Hong Kong.

The next thing that happens is his mother gets a terminal illness. It happened quite suddenly, and he's totally devastated. Before she died, she says to me, "Please look after my son. I know I'm going to die, but the only thing that's worrying me so much is my son. Make sure that he's OK." She's really begging me, one mother to another. So, I thought, all right, I'll look after him. It won't be too long now, he'll track the family fortune down, and everything will be OK. But it wasn't OK, it just went on and on and on and on. And it was bleeding me dry. I ended up mortgaging an apartment that I owned; taking out loans, everything, just to make sure that this guy didn't destroy himself.

At this point, I began to lose faith. Every time he needed more money, I remembered my promise to his mother and gave it to him, but thought to myself, "My family and my friends are right. I've been massively conned." I went through these highs and lows, and it affected my work and every other aspect of my life. Then he showed me his father's will and the bonds. That was good enough for me. The bonds were really old and falling apart, but they were also quite beautiful – very elaborate, all scrolls and fancy writing. He had to keep them in plastic sleeves. I had no doubt that they were genuine. So, for me this was proof. Because of this hard-core evidence, the will and the bonds, as well as the complete certainty of his family, I realized I hadn't been conned.

By this stage, however, he was in such a state of desperation, that he would be willing to basically starve himself, get into any kind of trouble, just so that he could provide for his family. This is difficult to explain, but he was in a very bad way. I couldn't get him to eat. He was just fading away. But now I had no doubt that supporting him financially was keeping him out of trouble and keeping him alive.

Also, at this time, he had problems with his young son. His ex-girlfriend was being difficult, which is an understatement. I never met her, but from the stories he told she was a bit of a psycho, and so that was another complication in his life that he really didn't need. Things were complicated enough.

Apart from me, he relied very much on his older sister who was also trying to look after him and also helping him to trace the family fortune. Then came the next blow. His sister was diagnosed with cancer. This was a very aggressive form. She was told she only had months to live. And just as his mother had done when she knew she was dying, his sister begged me to continue to take care of him. She'd seen how I was looking after him, and knew that I wasn't what you'd call a gold-digger or a fortune hunter. It was very sudden. Within a few months she, too, was gone. So now he's lost both of this parents and the older sister that he'd looked up to and relied on. He's only got two siblings left, or so I thought at the time. I found out later that there was another one, but she had deserted the family and disappeared. I also found out that his older sister, on her deathbed, had urged him not only to find the fortune but also to track down the missing sister.

Throughout all of this, he's in a great state of desperation. He told me many times, if it wasn't for me he wouldn't be alive. It's absolutely true. He really would not be alive. He wouldn't have made it, not after this long, long saga of – how can I say – drama after drama after drama. And a lot of it, with me not believing any more, having lost faith and thinking, "I've been conned."

After his sister died, I tried to get on with my own life. I started seeing someone I'd had an on-off relationship with a few years before. My work paid the rent, but it didn't excite me, not like it used to. I had a new boss, a total dickhead, and incompetent as well. I did some singing with a bunch of musicians who were trying to get a group together. I worked on repairing relationships with my parents and my sons. This wasn't easy. Like most expats, the family is scattered all over the globe. My parents have retired and are living in Australia. I have one son in London. The other one is doing his MBA at the Kellogg School of Management in Chicago. I called my father on his birthday. He didn't refer to my situation directly. All he said was "We love you, and we only have your interests at heart." How hard was that to deal with?

It was always just a loan. He said that many times. I'm totally expecting to get my money back and more. I gave him money, not expecting anything in return, but the irony in all this is that if it comes through, I'm actually going to be a lot richer than I ever was. His father was a Caribbean crook. He had a legitimate business, but kept the crooked money hidden under the business. The reason it's taken so long to get the money is that it's tied up in bank accounts all over the world. So his son is very, very wealthy and finally I think I'm going to get my money back – maybe by next week. And not only am I going to get my money back, but he's in my eternal debt, and going to look after me for the rest of my life. These are his words, not mine.

I've had so many doubts. I've had sleepless nights. I've had rifts with my family and the close friends I've shared the story with. They all think I've been such a fool. It's just such an incredible story. There have been many times when I don't believe it. If I were living in California or somewhere like that, I wouldn't have had this experience. Only in Hong Kong. It's a very Hong Kong story.

*

I bump into Dee almost a year after the interview and ask her whether she got her money back. She shakes her head, "Not yet," she says. "But it won't be long now. He called me the other night to say that he was in Kuala Lumpur dealing with lawyers. Then he's off to London. He's had to go all over the world to track the money down." I refrain from asking her where the money is coming from to underwrite his travel. Her young companion may have had a tragic personal life, but he's a very lucky guy to have found a friend like Dee.

12.

The shock of the new

I foresee death by culture shock. (Woody Allen)

Don is a little less than average height, but solidly built. Clearly, he keeps himself in shape, and like most men of less than average height, has the drive and determination to succeed at something; punching above his weight, as the cliché has it. What that something might be doesn't matter. As it turns out, he is an investment advisor; an important breed within the expat community – more important than medical practitioners. Medicos are merely entrusted with your physical and mental life: the financial advisor is entrusted with your financial life. Not surprisingly, Hong Kong is crawling with independent investment advisors. Like Don, most seem to be from the United Kingdom. Prior to the Handover in 1997, they were able to come to Hong Kong and set themselves up without the inconvenience of having to secure a work visa. They didn't have a particularly good reputation. Many of them were merely agents for mutual funds. They pushed clients into signing up for funds that paid substantial commissions, but did not necessarily secure clients the returns that were promised by the glossy fund brochures. In fact, in many cases, you were better off taking your money to the Happy Valley or Sha Tin race track. You'd lose your money either way, but at least at the races, you might have some fun in the process.

I first met Don through my friend Max in the lobby bar of the Shangri-la hotel, a space which also served as Don's office. Many of these independent advisors used pubs, coffee shops and hotel lobbies as informal offices. They were freely available, and if you bought a coffee or a beer, you could occupy a table for as long as you liked. Why pay stratospheric rents for a shoebox in Wan Chai or Sheung Wan (Central was out of the question) when you could conduct your business in the comfort of a luxury hotel?

He and Max are in a discreet corner of the bar, their heads bent over a pile of papers. For once, Max has a cup of coffee, not a glass of wine, at his elbow. Max sees me, calls me over, and introduces Don who is helping him develop a strategy for doing something more productive with his money than drinking it and spending it on relationships that go nowhere. Like most expats, Max makes good money, but unlike most, the money sifts through his fingers like water through sand.

Don turned out to be friendly and very generous in buying rounds of drinks, so he quickly gathered a large circle of friends and acquaintances in the various watering holes around Lan Kwai Fong and Soho. I was one of them. Although he became a permanent resident of Hong Kong, he made frequent trips back to the UK where his family lived. Eventually, as his children began to grow up, he relocated to the UK to spend more time with them, but made regular visits to Hong Kong to continue serving his substantial local client base. One of these visits coincided with my search for any informants who had returned to their home countries. I was interested in their life history in Hong Kong: the trajectory from first arrival as outsider, to insider and then outsider once more. Having been an outsider, what was it like once more to look at Hong Kong as an outsider? Don was happy to be an outsider informant, and ironically we met for the interview during a quiet period in the lobby bar of the Island Shangri-la. In the first part of our conversation, he told me about what led him to Hong Kong, and the culture shock that almost sent him scurrying home.

*

It was a couple of years before the looming event that the British wistfully referred to as the Handover, and the Chinese insisted on calling the Handback. The deal was sealed when British Prime Minister Margaret Thatcher unwisely suggested to the Chinese that she would be happy to accept a hundred year extension to their lease on the territory. Don had sold his business in England, and moved his young family to Italy for an extended 'sabbatical', but before long grew restless. After all, if you're not Italian, there's only so much pasta you can eat. He had never been to Asia, in fact had never been out of Europe, and thought that it would be interesting to see Hong Kong before it was lost to China. At about this time, he was walking down the Strand in London on his way home from a business meeting when he bumped into a former colleague whom he hadn't seen for years. They popped into a pub for a drink and a catch-up. His colleague had moved to Hong Kong and set up a financial services business. Before they had finished their second pint, Don had been offered a job.

"When I sold my business in the UK I thought, 'I've done with all that now. I want to do something different.' I don't know why, but I'd always had this desire to go and work overseas. A few years before that, I had the opportunity to go and work in Oman because another mate of mine was in the financial services sector there. I was all set to go. I had my tickets and everything was sorted, but then the Gulf War started. So I didn't go, but I'd always had that desire to work overseas. Then the Hong Kong job opportunity came up, and I jumped at it.

"Coming here from Italy was a real culture shock. The lifestyles were as different as chalk and cheese. I wasn't working in Italy. I'd decided to take a year out and just put my feet up, trying to figure out what to do next. I did actually have the opportunity to stay in Italy. I'd received the Hong Kong offer, and the salary and conditions were good. But then a neighbour of mine approached me and said that he had the rights to a section of beach just north of Rome. The problem was that he had no money. I did. He said to me, 'Do you want to go into partnership, and we'll have the rights to the deck chairs and the beach bar, and we'll do teas and coffees and all the rest of it. How'd you fancy that?' I must admit it was certainly quite appealing, but at the end of the day I didn't absolutely trust this guy and I thought, 'I really don't want to live my life as a deckchair attendant.' So putting those two factors together, I made the decision to come to Hong Kong."

Don stepped off the plane at the old Kai Tak Airport and was hit by the combustible combination of heat, humidity, the shit-stench of the nullah, and the screech of aircraft tyres thumping onto the runway. Never had he experienced anything so foreign, so exotic. His partners picked him up in a stretch limo, designed no doubt to impress him. And he was massively impressed. They drove through Kowloon, past crumbling tenement buildings festooned with drying laundry, then through the tunnel, and out the other side to the glittering fairyland of Central.

The contrasts all around him were amazing. He found it difficult to make sense of the sights, the sounds and the smells. At the beginning, he would set off from his office to meet a client, and find himself standing outside a strange building without having a clue as to where he was. He hadn't set himself a timeline for living in Hong Kong, and was incapable of thinking more than a few weeks ahead. He'd moved his family from Italy back to the UK, thinking it unwise to bring them to Hong Kong when he hadn't even seen the place himself. In particular, he was concerned for his children who were only seven and ten. Although he felt it had been the right decision, their absence only compounded the massive culture shock that hit him on waking up to his first morning in Hong Kong, and the disorientation stayed with him for weeks. His first thought was: "What the hell am I doing here?" He switched on the radio to be greeted by some strange Hong Kong news that made no sense to him: nor did the fact that the announcer would switch, seemingly at random, between English and Cantonese. His second thought, when he looked around the unfamiliar room was: "Why am I here?"

Despite having his senses constantly assaulted by unfamiliar sights, sounds and scents, he was also struck by just how friendly the expatriate community was. While he was looking for an apartment of his own, he stayed with a family who felt they had to look after him. Don, however, wanted to go out on his own and explore the place independently. One night he did just that. He followed his nose down a series of steep, twisting streets and alleyways, stepping aside for the tiny, shriveled women who inexplicably pushed trolleys piled with bags of garbage up the hill. Eventually, he found himself in a neighbourhood he came to know as Lan Kwai Fong, where he sat at a bar and ordered a drink. Several young men and women were sitting at the bar next to him. They struck up a conversation, asking him if he was new to Hong Kong, what he did, and how long he planned to stay. They bought him a drink, and then invited him to a party. He went to the party with them, and had the most fantastic night, meeting all sorts of interesting people – locals as well as expats. Several gave him their name cards and asked him to get in touch. As he remembers that first social foray, he says, "That says so much about Hong Kong. It's part of the Hong Kong way."

It took Don longer than he thought it would to adjust to his new life. In retrospect, he was able to identify events such as the ease of meeting people as part of the 'Hong Kong way', but at the time, being constantly confronted with behaviours that violated his sense of how the world worked came as a shock to him. The seismic shift in thinking required to navigate everyday life, and the time it took to adjust, surprised him. After all, hadn't he come to Little Britain in the Far East? There were the familiar red letterboxes on the street, the reassuring place names (Queen's Road, the Prince of Wales Building, Consort Rise), an underground train system of sorts. The latter was minuscule compared to the London Underground, but comparisons stopped at the fact that people were transported, largely below ground, by train. The trains were clean and modern and glided silently on their tracks; they were frequent and punctual; the passengers generally behaved themselves – the time that a middle-aged male produced a set of nail clippers and sent toenail clippings shooting all over the carriage was an aberration.

Don had travelled widely in Europe, and had smugly thought of himself as a sophisticated world traveller. Compared to his neighbours in England, who thought of a trip to Wales as foreign travel, he was. Therefore, the size of the culture shock and the time it took to adjust caught him off guard. It was partly a combination of missing his family and the shock of the new: new sights, sounds and smells, but above all, new ways of going about everyday life. Why, he could even buy beer and a bottle of scotch at the convenience store on the corner – and twenty-four hours a day at that.

Just when he thought that he was beginning to adjust, he was asked to go to China. One of the firm's clients was based in Zhongshan, a modestly pint-sized city of a mere three million people perched on the edge of the Pearl River Delta. Graeme, one of his office colleagues, volunteered to accompany him and show him the ropes.

Graeme was British and had been in Hong Kong for over ten years, which impressed Don, for whom ten years seemed an eternity. Graeme had done a lot of work in China and spoke some Chinese, which also impressed him. Naïve about many things, Don had a vague idea that the kind of Chinese they spoke in Hong Kong was different from the kind they spoke in China, but he wasn't sure what the difference was. Eventually, like most expats, he picked up a few phrases, but, like most expats, he never mastered the language to any great extent. He was too busy earning a living, and learning Chinese wasn't going to stand between him and his financial goals, so there was little incentive in investing time in mastering the language.

Don had moved from the family who had so kindly accommodated him on first arrival and was staying in a hotel prior to moving into an apartment of his own. Graeme had offered to pick him up from the hotel, which was a good thing because he didn't have a clue where to go. He knew that Zhongshan was somewhere up the Pearl River, but he wasn't even sure where the Pearl River was. (It took some time for him to learn that, by living on Hong Kong Island, he was in the middle of it.) From the hotel they took a taxi to Kowloonside. Don was beginning to pick up a bit of the lingo – Hongkongside and Kowloonside, not Hong Kong and Kowloon. He learned that they were to take a ferry at Ocean

Terminal, where the cruise ships docked. When he had to present his passport at Hong Kong immigration, it struck him that he really was going to a foreign country. Although Hong Kong was very exotic, it still belonged to Britain. China, on the other hand, was, well, China; and a very different proposition. The night before, he had called his parents, as his mother wasn't well. His father was scathing when Don told him he was going to China. "Dirty, dangerous place," he had said. "I wouldn't go there if I were you." His father was one of those people who never let lack of knowledge get in the way of a personal opinion. An old-school Brit, he thought the government was pathetic to be meekly handing Hong Kong over to the Chinese. He had no interest in visiting Hong Kong himself, but considered it to be part of Britain: like Gibraltar, like the Falkland Islands. Prime Minister Thatcher had gone to war with Argentina to retain possession of the Falklands, but was cravenly caving in to the Chinese. Don's father took this as a personal insult. It was tantamount to giving the schoolyard bully your bicycle.

Don was underwhelmed by the rusting vessel that was to ferry them up the Pearl River. It was a Sunday, but in Hong Kong business had no respect for the Sabbath. Apart from Don and Graeme and a small knot of Western tourists, the other passengers were old people. They were very different from the smartly dressed Chinese businesspeople Don had grown accustomed to seeing striding the streets of Central. Their clothing was shabby, and when they smiled, their mouths glinted with gold. As they looked around for somewhere to sit, one old man noisily cleared his throat and projected a lump of phlegm over the side of the ferry. "Let's sit on the other side," said Graeme.

Don found the trip to Zhongshan fascinating. They passed, or were passed by, boats of every conceivable size and shape, from massive container ships to unstable fishing boats that looked as though they could only be kept upright through divine intervention. Leaving Victoria Harbour, the ferry tracked a path to the east of Lantau Island and under the massive Tsing Ma Bridge which was still under construction. It was to connect Hong Kong to the new airport being built on landfill at the rear of Lantau. Graeme greatly admired the bridge, which was one of the longest single-span bridges in the world. One of his friends was an engineer in the construction. "It's being built by a consortium, but everyone knows it's basically the British who are building it," he said. "Of course," thought Don. Graeme told him that the Beijing government was massively pissed off at the building of the airport and its infrastructure. "They think Britain's parting gift is to run down Hong Kong's huge monetary reserves through projects such as this," he said.

It took about an hour and a half to reach Zhongshan. From the water, it was anything but impressive. While he had hardly expected to be greeted by the sight of a sub-tropical, Club Med style resort on the foreshore, he hadn't anticipated anything so shabby and industrial. The ferry nosed its way through small fishing boats and sampans and pulled in to the dock where Don set foot for the first time on Chinese soil.

The immigration hall was basically a tin shed. Inside, the uniformed officials outnumbered the disembarking passengers. All were armed, either with handguns or semi-automatic weapons, which made him vaguely uneasy. None of them seemed particularly thrilled to see a couple of white men in business attire emerging from the ferry. When they joined the line of passengers, time stopped, as it often does on immigration lines. When Don finally got to the head of the line he handed over his passport and documents to the official behind the counter. The official, who had teeth to rival those of an Egyptian mummy and possibly the worst haircut he had ever seen, took forever to process his papers. He seemed to be looking for the story of Don's life in the passport, flipping through the pages from front to back and then from back to front several times. Don finally realized that he was looking for his visa, which he had flipped past at least twice. In a gesture that was meant to convey helpfulness and cooperation, he reached across to indicate the location of the visa, but had his hand roughly pushed away. Finally, the relevant page was found and duly stamped.

Outside on the concourse, knots of people stood around with baggage at their feet. The baggage indicated that they planned on going somewhere, but they didn't seem to be in any great hurry to get there. Dozens of children of varying ages were hanging around, and Don wondered whatever happened to the one-child policy. Everyone, young and old, looked very poor, which was probably a pretty good indication that they were. In addition to the general sense of shabbiness, Don's other immediate impression was of dust, which covered every horizontal surface with a thin film.

They took a taxi away from the port to an industrial site. As they left the port, Don's unease increased. The river was like an umbilical cord connecting him to Hong Kong. He was tempted to share his concern with Graeme, but decided not to. Graeme seemed completely at ease with this mysterious, vaguely threatening place, and he didn't want rumours spreading about the office that he was a wimp.

At the site, they met their client, another Brit, and a long-term expat. An 'old China hand', Graeme had called him; who for some unaccountable reason seemed to prefer China to Hong Kong. Obviously, he was used to China and its ways, but Don, who was still new to Asia, was overwhelmed by the strangeness of it all. On his first arrival, Hong Kong had been exotic, but this was something else. The heat, the smells, the scenery and the people who looked at you as though you were from another planet before turning their back on you – it was difficult to take in.

After the business was done, they drove a short distance to a hotel, where a buffet lunch was waiting. Although by now he was hungry, he didn't fancy the sight or smell of the food that was set out on the buffet table. He'd have been more than happy with a steak and a glass of wine, but had to settle for a plate of salty, garlicky things, some of which appeared to shrink from his fork as it approached them. The thought came to him again, as it had, intermittently, since he arrived. *What am I doing here, when I should be at home eating a steak?* An image materialized of two small children curled up asleep in their beds in suburban Reading. He had an overwhelming urge to hold them. There was a lump in his throat. *What the fuck am I doing here?* he asked himself again. He blinked several times and looked down at the alien stuff on his plate.

He was relieved to be back on the ferry. This was a different one, larger with a first class cabin, which was really just a section at the front of the boat marked off from the main cabin by a glass panel and a bit of lace curtain. The seats were a bit more comfortable, so they sat in there. They were the only ones. It looked a bit elitist, but the old people in the main section didn't seem to care, or even to notice: no doubt they had other concerns. Graeme explained that as they were expats, it was expected that they'd travel first class, so that's where they sat and drank cans of Tsingtao beer.

As the ferry began its return journey, the anxious feeling in his stomach dissolved. Back to civilization, he thought. How odd that was, to think of Hong Kong, so recently unfamiliar and exotic, as civilization, as home. What he had learned of the old China hand and his way of doing business made him uneasy. He had his finger in various pies and was paying off local officials for the pleasure of doing business there. Not my cup of tea, he thought.

That night he tried to get the BBC World Service on his radio, but the battery was flat, so he poured himself a glass of wine, took out a pad and pen and began to write. He wrote and wrote, pausing only to replenish his glass, and when he had finished he had filled ten A4 pages with a memoir of his day. He wasn't naturally given to writing, and had no idea what had prompted him to put down in words the doings of his day, nor with whom he might share them. Anyone else, anyone who hadn't been there, would probably think the account was trivial, hardly worth writing about, hardly worth the paper. But he had been there, and to him it had been incredible.

*

"There were several reasons why I finally decided to repatriate myself to the UK, although to be honest, I've never really left one hundred per cent because my business is still here, my working life is still here, some of my best friends are still here. That said, I'll be totally honest, I don't think that, mentally and emotionally, I ever left the UK. My head, my heart and everything else has always been there. I used to think of coming to Hong Kong as a long journey to work. But then, that said, I gradually fell in love with the place.

"My reasons for eventually deciding to go back were entirely personal, not professional. I missed my wife and kids desperately, and wanted to spend my time with them. Modern technology helped a lot – email, cheaper phone calls, and then Skype, but they're not the same. Then the British government severely restricted the amount of time you could be in the UK and not be classed as a resident for tax purposes. They used to have a six-months-a-year rule like Australia, but then they reduced it to ninety days – you could only spend ninety days a year in the UK. That became a major issue for me because my mother developed a serious and chronic illness, and I had to be around more to help the rest of the family look after her. So, all in all, it was the right thing to do.

"I'm not one of those expats who whine about their home country and say how marvellous Hong Kong is. Sure, when you live abroad you start to see the failings in your own country – the bureaucracy, the shortcomings in the system and so on, but you can also see the other side; the shortcomings here. While things can be rigid, there's also a great deal of flexibility. I get very frustrated in the UK. Right now I'm having a problem with the Inland Revenue Department, and it's been dragging on for months. A similar problem occurred here just the other day. I walked down the road to the Inland Revenue Tower in Wan Chai, got an appointment, and sorted it out on the spot. On the other hand, life can be better in the UK. I think the lifestyle is healthier. Every time I come back, I notice the pollution getting worse and worse, and no-one seems to be interested in doing anything about it. You get letters in the *South China Morning Post* from gweilos complaining about it, but the government doesn't take any notice. They probably figure that it's blowing over from the Mainland, and that's way beyond their control.

"Overall, I love the energy of this place. Hong Kong is special, and a part of my heart will always belong here, even if I retired from business and stopped coming here. When I'm a little old guy I'll tell my grandchildren and great-grandchildren of the great experiences I had here, and I'll try to convey to them the enthusiasm, the energy, and the excitement of living here. It just gets in your blood."

13.

FIT FOR PURPOSE

Tolerance, inter-cultural dialogue and respect for diversity are more essential than ever in a world where people are becoming more and more closely interconnected. (Kofi Annan)

So, as usual, I head down to the fitness centre around mid-morning. In my day we used to call it the gym, but these days for some reason, they seem to favour 'fitness centre'. I like going around mid-morning when it's quiet, and after the wage slaves have gone off to their offices in Central. I get on a treadmill and set it at my sedate pace of four miles per hour. (Annoyingly, the machines are calibrated in kilometres, but I've always been good at mental arithmetic so it's not a big deal.) The only other people in the centre are a couple of young Chinese women, also on treadmills. The women seem to be friends. They're chatting to each other and strolling along at a leisurely pace. I don't know why they don't just walk around the block and leave the treadmills for people who want to do real exercise.

After about ten minutes, another young woman turns up. She's an expat, and absolutely stunning. I give her a sideways look as she gets onto the treadmill next to mine. She's tall and slim, almost skinny but not quite, tanned, blonde hair pulled back in a ponytail – Scandinavian, I'd say at a guess. A real beauty. I know it's politically incorrect to appreciate beauty these days, but, hey, I'm seventy years of age, I'm from New York. I have a licence to appreciate beauty. Anyway, she takes no notice of me, and why should she? I'm old and grizzled – invisible to the fairer sex. She gets herself sorted out, produces one of those tablet things and sets it on the ledge at the front on the treadmill. I guess she's going to read. This seems to be the thing these days – people are terrified of being alone with their thoughts. So, she stabs at the tablet, and this ear-splitting racket fills the fitness centre. It's a pop song by one of the hideous wailing women. I put up with it for a few minutes, thinking she's just getting things adjusted and that she'll produce some earphones, but she doesn't. She gets the treadmill going, and sets off at a cracking pace – I have to give her that. I turn my head, and give her a good long stare, but I remain invisible to her. I try to ignore the noise, but by the third song, my blood is at boiling point. I pause my own treadmill, and turn to give her a full-frontal stare. I can't believe that she's unaware of me, but she gives no indication that she is. Finally, I'm forced to get off my treadmill. I stand right in front of her and signal for her to pause her own machine.

She ignores me and continues with her jogging. The tablet continues with its intolerable shrieking. The Chinese women continue their strolling and chatting. Reluctantly I'm about to advance the agenda by reaching across and pushing the pause button on the treadmill when the girl looks up. There must have been something about the look in my eyes that causes her to push the pause button herself. As soon as the treadmill comes to a stop, I say: "Young lady, clearly you have no idea of the effect that your abominable music is having on the other users of this gym. I have to tell you that you are inconsiderate, insensitive, and selfish, and on top of that, your taste in music is appalling."

At this point, sensing an altercation, the Chinese strollers turn their heads in our direction.

"I am fluent in Cantonese, and have to tell you that the ladies on your left are equally as appalled at your self-centredness as I am. I heard their assessment of you with my own ears. They wouldn't tell you because it would be culturally inappropriate to do so, but I'm from New York, and I will."

I'm nonplussed when one of the Chinese women says with a West Coast accent, "Sir, I don't know how good your Cantonese is – we're both bilingual and bicultural by the way – but my friend and I were just saying to each other how much we were enjoying the music."

Of all the nerve! The young Hong Kong people are losing their cultural values, I have to say.

14.

A PERFECT COUPLE

You can never have enough. (Robert Kissel)

My friends Devon and Marie live at Discovery Bay, or DB, on Lantau Island. According to some of my informants, this fact alone would be enough to disqualify them as dinner guests in the eyes of many wealthy Mid-Levels dwellers. Soon after I arrived in Hong Kong, a British acquaintance gave me a short-cut to identifying potential candidates for friendship. "In most places, it can be done with a couple of questions. In England all you have to do to determine suitability is to find out where they went to school. In Hong Kong, just ask them where they live. The poor white trash live on Lamma Island. They're to be avoided at all costs. Those who live at Discovery Bay are a cut above the Lammaites – but not by much. They'll tell you that it's the perfect place to bring up children, but you're just as likely to find that they're childless, and best avoided."

Devon and Marie are childless and don't seek forgiveness for living at DB. As a number of informants have said, it's very easy to meet people in Hong Kong. You don't even have to go looking for friends, just stand around long enough and it will happen. It's also just as easy to lose them.

It's a Saturday evening at the Cultural Centre. I've just attended a concert given by the violinist Anne-Sophie Mutter. I have time for a glass of what they call champagne before catching the last Star Ferry back to the Island. I collect my glass and move across to one of the standing tables dotted about the foyer. "Mind if I perch my glass here?" I ask the couple standing at the table. The male, tall and of indeterminate age, wears a bow tie and a winning smile. "Be our guest," he says. His companion is petite with short razor-cut hair.

"Enjoy the concert?" he asks.

"I did, very much," I reply, thinking that at least they now know I'm not a music critic. "How about you?"

"Well, we were sitting in a box right above the stage, I spent as much time worrying about whether Sophie's strapless dress would defy gravity through the recital. It did – much to my disappointment." I titter politely at the impertinence of his observation, we introduce each other, and shake hands. Normally I'm suspicious of men who sport pink shirts and polka-dot bow ties, but there's something attractive about this particular person. Over a second glass of champagne, we become firm friends. As I get to know him, I learn that while Devon does a variety of things for a living, his real passion is collecting friends.

Then, realizing I've missed the last Star Ferry crossing for the evening, I suggest that we have another drink. Before we part that evening I find myself accepting an invitation for brunch the following day. It's then I learn that they live at Discovery Bay.

Their apartment is in one of the older blocks in the settlement. Older blocks have the advantage of being within walking distance of the ferry, and so there is no need to wait for one of the minibuses that feed the community. There are no cars at Discovery Bay, so transportation options are restricted to walking, minibus, or, for those who can afford them, golf carts. Older blocks do have disadvantages of course: lumps of concrete have a tendency to fall off them at unexpected moments, and the power supply can be unreliable.

Their one-bedroom flat, like Marie, is petite – a more charming adjective than cramped – and is crammed with furniture, books, artwork and decorative items assembled over many years of living abroad. As they are both blessed with good taste, everything works. Because they live on the top floor of the building, they have access to the rooftop terrace, which they wasted no time in annexing; and it is here that their Sunday brunches take place. In subsequent years, I attend many culinary and social events at which Devon holds court and dispenses acceptable wine, while Marie darts up and down the stairs producing astonishing plates of food that betray her Mediterranean background. The guests are just as varied as the food: on a given Sunday you might find yourself sitting next to the Turkish consul-general, a food critic, or a budding playwright. All have something interesting to contribute to the conversation of the moment. Devon is the glue that holds the day together until, in the late afternoon, it begins to unravel, undone by alcohol and, in summer, excessive heat.

On one particular Sunday in late April, I'm about to make my excuses and take my leave. As usual, it's been a pleasant day, but I have an early morning flight to Istanbul the following day and don't want to do it on a hangover. The party includes a visiting English architect who spent several years in Hong Kong learning how to squeeze impossibly tall buildings into astonishingly tiny spaces, his German girlfriend and a married couple, newly minted from the States. During a lull in the conversation, as I'm finishing my wine and waiting for an appropriate moment to extricate myself from the extremely late brunch, the newly-minted wife asks: "So, who is Nancy Kissel?"

There is silence for a moment. Some years ago, Nancy Kissel had her fifteen minutes of fame. Each day, Hong Kong expats followed her story as one astonishing revelation tumbled after another. It was intoxicating. The entire expat community was drunk on Nancy Kissel, and many claimed to have met her; even those who only arrived after her incarceration. And then, true to Hong Kong form, she is dropped from the collective consciousness.

Devon breaks the silence as I suspected he would. "Oh," he says, "she was the female half of one of the most successful and celebrated couples in Hong Kong: you could say they were the archetypical expat couple. These days, to the extent that anyone remembers her, she's known as 'the Milkshake Murderer'."

"Oh, I remember her," says the celebrated architect, "I was here during the time of her trial."

"It's just that I saw a piece about her in the SCMP," says the newly-minted wife. "It was reported that she had lost her final appeal against conviction for murder, and I wondered what it was all about. The paper didn't go into it, but it sounded kind of sensational."

"Oh, it was all of that," says Devon. "The whole sorry saga can be summed up in a single word – greed. Let me grab another bottle of wine and I'll tell you all about the Milkshake Murderer."

*

Devon launches in to his own version of the Kissel saga.

"As I said, if you're looking for a stereotype of the expat family, the Kissels were it. He was a rising star within the Goldman Sachs stable of brilliant bankers and money men. Goldman Sachs was the investment bank to which all investment bankers aspired. If you didn't work for Goldman Sachs, you were just fooling around. If you worked for Goldman Sachs, you were a member of the Inner Temple. If you lived outside the Temple, you merely made millions a year. Inside the temple, a million dollars was small change. There was only one problem for the ambitious investment banker. You didn't go to Goldman Sachs: they came to you. If they wanted you, that is. If they didn't, you sat and waited. That's what Rob Kissel did – he sat and waited. And on the day that they came to him on Wall Street, he didn't even pretend to resist. His mantra was: 'You can never have enough,' and he repeated it until his wife Nancy came to believe it too. When Joe McGinniss wrote his book on the Kissel saga, he appropriated the Kissel mantra for the title – *Never Enough*. It's a racy enough read despite being riddled with all sorts of errors.

"Rob couldn't wait to get to Hong Kong, the financial centre of the most dynamic and fastest growing region on earth. The Asian century was about to begin. Hong Kong was a sweet spot for the talented, the ambitious and the ruthless. Rob Kissel had an unfair share of all three.

Relocating his family from New York to Hong Kong was the right move, for the right man at the right time.

"When they got to Hong Kong, they made all the right moves. They took up residence at Parkview, high on the ridge at Wong Nai Chung Gap. For the Kissels, it was one of those 'people like us' places, a citadel within a city. It had a PARKnSHOP superstore, a cinema, tennis, swimming and golfing facilities, restaurants and even a Roman baths. For those who had started breeding, there was a pre-school. For wives who didn't work, there was no real need to ever leave this citadel.

"They slipped easily into the rituals of the investment banker family. No-one had to explain the rules to them: what car to drive, what suits to wear. The rules were obvious. BMWs were for boys, real men drove Porsches. Rob had always wanted a Porsche, and so it was one of his first purchases. It was all so seamless, so easy, so right. All you had to do was breathe, and the money rolled in. It would only be a matter of time before he made senior partner. He also wanted a son: someone he could mould in his own image: someone to inherit his billions. A son was an essential element in his plans to establish a dynasty. She didn't want another child: she had enough stretch marks. However, as he pointed out, she had nothing else to do. He was the one who put in the fifteen-hour days, the one who had created for her this life of privilege and ease. The least she could do was give him a son. And so she did, but it wasn't by choice.

"As they grew into Hong Kong life, they were also seen as the perfect expats: ticking all the boxes. A luxury apartment in one of the most highly sought-after complexes in the city. Two live-in maids who removed every last vestige of drudgery from their lives. A Mercedes for her, a Porsche for him. Wealth that grew faster than it could be counted. Mobility. He roamed the region to build a financial empire for his company and for himself. They could, and did, fly back and forth to the East Coast at the drop of a hat. Three gorgeous, if somewhat ill-disciplined, children. Social events where they rubbed shoulders with the rich and famous, including a former President of the United States. A luxury ski lodge in

Vermont. The list went on and on. Utter the word 'expat' in Hong Kong, and they were a perfect fit. The perfect fit, except for just one thing.

"Their immediate circle of friends were shocked, but at the same time titillated to pick up the *South China Morning Post* on the morning of November 2, 2003 and read that Nancy Kissel had been arrested and charged with the brutal murder of her husband. She had drugged him with a milkshake ostensibly made for the children, and bludgeoned him to death with a heavy-based statuette before rolling the body in a Persian rug and depositing it in a storage area belonging to their apartment. This was hardly the behaviour of a perfect couple. And it certainly didn't fit the stereotype of the archetypical expatriates."

I had forgotten most of the details of the Kissel case until Devon rehearsed them for his guests. The Kissel story, shocking as it was at the time to the expatriate community, had faded from consciousness. Newly-arrived expats have never heard of the case that riveted the community for a couple of years. Her name pops up from time to time at dinner parties and events such as the DB brunch; usually stimulated, as is the case today, by a newspaper report of yet another failed attempt on Nancy's part to have her conviction overturned.

The newly-minted wife and her husband are enthralled with the account that Devon has given and want to know more. What was it that had led the woman who had almost everything to throw it away by killing the goose that laid the golden egg, and end up in Hong Kong's Tai Lam Centre for Women with practically nothing? She is still there. And her husband is still dead. What made her imagine that she could leave a rug-wrapped corpse to rot in the Parkview storage facility and get away with it? Incredibly, the answer was that she saw a movie in which the wife dispatched her husband by the same means, and for the same motives as Nancy – money, and to be with a lover she had acquired back in the States. The fictional Nancy got away with it: the flesh and blood Nancy did not.

At the trial, one sensational revelation followed another. The public was enthralled. It was salacious, which was all the better. Sex and murder don't necessarily go together, but how delicious it is when they do. We can't believe what we're reading through the cracks in our fingers, but we read on, hungry for the next shocking detail.

It turned out that Nancy had never liked Hong Kong. Enslaved like her husband to Mammon, she saw herself as serving time. She made more and more frequent trips back to the East Coast. On one of these trips, she had a fling with a younger man. The fling, as flings so often do, evolved into a full-blown affair. She then made the mistake (fatal for her husband, as it turned out), of falling in love. Unbeknown to her, Rob had installed spyware on her computer, and was able to follow, at first with interest, and then with growing alarm, as the affair developed. He was meticulous and strategic in planning the divorce he intended to spring on his faithless wife. He secured the services of the most eminent divorce attorney in Duddell Street, and also consulted the other top attorneys who were thereby disqualified from representing Nancy if she learned of the impending divorce. Satisfied that all of the pieces were in place, he headed to Taiwan. He planned to have the divorce papers served on his unsuspecting wife on the following Monday, unaware that he would never make it to Monday; that on the Sunday he would be served with something far more lethal.

Nancy had plans of her own for severing the marriage, and they didn't involve divorce. Unfortunately for Rob, she didn't share the plan with her East Coast lover, and it was therefore beyond the reach of his spyware. Once her husband had been dispatched, wrapped in the Persian rug, and gone forever, she would return to the States for good and live happily ever after with her young and virile lover. She'd already checked on the details of Rob's life insurance and was satisfied that it would enable her to continue living in the manner to which she had become accustomed. When she learned that Rob had plans to move the family to Tokyo, the next step on his ladder to the top, she decided to advance her own plans. Rob was to return from Taiwan on Saturday, so Sunday would be the day.

It only took the Hong Kong police a couple of days to find the body. It took considerably less time to follow the clues to the killer – and there was no shortage of clues. Having brought Rob's life to an untimely end, she might as well have driven herself straight to Wan Chai police station. Clearly she was no fan of the plethora of 'true crime' shows that populate the media these days.

Had she pleaded guilty by reason of insanity, she might have got somewhere, but she pleaded not guilty on the grounds of self-defence and got nowhere. She claimed to have been repeatedly beaten up and subjected to anal rape over a five-year period, but there was no medical evidence to support these claims. She did go to the doctor on the day following the murder, but the superficial injuries she displayed could have been self-inflicted or caused in the course of bludgeoning Rob to death. She was found guilty and put away for life.

We sit on the rooftop as the light fades, the harbour in front of us and the green mountain rearing at our back; I can see the resort-like attraction of the place. If you like resort-style living, this would definitely be an option. I don't. Less isolating than a cruise ship, perhaps, but not by much. However, those who live here, either by choice or through necessity, endure the tedium of the ferry crossing and embrace the weekend barbecues and Sunday brunches.

I wonder what lessons are to be learned from the Kissel tragedy, in which the real victims were the children. The obvious one is that the Kissels, like many expatriates, led parallel lives, living out the metaphor of Hong Kong as a city of masks. Another is that the stereotype of the archetypical expat is partly true, but only partly so. They fitted the expat mould. They were here purely and simply for the money. They closeted themselves from the local community, much as the DB expats do, and seemed to have no interest in learning anything about the culture or the language. The hilltop citadel of Parkview could almost be seen as a city state. Hong Kong was nothing more than a massive slot machine in which, unlike real life, the punter always wins.

The American couple decide to accompany me back to Central on the ferry. As the winking lights of Central draw near, I ask the husband what he does. "I'm a merchant banker," he says. "J.P. Morgan, not Merrill Lynch." My poor-taste advice to him as we dock at the Central pier is to avoid drinking milkshakes at home: it fails to elicit so much as a smile. Honestly, I sometimes wonder whether Americans have a sense of humour.

*

Visitors to Hong Kong who happen to meet a family such as the Kissels will almost certainly admire them, and will also probably envy them: the perfect expat couple. Although an extreme example, the Kissel saga shows that the metaphorical adjective is a myth. Success and wealth mask secrets. Marital dissatisfaction among outwardly successful expats, if not rife, is widespread, as this and some of the other narratives have illustrated. This dissatisfaction can be resolved through reconciliation, resignation or divorce. Mrs. Kissel chose none of these, but did it in a particularly grisly way. When the story broke, and the events surrounding her husband's death began to unfold, members of the expat community, no doubt enjoying the delicious tremor of someone else's misfortune, would ask, "How on earth did she think she could get away with it?"

How indeed? According to those who knew her, she was not unintelligent. The media constructed her as an evil creature, a construction that was supported by the facts: the brutal and premeditated drugging and dispatching of her husband with blows to the head from a heavy brass statuette, the rolling of the corpse into a Persian rug which she kept in the bedroom until the stench became too much even for her to bear. Pure evil, one of the more oxymoronic collocations in the English language, was a convenient label for the perpetrator of the deeds. However, there is no evidence of evil in her life up to this incident. What was it about the Hong Kong lifestyle that led her husband into sexual debauchery, cocaine addiction and alcoholic excess, and to her own monumental brain fizz?

My sense is that neither Robert nor Nancy Kissel were inherently evil, but that they were congenitally unsuited to Hong Kong. It's a place that encourages and facilitates the best and the worst in people – locals as well as expats. If you have hidden weaknesses, Hong Kong will expose them. If you have strengths, it will bring them out. Robert and Nancy had both strengths and weaknesses, but unfortunately for them it was the weaknesses that were exposed. Ultimately, and unfortunately for them, Hong Kong was toxic.

15.

THE MAN WHO KNEW TOO MUCH

We all wear masks and the time comes when we cannot remove them without removing some of our skin. (Andre Berthiaume)

I'm in a bar in the area known to locals as Soho (South of Hollywood Road), one of the expat haunts I've patronized for many years. Outside of happy hour, when it's over-run by the suits from Central, it's a pleasant space where you can sit unmolested in a booth with a coffee (not recommended) or a Pinot Grigio (highly recommended) and do work that doesn't take up too much brain space. With complimentary wi-fi, you can answer routine emails, do research, or idly surf the net. On this day, just before the late afternoon rush, I'm chatting with Kirsty, the bar manager, a British woman in her early thirties. I've dropped by to give her a copy of my new book, a light-hearted travel romp through Latin America.

As Kirsty moves off to do her pre-dinner briefing with the wait staff, I'm approached by a man who appears to be in his early fifties. (I later learn that he is actually considerably older.) Handsome, bearded, with a hangdog smile, he addresses me in a quiet voice. So quiet, that I have to lean toward him to hear what he's saying.

"I'm sorry to bother you, but I couldn't help overhearing your conversation. I gather you're a writer."

"Of sorts," I reply.

Noticing that my glass is almost empty, he makes an apologetic hand gesture as though he's somehow to blame for this state of affairs, asks if he can treat me to a refill, then assuming that the answer will be 'yes', he slips into the bar stool next to mine.

"Leon," he says, offering his hand. I take it and tell him my name.

"So, what's your story, Leon?" I ask.

He shrugs self-deprecatingly. "I dabble," he says. "Do a bit of writing myself. Acting. This and that." He belongs to the army of invisible expatriates. These people do not live on the Peak. They do not drive fancy cars. In fact, it's most unlikely that they have a car at all. They don't have massive salaries plus benefits. They may have a mistress or two. However, that's about the only thing they would have in common with the stereotypical expatriate.

We became friends, as you do in Hong Kong; and, as you also do in Hong Kong, would meet from time to time in one or another of the expat bars in Central. One night, out far too late, and having consumed one vodka shot too many, I finally confronted him.

"So, come on Leon, confess. Why are you really in Hong Kong?"

"I'm a fugitive from US law enforcement. Or, to put it another way, I'm a self-imposed exile, fighting for justice."

"I'd like to hear your story," I say.

*

"Where should I start?"

"The conventional wisdom is to begin at the beginning, but beginnings, middles and endings are artifacts of story-telling. In life, there's only one beginning – birth, but let's not go back that far. Start wherever you think is appropriate. If I lose the plot, I'll let you know."

"It all happened at the time that I was at the top of my game as a radical lawyer in the United States. I had some notoriety, I had a public profile, I had prominence, and I'd managed to piss off people who you should definitely not piss off. A year before this, I'd been badly injured in an automobile accident, and was heavily medicated. I couldn't function without pain relief. I'd also been arrested and charged with menacing with a deadly weapon in a domestic violence context and was out on bail. This was a total stitch-up."

"Who were these people? The mafia?"

"No, not the mafia – quite the opposite. I'm talking about law enforcement agencies."

"And why did they want to stitch you up?"

"I'll come to that. I was out of prison on pre-trial release conditions that were designed to prevent me from pursuing the important case that I was working on. It was a case that had the attention of the whole nation. It had the attention of the international media. And it still pops up from time to time. Anyway, due to my pre-trial release restrictions, it was illegal for me to be in certain places, and to be in possession of certain hardware. That's a euphemism, but I'm sure you don't need me to spell it out."

"This is all going on in the US, right?"

"Right."

"So what's it got to do with Hong Kong?"

"This story explains how I come to be in Hong Kong now. It also ties in with my Native American background as a descendant of the Choctaw nation, and the whole Native American scene. I'd split with this Korean woman I'd been in a relationship with – the evil Korean as I call her – and was browsing in a bookstore in Boulder, Colorado, and I happened to notice this appealing young woman with long, jet-black hair. It was just before Columbus Day, a day that's anathema to Native Americans, and the Colorado Chapter of the American Indian movement was planning to demonstrate against Columbus Day. I was planning to take part in the demonstration, which I subsequently did, and was ultimately arrested next to Native American leaders including Russell Means, Professor Glenn Morris, and Ward Churchill, who had great notoriety later. And I don't know if he was arrested, but Vine Deloria Junior was also there. He was a professor at the University of Colorado, and someone who drew national attention to Native American issues. You may be aware of his book *Custer Died for your Sins*."

"No, I'm not familiar with the book – or any of these people."

"It doesn't matter. They're all in Wikipedia if you're interested. So, anyway, I walk up to this woman, whom I'm certain is an American Indian, and I say, 'Hey, what Nation are you?' And she pauses and looks at me awkwardly and replies, 'Um, Hong Kong?' I laugh and say, 'Oh, I'm such a schmuck. Let me buy you a cup of coffee.' And within the hour, I propose to her. I mean, I didn't for a second plan to follow through with it, but believe it or not, we did end up getting married. Impulsive. That's me. It's always been a tendency of mine.

"Anyway, after we were married, she was the ostensible victim in an allegation of domestic violence and I was the alleged perpetrator. Of course, she had not been a victim, and I did not assault her with a deadly weapon. The case was ultimately, and appropriately, dismissed. But in between the time of its dismissal, and my pre-trial release, the law enforcement juggernaut that I had managed to repeatedly embarrass in the national media took great delight in being able to interfere with the ordinary course of my business and relationships. I was followed, I was harassed, I was pulled over for no other crime than driving down the street."

"I still don't understand what all this harassment was about."

"It was all due to my involvement in the JonBenét Ramsey case. JonBenét was a child beauty pageant contestant who was found strangled in the basement of the family home in Boulder, Colorado on Christmas Day in 1996."

"Oh, I remember that case. It still comes up from time to time. Wasn't the father or the son supposed to have done it?"

"The family was initially implicated, but they were later exonerated. Then the notorious gossip magazine and scandal rag, the *National Enquirer*, claimed that a client of mine was the culprit. So blame shifted to him even though they knew damn well he hadn't done it. Actually, the Boulder Police never ever thought Miles had anything to do with it. They politely and perfunctorily took his DNA swab because they felt like they had to after the article came out and caused such a stir. Despite the police department's view, Miles still had to deal with the national obsession about the case and weather the negative publicity the article, which had been distributed at nearly every supermarket checkout lane in the United States, had created for him."

"And was he convicted?"

"No, he was never charged, but he was indelibly wrongly tarnished as a baby killer and a predatory paedophile. I managed to bring forward a witness who provided evidence that JonBenét had most likely been the victim of a paedophile ring. On the day in question, there was a Christmas party at a neighbourhood friend's home, a wealthy and prominent family in Boulder. The Ramseys were there, including JonBenét, who was six years old at the time. The last time she was seen alive by anyone other than her family was as she was leaving the party. Then she simply disappeared. The Ramseys' house was searched from top to bottom. Then there was a ransom note. And then, eight hours after the girl had disappeared, John Ramsey's close friend finds the body in the basement."

"What was this about a paedophile ring involving the wealthy and famous? It sounds like a story that the tabloids would love."

"As soon as I got involved in the investigation, and started collecting evidence, it became clear to me that there was a massive cover-up, and that the case was being deliberately mismanaged. There were also conflicts of interest between law enforcement officers. None of it was ever mentioned in the tabloids."

"The story gets more and more intriguing."

"We had sources who were prepared to name and identify prominent members of the business, academic and political community throughout the Colorado Front Range who had been engaging in the exploitation and abuse of children over three decades. It's wrong to view the JonBenét Ramsey case as an anomalous event. It wasn't. The violence and sexual abuse of children with impunity along the Front Range is a very old story."

"So, tell me about this witness you mentioned before."

"She was a woman who had years before been a victim of paedophiles with a nexus to the Ramseys. I had her in a safe house because she was reasonably terrified that she was going to be abducted. She described in graphic detail what these paedophiles did. They would twist a cord around the neck of the child they were raping and pull it tighter and tighter. The muscular spasms and twitches the little girl made as she was being asphyxiated resembled, to the abusing adult, the sensation of violent orgasm, and they got off on that. According to the witness, in the case of the Ramsey girl, whoever was abusing her had likely pulled the cord too tight. Or, if she hadn't been performing like she was told to, maybe he had hit her in the head too hard, as had been done to the witness when she had been abused as a little girl during other dark Christmas parties three decades ago. She explained that in addition to the simulated orgasm, the strangulation was also to exercise total domination. She also explained how the paedophiles threatened the children, by telling them that if the child ever said anything, the devil would come for them. She said, 'What better way is there to frighten a child into silence?' She was always making remarks like that. Her statements seemed to me to be exceptionally well-grounded and believable. She had no motive to lie. It was never intended that her story would be made public. We never wanted any of that."

"And her information was pivotal, because…?"

"Missing from the Ramsey case was any connection to child abuse and violence. They knew she'd been involved in these garish child beauty pageants where parents had a tendency to invite their pre-pubescent daughters to flirt and wear highly sexualized costumes and perform song and dance routines, but that was all. The witness said that she had been abused by adults from the time of her earliest memory, and she described in great detail how they did it. At Christmas time, they would throw a big party. At the end of the party, some of the guests would leave and some would stay, and the children would be handed out like party favours. This resembled, the witness said, the very party where JonBenét had last been seen alive."

"It all sounds a bit circumstantial."

"There's more – a lot more. I was running around, doing all sorts of high-profile stuff to redeem my client."

"The one who'd been accused by the *National Enquirer*?"

"That's right. I deposed the father, John Ramsey, for example. As a result, people who wanted to cover up and bury the Ramsey case were out to get me. I came under a lot of pressure from the District Attorney's office and the Boulder Police. In fact, at one point, the Chief of Police personally promised me that he was going to ruin my reputation. I was being seriously railroaded. And the people I knew within the system were telling me I had to get out. If I didn't get out, they said, bad things would happen. So we have this paedophile ring. We have this kid who'd been abused and strangled. We had this innocent guy, my client, who was being stitched up on the murder charge."

"Well, the question, surely, is who wanted the Ramsey case to go away and why?"

"When I deposed John Ramsey, I offered the District Attorney's office full access. And guess what? They heard my offer and sat there like the three monkeys: hear no evil, see no evil and speak no evil. I offered to ask any questions they liked on their behalf. They had none. They weren't interested."

"This story gets more and more fantastic. A Mad Hatter's Christmas Tea Party, a paedophile ring, and child murder case that enforcement doesn't seem to want solved. What's next?"

"What's revealing about this case is what we don't know, and the fact that certain people in law enforcement don't want us to know. John Ramsey had a consulting company, which was, at the time, the most profitable subsidiary of Lockheed Martin. No-one really seems to have had much of a clue about what his company actually did for Lockheed Martin. The other thing that no-one knows is who attended the Christmas party where his daughter was last reported to have been seen alive by others outside of her immediate family. If you were a police agency, wouldn't you interview every fucking person who was at that party? Wouldn't you? No-one knows. Or at least, no-one is saying. There was a person, or persons unknown at the party whose identity had to be protected at all costs. Why are the stakes so high here, that the whole justice system can't be brought into question?"

"I'm no lawyer, but I'd have thought a guest list would be the first thing they'd demand. I've watched enough reality crime shows to know that."

"The case was deliberately mishandled from the start, and everyone who tried to find out what was going on was destroyed in one way or another, including me. The responding officer who was first on the scene was the scapegoat for all of the initial case mishandlings. She thought something weird was going on. She was fearful of everyone in the house. She requested backup, made a record of counting all the bullets in her gun. Her career really suffered, and that was not fair because she tried to do everything by the book.

"Here's mystery number three. Why did the FBI remain so steadfastly uninvolved? When the kidnapping ransom note came to light, the FBI should have taken over the case. Kidnapping is clearly a federal matter. The Lindbergh kidnapping in 1932 was the FBI crime lab's first major case. It contributed to the national branding of the early FBI, and subsequently, kidnapping became a first right of refusal for the bureau. The FBI website states that even when interstate transport of the victim isn't suspected, they will initiate a kidnapping investigation involving a missing child 'of tender years'. The Ramsey ransom note purported to be from a group of foreign terrorists. An act of foreign terrorism directed against the CEO of a major defence contractor on US soil at Christmas. That's not federal? Think about it. Why didn't Lockheed Martin and other defence contractors go on alert? Other executives with small children would be contacted. Initially, ostensibly, it wasn't paedophilia, it was a kidnapping – abduction for ransom by a small foreign faction. That's how they identified themselves. And no one was in a position initially to reveal that as a fraud. That would be irresponsible. They hadn't time to establish that. And yet sources told an investigative reporter that the head of security at Lockheed Martin, a former FBI agent, by the way, had conveyed that everything was under control on the day of the incident before the child's body was found. It appears they knew from the start that it was murder, not kidnapping."

"This kidnapping note sounds like something out of a bad movie. Who would have written it? Who was it designed to deceive?"

"That, I don't know. People were winging it, they were deliberately fucking it up."

"Hang on, exactly who do you mean by 'people'?"

"Elements within various arms of the legal system whose job should have been to solve the case. They weren't worried about the things they should have been worried about. They weren't consigning this to the FBI whose job it actually was to try and solve crimes of this sort. The problem with this crime is that people don't want it solved. Solving this crime likely creates more problems, from a national security perspective."

"Maybe we can come back to that. But can you address the question of how these events resulted in your being in Hong Kong?"

"Sure. It was all a result of my efforts to clear my client, and the secret witness whom I had under wraps, and the cover-up. I was asking inconvenient questions and pissing people off. Once I suggested that the FBI were complicit in the cover-up, I began to look into the whole FBI apparatus in Colorado, and its relationship to the police. To begin with, why is there an FBI office in Boulder, when the regional office for Colorado and Wyoming is located in Denver, 30 minutes' drive away? Wyoming doesn't have an FBI field office. People have to drive down to Denver. Why would there be another office in Boulder? This question was put to me rhetorically by the sheriff of Boulder. Just so you know, the sheriff's department in Boulder has not been part of the problem. And there are others, too, like the Colorado Bureau of Investigation.

"I put the question of why the FBI weren't involved in the case at a meeting of the Boulder police department. There were no sheriffs in that meeting, no district attorney representatives in that meeting, just the police and the FBI. And they said nothing. I told them among other things that I planned to depose John Ramsey and that they were welcome to give me any questions that they wanted asked of him, and that I also planned to depose Lockheed Martin industrial security representatives because we had serious questions that we hoped they would answer. And the response of the Boulder police department was to pay good public money to a big Denver law firm to file a motion to dismiss my client's case against the *National Enquirer*. And the motion was successful. Surprise, surprise! My client suffered greatly because of the *National Enquirer's* allegations that he was responsible for the girl's death. And then they came after me."

"And how did they do that?"

"Here is how they did it, and how the Hong Kong connection came in. As I told you, I met my Hong Kong wife in a Boulder bookstore, mistaking her for a Native American. After I married her, I discovered she suffered from severe depression. Her psychiatrist was constantly tinkering with her medication, as they like to do, and she was having a negative reaction to a new anti-depressant that he had switched her to. At the time none of us knew that she was also bipolar, and that the anti-depressant medication he'd switched her to was contraindicated for people with bipolar disorder.

"One day we were packing up our apartment in preparation for moving to a new place when she suddenly had an anxiety attack and got extremely agitated. She grabbed a box of items I'd packed and threw it to the floor. The next box that she was going to throw contained my assortment of weapons and improvised weapons that my partner and I were experimenting with for our security business. I stood between her and the box and I said, 'You're not going to throw that box down. Calm down! Calm down!' And she charged into me and I protectively restrained her. I suffered scratches and bruises. She didn't have a mark on her. I got her to the floor and was holding her. My mother, who was staying with us and recovering from surgery, walked in and was quite shocked to see what was going on.

"My wife, whose English name is Bonnie, was struggling like a demon. I said, 'Look, Bonnie, I'll let you go if you just stop struggling.' She stopped momentarily, so I let her go. And the first thing that she does, being the Hong Kong girl that she is, she rushes to the telephone and dials for emergency assistance. I guess she was expecting that the friendly police officers would come by and help cool everything down as they do in Hong Kong. So as she's on the phone, I take my handgun, which was on the kitchen counter, and I hand it to my mother, and tell her to lock it in the safe. And then Bonnie immediately says to the police dispatch officer on the phone, 'Oh, he's got a gun'. As soon as I hear that, I go outside and stand under the street light to wait for them to show up. It's dark by now, but I'm under the street light so they can see me clearly and can see that I don't have a gun. I didn't want to give them any defensible reason to shoot first and ask questions later.

"So I duly get arrested and arraigned. At my pre-trial, a date is set for the hearing of domestic assault and threatening with a deadly weapon. I'm released on bail, and all sorts of conditions are set. I'm not to be seen within one hundred yards of my wife. I'm not to leave the State of Colorado. I'm not to be in possession of weapons of any kind: the usual stuff. My wife goes back to Hong Kong for medical treatment. I really wanted to go back with her to look after her, but because of the bail conditions, that was impossible, so I completed the task of moving out of our apartment."

"So your relationship with your wife was all right?"

"Absolutely fine. The minor incident in the apartment was just the excuse the authorities needed to muzzle me. They never even pretended to be looking after her interests. After Bonnie went back to Hong Kong, I moved into my business partner's apartment. In addition to my legal practice, I had a security consulting company on the side. My partner let me have his apartment because he was in Tel Aviv working as a contract embassy guard for the US Government. I didn't know it at the time, but he had less than a year to live. He was killed in the Gaza Strip while on duty. He was an expert in executive protection, and part of what he and

I were doing together was developing defensive apparel for prison guards and other people who face the peril of weapons, particularly improvised weapons, while on duty.

"My partner collected weapons of various kinds. Among other things, he had on his wall ceremonial swords. He had handguns locked in his safe. One of the things I had in his apartment was a hard, plastic photographer's case, used to carry light stands, microphone stands, and tripods. The brand name of that satchel or carrying case was 'Bazooka'. These items were to become highly relevant, as I'll reveal shortly.

"This was a dark time in my life. My wife was in Hong Kong. I was under all these restrictions imposed by the pre-trial release conditions. I was in constant pain because of head and neck injuries from the road accident and was on prescription drugs including morphine.

"Late one afternoon, I was preparing for my trial. I was writing to the former US Attorney General, Ramsay Clark, whom I'd met. I told him what was going on with me, and appealed for his assistance. On that particular afternoon, increasing pain told me that it was time for my next dose of morphine. I'd almost finished my letter to Ramsay Clark, a very personal and very sensitive letter, when there was a knock at the door. I went to the door and some asshole had put his notebook over the peephole so I couldn't see who was on the other side."

"You didn't know who was on the other side of the door, but you opened it anyway?"

"I was pretty sure who it was, and I was right. When I opened the door, ten or twelve Lakewood police officers filed in and interrogated me. Are you so and so? Yes, I am. I was immediately handcuffed. Then they began trashing the place, tossing stuff around in the apartment like the hominids at the beginning of the film *2001: A Space Odyssey*. They were there to arrest me, but they also used it as an opportunity to search the place. They took great glee in the Bazooka case, suggesting, incredibly, that it contained a bazooka. 'Unlock it. You got the key?'"

"So they were looking for evidence that you'd violated your pre-trial release conditions."

"Of course. And when they opened the case, guess what they found? Inside were toy blowguns that I'd purchased for my young sons by my previous marriage – you know, plastic dart guns. These, they said, would get me a year in prison. A year behind bars for being in possession of toy dart guns – they became an indictable count. I was indicted with that heinous offence. I couldn't believe that these men were taking themselves seriously. The next things they focused on were my partner's decorative swords. I tell you, these would be ineffective even as letter openers, but were treated in the same way as razor-sharp samurai swords. Plastic toys and decorative swords, and I'm being treated as though I'm in possession of weapons of mass destruction.

"But what did have me seriously worried was the fact that on the desk in the bedroom was an unlocked briefcase containing a World War II era fully-functional Thompson submachine gun. It was a collectors' item owned by a friend who'd asked me to look after it, and it could have sent me to federal prison for years. I'm thinking, 'There's no way they're going to miss that, and then I'm going to be in massive shit'. But you know what? They busted the apartment apart, broke open the safe and locked 'bazooka' case looking for everything they could find. And they ignored the machine gun."

"So maybe they just overlooked it."

"Oh, they knew all about it. There was a reason they overlooked it, as I'll come to. Partly to distract them, and also because I'm crawling out of my skin with pain, I asked for my meds, which they collected for me to take to the jail for my booking. I began to wonder what this was all about. Why had they turned up, and why had they immediately cuffed me? They hadn't yet seen the so-called 'weapons' at the time they slapped the handcuffs on me. I didn't have long to wait for an answer. They were there to arrest me, based on a warrant signed by Linda Wickman, one of the district attorney's investigators for the Ramsey case whom I had personally interacted with as I brought the witness forward. That district attorney had originally endorsed the witness, but then recanted under pressure from the police. Barry Hartman, the editor of the *Daily Camera*, and the person who had helped bring me and the witness together in the first place was discredited and forced out of his job as a result of this, even though he'd had a sterling career. Despite this, he never let go of his endorsement of the witness. So then the new DA came after me. Linda Wickman, who knew me very well, found a groundsman at the apartment complex where I was staying who was prepared to swear that he'd seen me with my Hong Kong wife in violation of the restraining order. This is despite the fact that on the day he claimed to have seen us together, she was in Kowloon and I was in Colorado. So here I am, arrested and charged with the heinous crime of being seen with my wife on a day when she was on the other side of the fucking planet. I was facing a minimum mandatory non-parolable twelve months' jail time. After my original arrest, a new statute was passed mandating jail time if pre-trial release conditions in domestic violence cases were violated."

"Do you mean that they changed the rules of the game to have you put away?"

"I'm sure the legislation was passed without paying attention to me. That doesn't speak to the DA's decision to charge me under the newly enacted statute. Even if I were cleared of the underlying domestic violence charge, I could be jailed and wind up doing even more time for violating the pre-trial release conditions."

"Why didn't your wife make a formal declaration that she was in Hong Kong when the alleged violation of the pre-trial release condition occurred?"

"Oh, she did that and more – she hired a lawyer who came to Colorado and demanded an audience with the DA prosecuting this charge against me. The whole point of that raid was to arrest me for being seen with my wife. Despite the lawyer telling them 'She's in Hong Kong'; despite presenting certified letters from the US consul-general's office in Hong Kong; despite showing airfare receipts; despite the letter that my wife sent to the DA's office, telling them, 'I'm here in Hong Kong. I wasn't there.' Despite all this, the deputy DA prosecuting my case stood up in court and said, 'We believe she's still in the United States.' There was no shred of evidence, and all the evidence was to the contrary."

"So there was no evidence to support their allegation."

"Only the statement by the groundsman. The lawyer my wife had retained, who had flown all the way from Hong Kong with a ton of compelling evidence, was there in court saying, 'She was in Hong Kong when this alleged restraining order violation occurred, and she's there now.' They didn't give a rat's ass."

"So finding the weapons, which was another bail violation, was a bonus?"

"Well, remember, they found two plastic blow dart guns and some ceremonial swords that wouldn't cut butter. The one thing that would have gotten me in deep shit was the machine gun sitting in an unlocked briefcase in the room they were turning over so thoroughly. What do you think happened to it? Absolutely nothing. After they had finished their search, the briefcase was still sitting where it had always been. In the United States, having an unlicensed machine gun is an extremely serious offence. It's a federal felony, and so having such a weapon throws the crime into the federal arena. There are minimum mandatory sentencing guidelines that have to do with having an unlicensed machine gun. They never mentioned a word about it."

"And why was that?"

"One possibility is that they simply didn't notice it – in an unlocked briefcase, that was on the desk right in the middle of the fucking room where they were tearing everything apart. Now that just defies belief. These guys may have been goons, but one thing they knew how to do was shred a room for evidence. No, they saw it all right, but left it sitting there. They simply didn't want to find it. If they'd turned the gun in as evidence, they have lost control of the case to the Feds, and that's the last thing they wanted. They hauled out of that apartment every pocket knife, every letter opener, and every child's toy that could be characterized as a weapon: everything except for the fucking submachine gun, the very weapon that would have put me into serious shit."

"I still don't understand. If they saw it, which according to you they clearly did, why leave it there?"

"If the case had been handed over to the Feds, different prosecutors would have been handling the case, and different issues would have arisen. And that's the core of the situation. These were issues that they desperately didn't want to see the light of day, because it would have thrown the focus directly back where they didn't want it to be – onto the JonBenét Ramsey case."

"How did they deal with the evidence that supported your position?"

"They simply ignored it. In the preliminary hearing of my case, the groundskeeper at the apartment compound gave his statement under oath that he had seen me in the grounds with a woman the prosecution claimed to be my wife. In fact, he had seen me with a woman who happened to be a friend of mine. Under cross-examination by my attorney, the groundskeeper gave a very accurate description of my friend. The problem was that she looked nothing like my wife. She was six inches taller, she had a different hairstyle, was a different age, and to top it all off, was Caucasian. And, as I've said, we produced all this compelling evidence that my wife was on the other side of the planet. But the prosecution was unmoved."

"If they wanted to get rid of you so desperately, wouldn't it have been easier just to have you eliminated?"

"There's a good reason why eliminating me was an option of last resort. That would have underpinned the credibility of the witness that they sought to discredit. In effect, I would have become a martyr. So the witness was the crux of the whole legal wrangle because she was the missing link between JonBenét's death and the child sex abuse ring. What she had to reveal could blow the whole JonBenét Ramsey case apart. However, if I were to disappear or be discredited, then so would she. She would certainly never come forward without me. It had taken me forever to earn her trust."

"There's a problem with the logic here, but let's move on. You're facing a lengthy term in prison for a crime you didn't commit, you're under a court order not to leave Colorado, and you turn up here in Hong Kong. How did you manage that?"

"No-one ever said to me 'Get out of the country and we'll leave you alone.' But the messages I was getting via third parties were clear enough, so it was a no-brainer. Hong Kong was the obvious choice. My wife was there and I knew that it was the perfect place for me to reinvent myself. The City of Masks, as I've heard it described: a place where everyone has something to hide; a can-do place where work is freely available to anyone who wants it.

"I flew out on my passport. I was triple-screened in airport security. This was not too long after 9/11, and security was tighter than it had ever been. I had lunch with a homeland security officer, a total stranger, by the way. I spent the entire lunch listening to him describe the inadequacies of their screening protocols, expecting he was pretexting me while waiting for backup to arrest me as I was waiting for my connecting flight out of Los Angeles. I wasn't supposed to leave the State of Colorado, so just by flying to California I was violating yet another of my pre-trial conditions. I had a rationale that provided an affirmative defence, but I didn't expect for anybody in Boulder to simply accept that without first inconveniencing me by arresting me. I never went by an assumed name. I flew to Hong Kong, exactly to where they knew my wife was living – where they would have expected me to go. Of course, this would have represented a logical conundrum for them, as they'd both asserted they believed she was still in the United States, while also refusing to cover her travel expenses when she offered to return to testify on my behalf. Within the first week I was here in Hong Kong I went to the American Consulate on Garden Road and renewed my American passport. Everybody knew where I was, but nobody did anything about it. They never revoked my bond. They never sent someone to knock on the door of my last known address. No-one ever went looking for me. Anyway, I'll stop now. I'm sorry, that's quite an answer to your question about how I came to be in Hong Kong."

*

Although Leon's story takes place in the States, I've included it for several reasons. In the first place, it illustrates the fact that many people in Hong Kong are not who they seem to be. It's a City of Masks, as Leon says. Many people, locals and expatriates alike, have something to hide. The City of Masks metaphor was to appear and reappear in various guises in a number of interviews.

Leon came to Hong Kong to reinvent himself, which he did very successfully. While the art of reinvention can be practised at home, there's a very good chance that you'll be unmasked. In Hong Kong, there's no problem in maintaining your mask, unless you do something to make yourself newsworthy. From time to time, this happens. The story mirrors other themes such as mobility. Leon, like other expats and locals, is constantly in motion. There may be other societies where the population roams the globe so ceaselessly, but I challenge anyone to name a place which outdoes Hong Kong. As another informant said, for many locals, modern Hong Kong was a staging post or, as the informant said, a refugee camp for Mainlanders who were on their way elsewhere. The restless spirit has infected the place, and these days, satellite families shuttle back and forth between Hong Kong and their other adopted homes abroad, or make frequent trips back to their ancestral roots. The mainly British expatriates who colonized the place also made frequent trips 'back home'. This was true even for those who were born here.

Finally, at the risk of appearing self-indulgent, I included Leon's story because it's simply a cracking good yarn. I'll leave you to draw your own conclusions on what it says about democracy and justice in the West. Elsewhere in the book, I include stories on the judicial system in Hong Kong. While far from perfect, it is no worse, and in fact in some ways it is more transparent than in the United States where justice is subverted by the 'national interest' which is invoked, as it was in Leon's case, to stop natural justice in its tracks.

16.

One little death

One little warm death comin' up
One little warm death with me tonight (Cassandra Wilson)

Although it's mid-morning on a working day, Eva sits on the sofa in her pyjamas. The pyjamas are warm, soft, fleecy, encasing and comforting her thighs. There she sits, her knees drawn up under her chin, clasping a cup of coffee in both hands. It's a nice sofa, and one she'd wanted for some time, but the opportunity to acquire it only came after the split, and he'd moved out taking the old sofa with him, among other things. Her friend Mai, who had come around for coffee and a viewing of the new sofa, had spoiled things by pointing out how impractical it was to have cream covers. Was it envy? She certainly couldn't afford something of this quality herself, and anyway, there's no way that it would fit in her cramped little flat. She had deliberately chosen the cream-coloured sofa because it brightened up her flat and showed off the Thai silk cushions she had bought in Bangkok.

She had decided to work from home because there was nothing pressing happening at work. She has a slight headache, which she could have dealt with by taking a pill, but the dull pain gives her an excuse not to confront the outside world. Like many Hongkongers, she is feeling beleaguered. The protest movement has dragged on for over a month, and while it wasn't really that much of an inconvenience to everyday life, the social fabric was beginning to fray. The international media, particularly CNN, gave the impression that locals were solidly behind the courageous young people and their 'protest with peace and love', but nothing could be further from the truth: the protest was tearing apart the place she loved.

Removing a hand from the coffee cup, she feels for the remote control and switches on the television, then flicks to a local channel to catch up with what has happened overnight. The crowd has thinned a little during the night, but still numbers in their thousands, and will swell again during the day. The camera pans across the placards and posters plastered on the wall behind the protesters. These are written in traditional Chinese script, which serves two purposes. Firstly, it makes them difficult, if not impossible, to decipher by Mainlanders schooled in the simplified script. Secondly, it is an act of defiance, challenging Beijing dictum about what language to speak and what script to write. There would be no misunderstanding in Beijing about the real meaning of the posters.

The television feed switches to Mong Kok, showing violent clashes between the police and the protesters. The voice-over announces that the police are carrying out an injunction ordered by the high court to clear Nathan Road, and they do so with pepper spray and tear gas. The umbrellas carried by the protesters, which have given rise to the label 'Umbrella Revolution', are no protection against the gas attack. One young protester, blinded by the gas, stumbles to the ground not far from the camera, where he is jumped on and kicked. Horrified, Eva loses her grip on the coffee cup, which falls onto the sofa leaving a dramatic brown stain on the cover. Mai's vindictive prediction has been fulfilled. Dabbing at the stain with a damp cloth only makes it worse.

The rumblings had been going on for months. In the beginning, she hadn't taken much notice. It was like distant thunder that was too far off to be concerned about, a storm that you knew was going to pass. Besides, she had her own problems: personal ones, and therefore far more significant than some political spat. Protests came and went, but they never amounted to much. Each year since the Handover, on the July 1 public holiday to mark Establishment Day, there was a protest march organized by the pro-democracy movement, but the protesters got very little except heatstroke. During 2014, the rumblings grew louder. There was talk of an Occupy Central movement. A couple of years before, she had been visiting her sister June, who worked as an attorney in New York, when the Occupy Wall Street protest came to a head. Her understanding from June was that it had "something to do with the anti-globalization movement." She only visited the Lower East Side once for lunch with June and a couple of June's friends, but saw nothing of the protest. From her point of view, it might never have happened. She assumed that the Occupy Central movement, if it ever happened, could be similarly ignored. Leaders of the movement seemed to be all talk and no action. In any case, the vast majority of Hongkongers were more interested in getting on with their lives and providing for their families than involving themselves in movements for political change.

But she was wrong. The spark that ignited the passions of the pro-democracy movement and turned the all-talkers into activists was the electoral reform legislation. She asked her father, who took an interest in these things, what it was all about. He explained that it had to do with the provisions for electing the Chief Executive. She knew that he (it was always a he, of course, despite the attempts one year to get the much admired Anson Chan onto the slate), was elected by an Election Committee: a hand-picked group of Beijing-friendly locals. Beijing agreed to honour the provision in the Basic Law for the 2017 election of the next Chief Executive by universal suffrage, but the three candidates to present themselves to the electors would be vetted and approved by the Beijing-friendly locals. It was this that finally got the pro-democracy activists on to the streets. She didn't get it. Her father, ever patient, enlightened her. "Electing one of three stooges approved by Beijing – where's the democracy in that?"

Drawn, like many people, more by curiosity than a sudden political conversion, she observed the swollen crowd from well behind the safety of the barricades. There seemed to be almost as many police as protesters. Where had they come from? And what had happened to them? The benign, smooth-faced young men had morphed into fighting machines with guns, batons and riot shields. She was fascinated and horrified. You could smell the aggression. What was happening to Hong Kong, her beloved Hong Kong? As she backed away and trudged home, a storm was brewing. Many of the protesters were carrying umbrellas which might protect them from the rain, but not from the riot police.

In the morning, she watched the news: the baton charges, the beatings, the tear gas. The CNN reporter brought the free world up to date with a theatrical account of the evening's events. Seen through the lens of the camera, it did look like a piece of theatre, but to her there was nothing theatrical about it. She found it profoundly depressing.

At five o'clock, she receives a text message from Dan. He had noticed her absence from work and wonders if she is all right. She texts back that she is OK. He is in the neighbourhood and wonders if it would be all right if he dropped by for a while. Reluctantly, she sends him another OK. Ever since rumours of the breakup had leaked into the corridors of the college, his attitude towards her had changed from colleague to caring friend. The first thing he wanted to know was whether he left her or she left him. She was the one who had ended the relationship, a fact which seemed to please him. How had she done it, he wanted to know. She deflected the question, as it was really none of his business. She'd taken the coward's path, waiting until he was away on a business trip, and then removing herself and her possessions to Mai's place, but she had no intention of sharing the messy details of the breakup with nosy Dan.

No doubt his concern and that of her other colleagues was genuine, but she could also detect a hint of pleasure in her misfortune. It was only natural. She remembered how she felt at the news that her former school friend, now in Vancouver, had been diagnosed with breast cancer and had subsequently passed away at the age of forty. There was choking grief, of course, but also the relief that it had happened to someone else.

The intercom startles her with its annoying intensity and persistence. When he sent the text message, he must have been lurking right outside her building. She buzzes him in, flips the sofa cushion to hide the coffee stain, and hurries to the bedroom to pull on a pair of jeans. When she opens the door to him, he steps inside, kicks off his shoes and gives her a hug that lasts a few seconds too long. She backs away and retreats to the sofa. "Mind if I help myself to a beer?" he asks, heading to the tiny kitchen without waiting for an answer.

Dan is sweet, all her colleagues agree on that. He has that charming American incapacity to believe the world could possibly be different from the way he imagines it. When he arrived at the school, she had taken him under her wing and shown him how things worked, but he persisted in doing things his way. A panel chair, she was nominally his boss, but there was no way of establishing any kind of hierarchical relationship over him. At work, they had slipped into a comfortable friendship: an occasional beer after work and one or two social events. His lack of maturity was compensated for by his relentless good humour. Because of her years abroad, as a graduate student in the UK, and the long visits to her sister in New York, she'd had plenty of contact with foreigners and was comfortable in their presence, but she had never dated one.

He drops onto the sofa beside her, swigs beer straight from the bottle, and sets it on the coffee table. It will leave a ring, but she makes no move to place a coaster underneath it. The television flickers, but there is no sound as she has it on mute. Dan rests a friendly hand on her knee and asks her how she is. "Fine," she replies. Why tell him how she's really feeling? His attention wanders from her to the television. "Oh, look," he says, pointing to the screen. "It's that pro-Beijing dude. Turn it up, I want to hear what he has to say." On the screen, a talking head obliterates most of the long shots of the protesters.

That 'dude' is a prominent Hong Kong businessman and convener of the mischievously misnamed Alliance for Peace and Democracy. "This is not civil disobedience," he says, "but a direct challenge to the law and disruption of public order. What Gandhi did was refuse to pay salt tax to the British government to protest against the laws. What Martin Luther King led was a bus boycott campaign to protest against the reservation of seats for whites. They were not hurting anyone. They weren't inconveniencing anyone, but what the Hong Kong protesters are doing is inconveniencing people and hurting our businesses."

He leans across and returns the television to mute. "So whose side are you on?" he asks. It's the question on everybody's lips. Are you yellow or blue? It's a ridiculous question. Today the answer might be yellow, tomorrow it will be blue. Giving the wrong answer could have serious consequences. Just the day before, her friend Mai had called her in tears – she had been removed as a Facebook friend by two work colleagues and a close relative, and is devastated. There is only one answer to his question, and finally she gives it to him. "Hong Kong," she says. "That's whose side I'm on. And Hong Kong is losing."

"All sorts of crazy theories are going around," replies Dan. "Yesterday, I heard someone saying that it was a CIA plot. There's always someone who wants to blame the Americans. If you ask me," he says (she hasn't but is going to be told anyway), "if you ask me it's a communist plot. Think about it. The longer this goes on, the more Hong Kong gets damaged. Beijing wants Hong Kong to become just another minor city in the South China Sea. They don't have to do anything to you to achieve this, you're doing it to yourselves. Democracy? You're not ready for democracy. It has to evolve over many years; it can't just spring up overnight. It doesn't matter who you vote for, you'll just end up with another C.Y. Leung."

She's growing tired of Dan. It had been a mistake to let him invite himself up. Today was her day to be alone. She wants him gone, but doesn't know how to make it happen without offending him (hardly likely), or, more likely, hurting his feelings. He hasn't even finished his beer. But then he provides a solution. She knows it's coming. You always do, you can feel it. It's something men will never understand. She turns her head away as he leans towards her and his nose collides with her cheekbone. It must have hurt, but he says nothing. Unperturbed, he reaches for his beer. She realizes that it isn't his first for the day. She stands up. "It's time for you to go," she says.

Eva, alone among her close friends, is the only one whose father was born in Hong Kong. The others, like most of their generation, are the offspring of refugees from the Mainland. Her grandfather was a wealthy merchant who owned tea houses, restaurants and wine shops in Guangdong, Macau and Hong Kong, and divided his time between all three. Her father, the second of seven children, was born in Hong Kong in 1939, a time of global upheaval, and grew up there living a privileged existence under the noses of the Japanese occupying forces who were paid off by his father to leave them alone. In 1947, when he was eight, his father moved him to Guangzhou to complete his education. He was passed around the extended family in which uncles and aunties looked after each other's children. In time, he would come to look back on that decision to move to China as a masterstroke of mistiming. The communists came to power, and confiscated his father's money and properties. He and his father were looked on with great suspicion by his father's siblings, who were indoctrinated by the communists and taught that Hong Kong and its inhabitants were corrupt and degenerate. On leaving school, he wanted to study medicine at university, but was denied a place because he had been born in Hong Kong. He had to settle for a science degree. When the Cultural Revolution began, he was one of the first to be denounced, displaced from urban life, and sent to the countryside to learn what real hardship was all about. His biography ticked all the wrong boxes. He was a member of the middle classes. He had a university degree, and was therefore considered to be an intellectual. He never said much about the years he spent living the life of a peasant, but Eva could well imagine it. Risking his life, he escaped to Macau, and from there made his way back to Hong Kong.

After the National People's Congress adopted the Basic Law in 1990, he became increasingly anxious. One evening, he gathered Eva and her sisters together in their apartment, and said to them, "We have to get out of Hong Kong. We need a new identity." Like many Hong Kong residents who had suffered at the hands of the communists, he had no faith whatsoever in the guarantees enshrined in the Basic Law that had been forged between England and the Chinese government in 1984. More than that, he saw it as a betrayal on the part of the British government.

When Margaret Thatcher, the prime minister of the day, had suggested to the Chinese that the treaty be extended, the Mainland government was highly offended at her arrogance. He knew that it would take its revenge against Hong Kong at a time of its choosing.

He narrowed his options to Vancouver, London and Singapore and, after due consideration, settled on Singapore. Vancouver and London were too distant and both had unforgiving climates. Singapore had its faults, but it was close, it was warm, and you could mind your own business. He bought a government flat, and they spent each summer there, trolling around to various government departments collecting stamps in their passports that made little sense to Eva, but kept her parents happy. Like other Hongkongers who had embraced the Singaporean solution, as soon as they had collected the requisite number of stamps, and had been granted permanent residence, her father sold the flat. However, unlike most Hongkongers, who were dismissive of Singapore's stultifying lifestyle, they developed affection for the place, and continued to spend part of the year there.

After completing a graduate degree in England, Eva got a job in Singapore. However, she never developed anything remotely approaching affection for the place. Despite her status as a permanent resident and the fact that she spent five years working there, she never saw herself as anything other than an expatriate. To save a couple of dollars, her colleagues would rather endure the heat of a hawker stall for their morning coffee than the air-conditioned comfort of a Starbucks. Occasionally, she would put up with the hawker stall heat, not to save money, but because she enjoyed the food. On her first 'winter' in Singapore, to the amazement of her colleagues, she insisted on wearing boots to work as a reminder to herself that the rest of the world had four seasons, even Hong Kong, and that she wasn't going to be in Singapore forever. There was no way that she was going to lose her sense of the seasons.

Despite her dismissive attitude at the lengths the locals would go to save a dollar, when she discovered that if she had expatriate status in Singapore she would be eligible for a housing allowance, which she could use to supplement the purchase of a property in Hong Kong, she promptly renounced her permanent residency. As well as making her better off financially, she was happy to be an expat in a legal as well as a spiritual sense. Now she could disparage Singapore and the Singaporeans to her Hong Kong friends without carrying a burden of guilt. It no longer bothered her when her Singaporean colleagues criticized her defective Putonghua or the fact that they thought she was showing off by speaking English without a Singaporean accent. She was advised by a number of people at the University, including her favourite Indian student, that she should try to pick up the Singaporean accent in order to have an easier life there, but she just couldn't do it. It wasn't that she didn't try; it simply wasn't her. As an expat, she considered that she could bring something different to the students, who were mainly Singaporean. Having given up her permanent residency, she was officially, and happily, an outsider. During her time as a graduate student in England, she had not thought of herself as an expat, but now, in Singapore, she did. She limited her contact with locals, and spent more time with expats, joining a women's badminton team and frequenting the expat bars along Clarke Quay.

The truth was, she had never fitted in, and the local colleagues had never wanted her to. There was one telling incident that occurred shortly after she started teaching at the university. It happened at the end of her first staff meeting. She and several colleagues were walking back across the campus to their offices. Two of the Singaporean women walking behind her pretended to be talking to each other but their remarks were directed at her. One said, "Why do we need to have someone coming from Hong Kong to teach our Singaporean students English? Don't we have talented, educated people here in Singapore to do that?" The other one replied, "Of course we do. I don't know why we have to have these people from Hong Kong." She neither reacted nor responded, but she never forgot.

When she eventually returned to Hong Kong, she saw the expatriate community in a new light. In her younger years, she had had limited contact with foreigners, and thought of them, if she thought of them at all, in stereotypical terms: rich, white guys, who were here for a limited time to get even richer. In her new job, she had worked with several of them. These were mainly young teachers such as Dan who were not particularly wealthy. She began to socialize with them, and realized that they made Hong Kong a more interesting place.

She had a way of differentiating between gweilos according to where they hung out and where they lived. The ones who hung out in the Wan Chai bars were not the ones she wanted to associate with: they wanted cheap beer and cheap girls. She and her friends would categorize them: "Oh, there's a Lamma gweilo" or "There's a Discovery Bay gweilo." Even though they were university-educated and had studied overseas, she and her friends were not interested in dating gweilos. They found talking to gweilos too much of an effort. They had decent jobs and their own apartments, so why bother with gweilos? At one point she may have been interested in Dan – after the breakup, when he was being nice to her. But then the moment passed. After his visit to her in her apartment, she realized it would have been a mistake.

It's lunchtime in the college cafeteria. A group of her colleagues are occupying one of the long central tables. She is about to join them, but the group includes several of the expat teachers, including Dan, with whom she doesn't particularly want to socialize today. On the other side of the room, she notices Chelsea, one of the office assistants, sitting by herself some way apart from the other assistants. On a whim, she takes her tray and joins the girl. Unlike some of the other assistants, who respond to requests for help with a resigned, put-upon attitude, Chelsea is unfailingly helpful: quick, willing and smart. Whenever Eva has some copying to do in a hurry, or grades that need to be entered into the system before a looming deadline, she seeks out Chelsea. It's unusual, although not entirely unheard of, for a teacher to sit with a member of the support staff over lunch. It's one of those cultural rules that determine how things are done. But Eva has never been big on rules, cultural or otherwise.

Why is Chelsea sitting all by herself? She hasn't touched her food. Is she feeling unwell? Chelsea, usually bubbly and fun-loving, is reluctant to talk. But Eva has ways and means, and Chelsea has little resistance to her relentless kindness. Of course, it's all about Occupy Central. When she refuses to join in the universal condemnation of the government, her office colleagues become suspicious, and then, the previous day, the inevitable question. "Are you yellow, or blue?" Why does she have to be one or the other? "You're either with us or against us." She refuses to either confirm or deny. That afternoon there is a whispering campaign and she discovers that, like Eva's friend Mai, she has been removed as a Facebook friend by the other assistants.

Chelsea's mother owns a little shop in Mong Kok, epicentre of the worst excesses of the crowds and the police. She is clinging to the place by her financial fingernails. If the protest goes on much longer she will lose the shop, and to lose the shop will be to lose everything. Yellow and blue are meaningless. You can't eat democracy. You can't sleep on it. Her mother will end up back in Guangzhou with Chelsea's father and his other wife.

Eva's anger burns slowly as, late in the afternoon, she joins the conga line of commuters at the express bus stop. According to the Occupy Central manifesto, developed over a year before the start of civil disobedience, the aim of the campaign was to "establish a society embracing equality, tolerance, love and care." Where is the tolerance here? she asks herself. Where is the love? Where is the care? Where is the decree dictating that the universe shall consist of only two colours? She thinks of her friends who are yellow one day, and blue the next, blue one day and yellow the next: the relentless pressure to conform to this side or that side. It seems to be going on without end.

She stops off in Central to have coffee with a male cousin. They are a similar age, and have been very close since they were children. It's all because of your birth signs, says her mother, who has read books on these things. Things are not good at home, says her cousin, half the family is yellow, the other half is blue. Her cousin is unwaveringly yellow and has spent many hours at the protest site. However, one of his uncles, just five years older than he is, and someone he has looked up to most of his life, has hardened his position into an unwavering blue. A very gentle man, he had shocked her cousin when he burst out, "I just want to drive my van into the umbrella movement people. I just want to bring them to their senses." Eva tells her cousin that she can understand. Although she refuses to take sides, if there was anything she could do to bring it to an end she would do it. Anything.

Later that night, lying in bed and unable to sleep, an idea begins to harden in her head. It is a crazy idea, but once it has taken hold, she is unable to shake it. She rises early, makes her morning coffee, and thinks. It's not that she doesn't value her life, but she doesn't have a partner or children. It would be worth a life to bring all this mess to an end. Would she have time? Ideally, she would like to do it 689 times – one for every vote he got in his rise to Chief Executive.

At Wing On, she goes first to the furniture department to buy a replacement for the vase her mother broke on a visit the previous week. Then she takes the escalator to the basement and finds her way to the kitchenware department. The most suitable one is the smallest in a boxed set of three. She turns the box over in her hands while the shop assistant hovers.

The blade flexes slightly at the pressure from her palm. She winces at the needle prick of the pointed blade that draws a bright spot of blood from the tip of her finger. It will certainly do the job.

*

"What made you think that you could get away with it?"

"Listen. Only someone like me who appears very gentle, very timid, and very conservative on the outside would be able to get close to him. I thought that if I could bring a halt to something that was destroying Hong Kong, I wouldn't mind other people taking my life."

"So why did you decide not to go through with it?"

"I told my cousin, the one whose uncle wanted to drive his van into the protesters. I told him because I thought it might help him to understand a little more where his uncle is coming from – maybe all he wanted to do was bring the whole thing to an end. My cousin just laughed and said that driving a van into the crowd or stabbing C.Y. Leung isn't going to change anything. Those people from the north will just bring in another C.Y. Leung, so what's the use? There's no use, no use at all."

"It sounds as though you've given up."

"It's not going to make the Beijing people change their mind. So we need to do things more strategically, I think. If negotiation, or talking, or some kind of compromise is the strategic way to go then we go the strategic way. The whole Occupy Central thing hurts a lot. It hurts, it hurts a great deal."

"Because you love Hong Kong?"

"Yes, yes, it hurts because I love Hong Kong. It hurts because it's hurting Hong Kong so much so that I seriously thought about moving away from Hong Kong."

"If you moved, where would you go?"

"If you leave somebody whom you really love, does it matter who is going to be your next lover? I think it doesn't really matter. Anywhere else doesn't matter. And because it doesn't matter, it isn't going to hurt."

17.

GO BACK TO WHERE YOU CAME FROM

*Society, as we have constituted it, will have no place for me, has none
to offer; but Nature, whose sweet rains fall on unjust and just alike,
will have clefts in the rocks where I may hide, and secret valleys in
whose silence I may weep undisturbed.* (Oscar Wilde)

To say that since he arrived in Hong Kong life has been tough for
Michael would be a considerable understatement. While his application
for political asylum is being considered, he is not allowed to work, and he
has to rely on the charity of friends who do have work. It was unfortunate
that before his status had been determined, responsibility for processing
applications had passed from the United Nations High Commission for
Refugees to the Hong Kong Department of Immigration. The UNHCR
was overwhelmed by the global tide of displaced humanity that was
coming to define the early part of the twenty-first century, and had run
out of solutions. So the government took over the problem, and it didn't
take them long to come up with a solution. They would make life so
difficult for those seeking asylum or refugee status that they would go
back to where they came from. Although they make minimal demands
on the public purse, any money spent on what are considered 'second-
class potential citizens' is resented.

Hong Kong doesn't look kindly upon refugees or asylum seekers. This
is ironic given the fact that modern Hong Kong is a post-World War II
creation, made up of the masses who flooded into the colony after the

communist takeover of the Mainland in 1949. For them, Hong Kong was a refugee camp, a staging post. They were on their way to somewhere else: somewhere called freedom. The vast majority ended up staying, and they and their offspring became the gene pool for the Hong Kong of today.

At the end of the Vietnam war, another wave of refugees arrived from the south. Hundreds of thousands of them flooded into the colony. Prior to the 1997 Handover, almost 100,000 of these were repatriated to their place of origin. By the time Michael arrives, no new asylum seekers are being accepted into the territory. This doesn't stop them turning up, mostly from Africa and South Asia. They slip under the radar and work illegally, often for years. A common plot, if caught, is to claim they are the victims of torture and will be killed if sent back to their home country. This strategy has a low rate of success. In fact, only about one in 400 applicants succeed.

Michael's waiting time turns from weeks into months. Although he is not confined to a detention centre, with very little money every day is a struggle. Then he is informed that his application has been misplaced, and he would have to reapply. On the second occasion this happens he is tempted to give up. But then what would he do? He knows he is being tested, but by whom? And to what end?

While his application is being considered he is not allowed to work. Survival options are limited. Some of his friends had taken to peddling drugs on Hollywood Road. This was a high-risk strategy, because if you were caught, you were instantly deported. A second strategy was to marry a local. The problem with this strategy was finding someone who was prepared to marry you. A Nigerian he met in Chungking Mansions on Nathan Road had found someone and married her. The Nigerian's wife had a sister who evinced interest in meeting Michael with a view to marriage. Michael was also interested until he met the Nigerian's wife, which prompted an instant change of mind.

In Somalia, his treatment at the hands of Al Shabaab, the Islamist militant group which captured him, gave him constant nightmares.

The physical torture that left his body permanently mutilated was bad enough, but not as bad as the mental torture of the wait: the wait that ended with the clatter of footsteps in the corridor, the slamming back of the bolts. It was a day he had known was coming, and as the days mounted the terror of anticipation reached a point where even beheading seemed preferable to the wait. He began to wish for the day to come: and then he got his wish.

He had squeezed his eyes shut when he heard the footsteps and realized what they signified. Those sounds had been a constant presence in his nightmares: those and the smell of his own fear. Now and then they would enter the cell and take him off to the interrogation room where he would be questioned and beaten unconscious. On this morning, they dragged him not to the interrogation room, but to a small yard with high walls – the killing ground. He knew what was coming, and wondered which of them was to be his executioner. He thought of his family and their frantic attempts to raise the ransom. His torturers took pleasure in keeping him updated on those futile efforts. If they managed to secure the ransom, he would be freed. If they failed, he was a dead man. Either way, the torturers won.

His hands are bound and he is prepared for death. On his knees, they tell him to be still. He wants to be still. His mind wills his body into stillness, but his body refuses to listen. The steel blade has come to rest across his neck when he hears shouting. There is a brief conversation, he is hauled to his feet, the blindfold is removed, and he is led back to his cell. At the eleventh hour, his family members, by sacrificing everything they own, have managed to meet the ransom demand.

He wasn't free for long. A short time after his release, he was captured by another Islamist group, just as radical as Al Shabaab but less organized, which had seen some of his news reports. This time, there was no ransom demand. For a second time, he faced imminent death. However, his new captors were a disorganized rabble, and security wasn't as tight as it had been with Al Shabaab. One night he managed to escape by climbing a wall. Although he was free once more, Somalia was a perilous place. Not wanting to place his family at further risk, he made his way to Hong Kong and applied for refugee status. During an interminable series of interviews, he stripped himself naked and provided graphic evidence of his torture. He showed them his news reports, samples of his video footage, some of which had made its way on to international media outlets, even as far as CNN. He didn't want their sympathy, and they didn't disappoint him. What he wanted was asylum. He didn't get that either, although they didn't reject his application outright. Instead, he was left in limbo. These people, who hadn't occupied this territory for very long themselves, were sitting there deciding who to let in and who to turn away. They told him to go away and wait. Not knowing what more he could possibly do to convince them of the legitimacy of his claim, that is what he did.

It was only on rare occasions that the racism manifested itself overtly. Like the way that people pressed themselves away from you when you stepped into the elevator, covering their mouth and nose as they did so. Like the time on the MTR: he was standing near a mother and child minding his own business when the child looked him up and down and started crying. "You'd better behave," said the mother in English for his benefit. "Otherwise he'll come after you and take you away." No, most Hongkongers were more subtle than that. In general, they were pretty tolerant, he had to admit, but the racism was always there. You could smell it.

Michael had long ago come to believe luck was something that happened to other people, and he had plenty of evidence to support the belief. Meeting Mona, an American expatriate and volunteer aid worker, was pure coincidence, and he later had to add luck into the equation. There was nothing earth-shattering about the meeting, although it was a little out of the ordinary. Hong Kong is one of those places where people meet often and effortlessly. Two pairs of eyes meet in a bar and lock on: in most other places they alight briefly and slide on, eye contact lasting more than a nanosecond being an embarrassment. But here, more often than not, a drink is offered and accepted and a friendship is born. The friendship may last for a lifetime, for days, or for hours – not unexpected in a city as fluid as this.

Their meeting happens not far from the MTR exit on Lockhart Road. An ancient woman has collapsed on the street. Hong Kong is full of ancient people, invisible to the rest of the population unless they happen to be a relative, or unless they get in the way. Michael notices them because in the anonymity of the street they are outsiders, just like him. He marvels at their ability to remain more-or-less upright at their crepuscular pace along the street, at the way they negotiate potentially life-threatening tasks such as crossing the road.

They are approaching each other from opposite directions when the old woman subsides to the ground. She doesn't drop like a stone, not like people do when their heart decides it's had enough, but slowly, the way that ballerinas are taught to do. Unbelievably, people step around her. Hong Kong people don't lack compassion, but minding their own business is part of their DNA. Of course, soon enough people would have stopped, when the old woman on the pavement had pushed other busy thoughts from their minds. But on this day, it falls to the white woman heading west, and the black man heading east, to be the first to stop.

Mona, by instinct and nature, stoops to attend to the old woman who has collapsed on the pavement, so close that she almost trips over her. As she bends over she almost cracks craniums with the black man who had vaguely registered in her consciousness as she pushed her way through the pre-lunch crush. She looks up, face inches apart from an extraordinary pair of eyes. She registers the eyes before turning her attention to the old woman. The black man places slim fingers against the carotid artery. "She still has a pulse," he says. She wonders if he's a doctor.

By this time, a small crowd has gathered around them. A man crouches down and speaks to the old woman in Cantonese. Her eyes flutter open but she doesn't respond. Mona looks around for the police, who patrol in pairs and are ubiquitous on the streets, disappearing only when you need them. Eventually, two young officers push their way through the bystanders. Mona explains what she saw, and the police take charge.

Mona stands back and looks at the black man. The look in his eyes tells her part of his story, but she needs to know the details. There's nothing more that they can do for the old woman – not that they did much in the first place. She asks him if he has time for a drink. He smiles and nods. It's clear that being picked up by a white woman on the streets of Hong Kong is a novelty.

In a coffee shop in Ship Street, away from the crowds and the sleaze of Lockhart Road, they sit and drink Coke. She thought she had heard it all, but Michael's story touches something in her. It was a source of wonder to her that human beings could endure physical and mental torture, stare down death, survive on practically nothing in the midst of Hong Kong's obscene plenty, and yet still be capable of going about daily life, still be able to walk down the street, to smile, to stop and try to assist an old woman in distress – something that not even her own race could be bothered to do. Mona had a moral code which she applied uncompromisingly to individuals and societies alike. Hong Kong society didn't measure up too well against that code. For her, the human in human being came first: race, religion, and social status a distant second, third and fourth.

He knows about the refugee centre but so far has avoided it, doesn't want to get sucked into the asylum seeker underclass and then pigeonholed. He doesn't want to become institutionalized: it goes against all of his journalistic instincts. He knows a number of refugee and asylum seekers. Walking on the street, they sniff him out, he tells her. Some of them go to the centre. He mentions several names she recognizes. "Come along tomorrow," she says. "In the evening. I'll be there."

And against his better judgment, he does. She's surprised but pleased to see him. She introduces him around and tells him what the centre can do for him. It's not at all like the place he had been avoiding in his imagination. She's quite hungry, and she imagines that he might be as well, but when she suggests that they go for a meal, he hesitates. "It's all right," she says. "And if it's about the money, well…" In the end, he lets her buy him dinner, and then she offers him some cash. "Just to tide you over," she says. At first, she used to be embarrassed when they refused, but no longer. She knows he'll come around in the end. They always do. Then she takes him to a bar. It occupies a large space in a basement, and has a vaguely African theme. A group of black musicians is playing the kind of music that used to be familiar to him. They all seem to know her. When she offers to buy him a drink, he accepts a Coke. He doesn't touch alcohol. Now and then he goes to bars for one reason or another, he says. Someone will always offer him a drink, but no one ever offers him food.

Tired of living rough in squalid apartments or in public spaces such as the Star Ferry concourse, and scavenging for food, he eventually gives in and accepts her assistance. But she knows that it isn't only the money, or even primarily the money, it's her friendship and support, with no strings attached. He never asks her what is in it for her: he doesn't need to. But their relationship only gives him a temporary lift. His growing frustration, bordering on anger, worries her. He is just a number, one of hundreds claiming refugee status or political asylum on the grounds of persecution and torture. His cause isn't helped by the fact that not every claimant is genuine, nor by the fact that Hong Kong isn't a signatory to the United Nations Refugee Convention.

Late one afternoon she receives a call. Michael has been arrested and charged with the wilful destruction of public property. Even the mildest of men has his breaking point, and Michael reached his when he learned that his application for asylum in Canada had been approved, but the paperwork had been lost and the process had to be started all over again. He began shouting at the official who informed him, and then began hurling objects around the office. Damage was minimal, and he was quickly restrained. The charge of destruction of public property was laid when it was discovered that a pen-holder had been broken. Incredulous, Mona is tempted to laugh, but she knows that this will only exacerbate Michael's already precarious situation. It's no secret that Hong Kong officials are short on humour, a characteristic of officialdom in general. They wouldn't show their irritation outwardly. There'd be furrowed brows, no scowl. They would do it in other ways – like delaying his release as long as they liked.

"They have contempt for me," he says later when the paperwork has been completed and she has paid his bond. "They have contempt for all of us. They don't want us here. They give us just enough to keep their conscience clean, but not enough to live on. They don't want others to come."

"At least they let you stay," says Mona. "In Australia, they dump their refugees and asylum seekers on barely habitable offshore islands and leave them there to rot."

*

When Mona first told me Michael's story, I asked her to arrange a meeting. She called me a couple of days later and said that he had consented to meet me, although he was somewhat reluctant. He family still lived in Somalia, and he was worried that if he were identified as the source of the story, there might be reprisals. I was surprised. Michael's horrendous treatment at the hands of Al Shabaab hardly counted as a state secret. In fact, I was under the impression that they wanted stories such as this to be told to strike fear into people at home and awe abroad. Mona shrugged. She said that they'd use any excuse: she'd get back to me when a meeting time had been arranged.

Weeks pass. I don't like to hound Mona for a meeting with Michael. When I bump into her at a party, I pull her aside and ask her about the meeting. She looks embarrassed and says there won't be one.

"Why did he change his mind about the interview?"

"He didn't. But he isn't here any more."

"What happened?"

"He decided to go back to Somalia."

I'm not sure why I'm shocked. Hong Kong has a knack for messing about with people's thought processes, and from time to time friends and acquaintances make choices that defy logic to the outsider. "Didn't he know the risk he was taking?"

"Of course he did. I spent hours trying to persuade him to change his mind, but he said, 'In the final analysis, I'd rather be dead in my own country than alive here where nobody wants me.' I could kind of understand it. For people like Michael, Hong Kong is a living death. In the end, the support I gave him wasn't enough to keep him here."

Although I never got to meet Michael, I decide to include his story in this collection. His story was a compelling one, and there were many other asylum seekers and refugees in Hong Kong with similar experiences.

18.

I JUST WANTED TO GET HIM FIRED

*Justice will not be served until those who are unaffected are as
outraged as those who are.* (Benjamin Franklin)

I'm nursing a late afternoon beer in the Globe when, unexpectedly, they
push their way through the heavy swing door. This is the old, intimate
Globe on Hollywood Road, before it got big ideas about itself and
relocated to a much grander venue up the hill. Never a big man, Patrick
now seems to have shrunk into himself. Toby steers him towards my table
where he sinks into a chair. They're both wearing suits. I've never seen
either man in a suit. Toby's suit, like Toby himself, has seen better days,
but Patrick's is new – a shiny number that can be picked up cheaply from
one of the tailors in World Wide House.

"Hello, boys," I say. "You look as though you've been to a funeral."

"Haven't you heard?" asks Toby.

"Heard what?" I retort.

"It's all over the *South China Morning Post.*"

Patrick says nothing. He gives me a nod, and sits clenching and
unclenching his fists, his head hanging like a schoolboy caught doing
something unmentionable. Toby goes to the bar and returns with two
pints of Guinness.

Patrick lowers himself into his Guinness and comes up with a line of
froth on his upper lip. "It isn't looking good, is it Toby?" Patrick asks in
his Irish lilt. It's a plea for denial, for a glimmer of hope, dressed up as

a question to confirm what they both already know. He wants Toby to throw him a bone, but that's not Toby's style.

"Well, it didn't help that your barrister was clearly alcohol affected," says Toby. "Anyway, it's day one, so anything can happen."

Can one of them tell me what's going on? The *Readers' Digest* version will do just fine.

Patrick, however, holds up his hand and shakes his head. He's downing the Guinness like it's medicine, and doesn't need a rerun of the day right now.

"Later," says Toby, and fetches two more pints even though he's hardly begun on his own. Patrick makes short work of the second pint, and gets to his feet. He looks as though he might slip out of his shiny charcoal suit at any moment. It has either been borrowed or purchased in haste, without benefit of a second fitting.

"I'll come with you," says Toby, but Patrick won't hear of it. "I need some time with Esther," he says. "I'll see you tomorrow." Like a condemned man, he leaves the bar in his own bubble.

As soon as he's gone, I turn to Toby. "So?"

"Well, I knew nothing about it because it was late August, the middle of the summer vacation, and I'd been away," he says. "We live in the same apartment block, and he's on the floor below me. So when I returned to Hong Kong I called in to see if he wanted to go for a drink. Anyway, he opens the door and the first thing he says is, 'You'll have heard then.' And I say, 'Heard what?' 'That I've been arrested,' he says. And I reply, 'What on earth are you talking about?' I hadn't heard anything at all.

"So he tells me what happened. It was mid-afternoon, and the Dean asked him to come down to her office, which he did, and then she said, 'I've got to leave for a few minutes.' So she left, and in came quite a few policemen, and he was arrested on the spot and handcuffed, and escorted to a van parked behind the University building in full view of everybody who happened to be around. Don't ask me which day of the week it was. And he was taken down to the Western Police Station just next to the Macau Ferry Terminal and charged with sexual assault. Oh, yes, it would have been after a weekend, because the incident allegedly occurred on the previous Thursday or Friday. However, the police weren't alerted until the beginning of the following week, a fact that the defence counsel never exploited. It seems strange that they did nothing for three or four days. Two girls were involved, both undergraduates, one of whom had been in one of my classes. Both of them were having trouble with their courses, and, to be honest, the one I had taught was having psychological problems."

I'm shocked by what Toby tells me. It's one of those incidents you hope never happens to you. You also hope that it doesn't happen to anyone else, but if it has to happen to anyone, let it not be you. I know Toby well. Patrick is one of the many nodding acquaintances I have in Hong Kong – someone with whom to have the occasional jar. He's good-natured, ebullient in the Irish way, and respected as an academic. The accusation seemed out of character. He was in a stable relationship with Esther, an attractive and quick-witted Chinese woman who kept a close eye on him, and to whom he seemed devoted. But then aren't we forever being reminded that the rapist looks just like the inoffensive bloke who lives next door, the murderer the exact image of the elegant woman in the coffee shop at the Peninsula Hotel? In most places, appearances can be deceptive: in Hong Kong, it's almost guaranteed.

"Anyway," says Toby, "It will be all over the newspapers again tomorrow. It was a feeding frenzy in the press gallery today. I believe that the Clerk of the Court tips off the media when there's a juicy case listed for hearing."

In this town, everyone loves a scandal, and baiting someone who has stepped beyond the bounds of respectability, allowed themselves to be caught with their hand in the till, or up the skirt of someone else's wife, will be tried in the court of public opinion long before they come before the magistrate. All the better if it's a celebrity rather than a no-account academic, but in the off season, someone like Patrick will have to do. The daily newspapers are fully dedicated to encouraging the social sport of ruining reputations and humiliating alleged transgressors. On the morning following the first day of Patrick's trial, the English as well as the Chinese press outdo themselves. Lurid sketches and imaginative reconstructions by court artists of the events that supposedly took place in Patrick's office feature prominently in the newspapers. Even the illiterate are left in little doubt as to what had occurred. Here he is with a leer on his face and his hand up one girl's dress while the other alleged victim, hands raised to her face, looks on in horror. Laughably corny, but not for Patrick.

On the afternoon of the second day of Patrick's trial, I meet Colin for a drink. Colin is an expat dentist. For some reason, Hong Kong is a magnet for expat dentists. The cynic might think that this had something to do with their skill at extracting money along with teeth, and the cynic would probably be right. Colin is fondly thought of as a semi-entertaining bore. He has a story for every occasion, most of which revolve around his heroic feats of dentistry. On entering whichever drinking hole we had agreed to patronize on a given day, he would prop himself against the bar, run a hand wearily through his thinning hair, and say "I nearly lost one today. It was touch and go. It started out as a simple extraction, but the tooth sheared in half, and shot up through the nasal cavity. It could have gone all the way into the patient's brain, and that would have been the end of her." He then launches into a technical narrative that involves some highly improbable procedure such as removing the tooth through the eye socket. You didn't have to make an effort with Colin apart from listening and being suitably awe-struck.

On this particular afternoon, there are no heroic tales. On entering the bar, he waves a copy of the *South China Morning Post* at me and asks, "Have you seen this?"

"I have."

"Is he a colleague of yours?"

"A former colleague," I reply. "Why?"

I can sense that bad news is on the way, and I'm not wrong.

"I don't know the ins and outs of the case," says Colin, "But your colleague doesn't stand much of a show, I'm afraid. He's up against the Hanging Judge." He then goes on to tell me that the magistrate assigned to Patrick's case had started his professional life as a dentist. "He was hopeless at that, so he became a magistrate."

Given Colin's assessment of himself as an oral surgeon, I was pretty sure that few others would measure up. And the fact that the magistrate had a one hundred per cent conviction rate was no indication that he was either inept or corrupt. (Although, as it turns out, Colin's assessment was accurate.)

Later, I catch up with Toby, who has attended the second day of Patrick's hearing. It has gone no better than the first. His counsel was slightly alcohol affected in the morning, and clearly inebriated after lunch. The prosecutor, a young woman just out of law school, had very poor English, and long stretches of the proceedings were conducted in Chinese, a violation of the legal right of the accused to be tried in his or her first language. "I asked Patrick where he'd dug up his counsel. Apparently he'd come on the recommendation of one of his drinking pals. I checked with a couple of lawyers I knew." Both confirmed Toby's assessment of the counsel, saying that they wouldn't touch him with the proverbial barge pole.

"Is there anything that can be done?" I ask.

"Not at this stage of the game. In evidence given during the morning, the girls clearly perjured themselves, as did a couple of other students who claimed to have witnessed the assaults. I had full access to their written statements, and they didn't add up. During a break, I spoke to the counsel and said that the evidence was clearly bogus. Patrick's office is on the fourth floor. The students who claimed to have witnessed what had been going on were in class on the second floor. And they were also on the other side of the building, so even if they were on the same floor, they couldn't possibly have seen what was taking place in Patrick's office, and they couldn't have witnessed the two students leaving his office and supposedly crying and screaming and so forth. He was supposed to have done one, then the other. But in court, it was recounted with such accuracy and detail that it wasn't believable. If you'd been assaulted and were traumatized, you wouldn't say 'He played with my genitalia,' or, 'He tried to do this to me.' They'd clearly been coached by their counsel as to what to say, which of course is illegal.

"The whole thing was a farce. As I say, the defence counsel was clearly under the influence after lunch, and the counsel for the prosecution could hardly string two words together in English. She was incoherent at times, and there was no proper cross-examination. There was no real questioning of the witnesses. But despite the fact that the trial is a total shambles and all that's been said about the Hanging Judge, I'm pretty sure that Patrick will get off. It's clear that the so-called 'evidence' against him has been concocted by the girls. He was pretty depressed by the end of the day, but I did my best to cheer him up. You know, despite its faults, the legal system in Hong Kong is a pretty good one – it's one of the few things the British got right, and I say that as a Brit."

This was the first time that I'd ever heard Toby say anything positive about his country of birth and its role in the development of Hong Kong. On first meeting him, you might think that he was a member of the British Establishment. He had an accent so rich you could see the words rolling off his lips like plums. In reality, he had come from a lower middle class background, son of a cockney from the East End of London. He had no tolerance for Britain and its ways, and had spent most of his adult life living and working abroad. Only a native of the country could have lambasted Britain and its role in the world in the way that Toby did, so his praise for the Hong Kong legal system was praise indeed.

At the beginning of the trial, most colleagues and acquaintances who know Patrick were prepared to believe in his innocence, but then a rumour circulated that 'he'd done this sort of thing before'. When Toby asked him about this, he said there had been a student at one of his former universities who had started a rumour that he had been 'rather forward'. There was never a formal complaint, and nothing ever came of it, but it marked a turning point in public sentiment. There is nothing harder to kill than a rumour, however baseless, if people want to believe it, and as the trial progressed, only a handful of people continued to support him. Of those, Toby was the most steadfast, attending each day of the case, and doing his best to maintain Patrick's morale.

When the trial ended with a guilty verdict, Toby quickly changed his tune on the virtues of the Hong Kong judicial system in general and the presiding magistrate in particular. Patrick was incarcerated in the Lai Chi Kok Detention Centre. Toby went to visit him there the following day. Patrick was alternately distraught and seething with anger – emotions which were entirely understandable. He was adamant about going to appeal, despite receiving legal advice that this was not to be recommended because it demonstrated a lack of remorse and, in any case, appeals were very rarely successful. Apparently, this was because a successful appeal would be a not-so-tacit admission that they'd got it wrong in the first place. This was very curious logic, if logic was a term that could be applied in the first place. Toby fully supported Patrick's decision and consulted friends within the legal fraternity to see whether they could recommend a counsel who could be relied upon to stay off the bottle for the duration of the appeal.

At the end of the trial, as Toby was leaving the court, one of Patrick's accusers came up to him, visibly upset, and said, "You've been here every day. Why is that?" Toby suppressed the urge to call her a lying little shit, and replied that Patrick was his friend, and, as such, was there to support him. At that she broke down and said, "I never wanted him to go to prison, I just wanted him to lose his job."

"Mission accomplished," said Toby. "For trying to help you keep your university place, he lost his job and a great deal more. Think of the prison stretch as an unfortunate side effect." The girl asked Toby if she could see him in his office to discuss the case, but he wisely refused. "I saw no purpose," he said. "And besides, I didn't want to run the risk of ending up in the same situation as Patrick. That young woman might have been failing her bachelor's degree, but she could have done a doctorate in playing the victim."

With the help of a senior magistrate whom he knew, Toby managed to secure the services of a competent lawyer who was appalled at the way the case had been conducted as well as the eventual outcome of the trial. He was also scathing about the presiding magistrate who was notorious for writing his judgment during the course of the trial. While this practice was a fabulous time-saver for the magistrate, legally it was considered to be extremely dodgy as it indicated that his judgment was reached with a mind uncluttered by evidence.

"What he does is to write out his judgment as he's listening to the case," said the lawyer. "When you're trying a case, you make your notes, but you don't start pre-judging the issue. When you've got all the evidence, to the extent you can get it, on that basis you make a judgment. And it needs to be borne in mind that the magistrates here in Hong Kong are not all legally trained very well." Apparently, Hong Kong has the highest conviction rate outside of North Korea – although where they get the conviction rates for North Korea from, God only knows.

With Patrick languishing in the Lai Chi Kok Detention Centre, Toby busied himself helping out with the defence. He took a junior member of the defence team on a tour of the university building where the alleged offence had occurred, pointing out that unless the witnesses had X-ray vision or other superhuman powers, there was no way that they could have seen the supposed assault on their classmates and their subsequent distress.

In addition to helping out the lawyers, he made frequent visits to Patrick to keep his spirits up until the appeal hearing took place. Now, however, he had to fake his optimism. During the original hearing, he'd have put money on an acquittal, but knowing what he now did about the mysterious workings of the legal system, he felt pretty sure that the appeal would be dismissed. During his visits, Patrick told him about the goings-on among fellow inmates. Entertainment options were non-existent, so the prisoners took matters into their own hands. Self-abuse was rampant, and went on day and night, regardless of who was around. As the centre was a semi-secure one, the inmates also had ready access to one another, and many took full advantage of the opportunities that presented themselves. At first Patrick was shocked. However, he soon became inured to the nocturnal grunts, growls, and howls of release. For his part, during the weeks of waiting for his appeal, Patrick amused himself by attempting to teach English to those inmates and guards who were interested.

Toby learned that lawyers can sometimes appear to be slow on the uptake. They would take Patrick through the events of the day of the alleged assaults many times and from different angles. They continued to ask questions that had already been answered. The only question that Patrick wanted answered was, "What are my chances?" No-one wanted to provide the obvious answer, which was, "Not very good."

The ink had barely dried on the magistrate's original guilty judgment when the university regretfully decided that Patrick's services were excess to their requirements, and he was dismissed with immediate effect. The government also revoked his visa, and informed him that he would be deported on completion of his sentence. The one piece of good news was that his house in the UK sold quickly (price reduced for quick sale). The not so good news was that the proceeds were quickly consumed by his legal costs. The fact that the government and the university moved so swiftly and decisively against him while his appeal was pending confirmed in Toby's mind the belief that Patrick's chance of winning the appeal was slightly shy of zero.

By the time the appeal finally got under way, Toby, and the rest of us who were vicariously following Patrick's ordeal, were resigned to the fact that the appeal was futile. From several comments he dropped to Toby, it seemed that Patrick had also come to the same conclusion. When the judge hearing the appeal set aside the conviction, it therefore came as much of a shock as the original judgment. Patrick was a free man, but there was no dancing in the streets because he was also ruined. Financially ruined, professionally ruined and personally ruined. He got no compensation from the university for unfair dismissal, nor was his right to land restored by the Hong Kong government. He did not sue the university, or the government for his ruined reputation, or the students for committing perjury. Being broke, he lacked the resources to seek financial compensation.

Although once the original conviction was overturned, he had no criminal record, and anyone who sought to refer to the case would be guilty of libel or slander, his reputation remained in tatters. Restoring a ruined reputation is futile.

Once released from prison, Patrick made his way to Macau to lick his wounds and figure out what to do with the rest of his life. He would have gone further, but Macau was as far as his funds were able to take him. Even if it had been possible, he had no taste for a future in Hong Kong. He stayed with a friend for a while until a relative in the UK provided temporary financial relief.

The students had a remarkable reversal of their academic fortunes. Guided no doubt by divine intervention, their grades dramatically improved, and they drifted inexorably into the second year of their studies, and from there into oblivion.

While the dentist-turned-magistrate came in for harsh words from the judge who overturned the conviction, he remained on the bench. Patrick wanted to put as much distance between himself and the magistrate as possible. Reassigning him to Mars would do just fine. Toby thought there might be grounds for going after the magistrate, but upon consulting one of his seemingly inexhaustible supply of legal experts, he was told that there was "no way you could go after the magistrate for misconduct." When Toby pressed him for a reason, his source rather enigmatically replied, "He was just following the script."

*

What is to be learned from Patrick's misadventure at the hands of the Hong Kong judicial system? Not a great deal. The title of a sentimental self-help book sums it up: *When Yucky Things Happen to Good People*, or, more succinctly – shit happens! The Hong Kong legal system is just as capable of screwing up as comparable systems in other parts of the world.

Patrick was the victim of a malicious accusation, sloppy police work and an incompetent magistrate.

III.

CULTURES IN CONTACT

*Difference is the essence of humanity. Difference is an accident of birth
and it should therefore never be the source of hatred or conflict. The
answer to difference is to respect it. Therein lies a most fundamental
principle of peace: respect for diversity.* (John Hume)

*The love of one's country is a splendid thing. But why should love stop
at the border?* (Pablo Casals)

*It is not easy to be stranded between two worlds. The sad truth is that
we can never feel completely comfortable in either world.*

(Sharon Kay Penman)

The chapters in this section pick up several themes that recurred in
the course of interviewing a wide range of people. Not surprisingly,
the British occupy a special place in Hong Kong. Their legacy, and
their feelings about Hong Kong in the aftermath of decolonization,
are captured in the first chapter. Other themes include identity and the
notion of the Other: racism, perspectives of locals and expats on each
other as well as Mainlanders who are becoming increasingly visible in
Hong Kong. Language, the law and interracial contact and conflict are
also woven into these pieces.

19.

AFTER THE BALL IS OVER

It is a little after midnight. The night of June 30 / July 1, 1997. It has been a long, steamy evening, with fireworks dampened by rain, and crowds of people in the street. I lean on the weathered, varnished wooden rail of the Star Ferry as it ploughs back across Hong Kong Harbour. Over the dark, choppy water, beyond a ring of protective boats, the Britannia is pulling slowly away from the quay. On board, Prince Charles and Governor Patten are signalling this symbolic end to colonialism in Hong Kong. The Royal Yacht swings round and moves quietly past the brightly lit Convention Centre, full still of many of the world's dignitaries, where soldiers had marched back and forth, flags had been hoisted and lowered, speeches made. The Handover. The Handback. A great piece of political theatre.

(Alastair Pennycook)

*

For Dave, the run up to the Handover, and the Handover itself, left indelible imprints. A short time before the event, he took a trip to the border crossing, where a huge electronic clock counted down the months, days, hours, minutes and seconds to the moment that Britain would lose Hong Kong. Those seconds were going by at a frightening speed. It was like the sands of time running out. He returned to Hong Kong Island overwhelmed with sadness. The clock had said it all. Being British, he felt that he owned a little piece of Hong Kong and was losing it. He remembered an incident that happened when he was a small schoolboy.

Two of the school bullies had taken from him a pen that had been given to him as a birthday gift. His father had flown into a rage, not at the bullies, but at Dave. "Never let anyone take from you something that is yours," he had shouted. But what was he to do? The bullies took his pen and he never saw it again. And then, many years later, the Chinese just took Hong Kong, and it seemed that there was nothing anyone could do. He often used to go to a bar in Lan Kwai Fong called *1997* near *Dolce Vita*. It was all about the Handover, and of course it closed once Hong Kong was handed over.

He remembered the day itself like it was yesterday. It had been raining non-stop for ten days and it felt as though the weather was in mourning for what was about to happen. He and a number of his British friends went to a theatre to watch a concert modelled on the Last Night of the Proms. (Or, as his cheeky Antipodean friends said, "the last night of the Poms.") It was an excellent concert, but also very, very nostalgic. When the band played Elgar's *Land of Hope and Glory*, there wasn't a dry eye in the house.

Later, he went to a Handover party at a friend's place, and watched the ceremony on BBC World and CNN. On the stroke of midnight, the television cameras cut to the border, and they watched in horror as truck after truck carrying PLA soldiers rolled into Hong Kong on the orders of the Chinese president, Jiang Zemin. He'd promised he wouldn't do it, but he did. That was a chilling moment, a chilling message that passed over the heads only of those mired in denial, those who in succeeding years would tell visiting friends and relatives that "nothing much has changed".

A short time after the event itself, he returned to the UK to visit friends and relatives and everyone asked the same question: "What do you think of Hong Kong after the Handover?" Some years later, when he returned permanently to the UK, the question was, "Has Hong Kong changed?" It was a question he came to dread, an impossible question, because Hong Kong was constantly changing. It was a defining characteristic of the place. Each year he returns to Hong Kong to visit friends and maintain his status as a permanent resident. For a few years, on the surface, there did not appear to be much meddling from Beijing, but then that, too, began to change. On the whole, however, he had to say that looking back, the Handover had been carefully and cleverly stage-managed by Beijing.

*

"What were your feelings about the Handover?"

"What do you mean?"

"Well, were you sad at all? Did you have a sense of nostalgia?"

"I think you're forgetting something."

"What's that?"

"I'm Irish – a County Cork man. Why would I be feeling nostalgia? I'll tell you what I was feeling. For once you lot are doing the right thing, giving something back that never belonged to you in the first place. The Handover? It should be called the Handback – that's what my Mainland comrades call it. They never had the decency to do the same for Northern Ireland, now, did they? No, they colonized it with their rubbish, and that's the way it will stay. So no, in answer to your question, I don't have a sense of nostalgia – none whatsoever."

*

Getting out of bed the morning after was less of a struggle than Nicholas had anticipated. He might have been tempted to lie in bed a little longer, had the dog not come pawing at the bed sheets. She was a very good dog, when you came down to it: wouldn't think of soiling the carpet just to give him an extra lie in. It would normally have been a working day, and the maid would have been available to do the walking and the pooper-scooping, but they had declared it a public holiday and the maid had evaporated as all but the most dedicated of maids tended to do. Genevieve would have done the walking. It was her dog, after all, but Genevieve wasn't around any more.

The rain had let up temporarily, so he pulled on a pair of shorts and a tee shirt emboldened with a single word: *ENGLAND*. Although he had lived abroad for most of his life, he was a very proud Brit, and was happy to let the rest of the world know. That said, he was pretty disgusted with their sporting performances at the moment. Over the last week, he had watched the football, the cricket, and the Formula One, and they'd screwed up in every one. You couldn't have expected them to do any good in the tennis, of course, so no upset expectations there, but fancy losing the rugby to the loathsome Wallabies.

His plan had always been to retire to Mother England, but Genevieve's unexpected departure upset all that. How ironic that had been. The marriage had long since run out of steam and was held together by nothing more than inertia, but the suddenness and circumstance had found him unprepared. He'd started making plans with his financial adviser and had set up one retirement package for the UK and another one offshore for taxation purposes, but with Genevieve out of the picture, all that had to be recalibrated.

All his family, apart from a daughter who had married a New Zealander and moved to Dunedin, were in the UK, so that was the logical place for retirement. Not that he got on particularly well with his siblings, or his son for that matter. Some of his friends were opting to continue the expat life on the Costa Brava or in Portugal, but for him this was out of the question. When all was said and done, he was, and would remain, a proud Brit who loved British Asia, having spent part of his childhood and most of his working life in Hong Kong and Malaysia. The one possession he valued above all others was his British Asian stamp collection.

The dog, all questing nose and wagging tail, pulls him up a side street. It's not a route that he had planned to take on this post-Handover morning, but it doesn't really matter. There is something odd about the street this morning, something different – out of whack. Then he realizes what it is. The pillar-box where, for over thirty years, he has deposited letters and postcards, is no longer crimson. Someone has painted it green – of all the cheek! It looks so wrong. It must have happened in the small hours of the morning. Tut-tutting at the indecent haste, he jerks on the dog's leash, and returns to his original route. "What next?" he wonders to himself. "Dynamiting the Prince of Wales Building?" He knew all of this was on the cards, which was why he'd spent the two days prior to the Handover taking pictures of every British insignia he could see. On the very day prior to the momentous event, he'd been lurking in the bushes just outside Government House and caught the Governor, Chris Patten, going past. Now, that snap is going to be worth something one day, he thinks to himself.

He had also sent out postcards around the world to family members and friends. On each postcard he had written one of his favourite quotes from Shakespeare, "We band of brothers, we chosen few." Some wrote back, even his son who rather unkindly suggested that it was time he made the move to the twentieth century in preparation for the twenty-first, which was just around the corner.

It was physically painful to watch the Britishness being leached out of the colony, but when all of the royal clubs in Hong Kong proposed to de-royal themselves, that was the last straw, as far as he was concerned. Action was required. As a member in good (and of extremely long) standing, he attended the extraordinary general meeting of the Royal Hong Kong Yacht Club at which it was proposed that the 'royal' be given the boot. Temporarily putting aside his very British diffidence and preference for understatement, he got in line to speak. He remembered with some satisfaction the speech he had given: "If you're going to rebadge the club, why don't you rebadge your kids? Should I call my daughter Miss Wong or Miss Lee? The thing about the Chinese is that they love prestige, and I guarantee that if we drop the 'royal', there'll be royal yacht clubs all the way up the China coast. We have to make a stand. Dropping the 'royal' will be the thin end of the wedge. What will be next? Dropping the 'Queen' from Queen's Road Central? If you work out how many addresses, how many offices, there are on Queen's Road, just imagine how much it would cost to change the name – millions and millions of dollars." His speech had carried the day, of that he was certain, but it had been a close call with only a couple of votes in it.

But now, with the sun having set on this part of the British Empire, who knew what was going to happen? The overnight redecoration of the iconic red pillar-box was a sign, a sign that the new regime was intent on obliterating the old. "It's time for us to go," he said to the dog. But at the sound of his voice, all the dog did was wag its tail and grin.

Although they had retired him before he was ready to go, as a former senior civil servant he got a decent seat at the Handover ceremony in the Convention Centre – not that it was an event he particularly wanted to attend. He went because it was the right thing to do. He hadn't been happy though, not happy at all, and there were times during the ceremony when he had been forced to turn his head aside so his neighbour wouldn't see the tear that trickled down his left cheek.

The last words she had ever said to him were, "Sometimes I wish you would just drop dead." With that she had taken herself to bed, and he had returned to his whisky glass. She was always an early riser, and when, by ten o'clock in the morning, she had failed to appear, he took the unprecedented step of knocking on her bedroom door. When that failed to elicit the anticipated tetchy response, he opened the door. She was dead on the bed, her arms folded peacefully across her chest.

His first thought was that she would miss the Handover, which was only weeks away. "So like her," he thought. "No sense of duty."

*

As part of preparations for the Handover, the British government conducted a study into what to do about the Hong Kong people problem. The Hong Kong people wanted right of abode in the UK. When the Malay states were federated in 1957, individuals designated as the "Queen's Chinese" were given British citizenship, and loyal Hong Kong Chinese expected no less. As part of the study, a survey was conducted into the question of which citizens of former colonies would fit in best in the United Kingdom. Hong Kong won hands-down.

Respondents gave three reasons for their choice. In the first place, Hong Kong people would keep to themselves rather than wanting to assimilate. Secondly, they were clean and law-abiding. And thirdly, they had money. The right to a British passport was refused, however, for the simple reason that there were too many of them. (There were exceptions, of course. The embarrassingly winsome David Tang got not only a passport, but a knighthood to boot.)

"A particularly weak reason," said Nicholas, who had had something to do with the survey. "Such a shame. If we sent the Romanians back to Romania, and a few of those other Eastern European types back to where they came from, we might have been able to accommodate the Hong Kong lot."

20.

The letter of the law

"Are you planning to follow a career in Magical Law, Miss Granger?"
asked Scrimgeour.
"No, I'm not," retorted Hermione. "I'm hoping to do some good in
the world!"   (J.K. Rowling)

If you happen to be in Hong Kong, in the unlikely event that you have a day to spare from eating, drinking and shopping, take yourself to one of the magistrates' courts, and get an insight into the way the legal system works. You will observe a cross-section of society, from its underbelly to its leaders, although, not surprisingly, the former are in the preponderance. Expats are well represented in the population of plaintiffs, as are Mainlanders and domestic helpers – more often than not for overstaying their work visas.

The Hong Kong court system is frighteningly efficient. If a magistrate has a good run, he or she can get through forty or more cases in a day. The charge is read, and the accused is asked how he or she pleads. The vast majority plead guilty, mainly because they are guilty. They know it, the court knows it, and they know the court knows it. As a further inducement, all those who plead guilty receive a thirty per cent discount off their sentence. Six months in detention is thus reduced to four. A nine thousand dollar fine is cut to six. One hundred and twenty hours of community service is reduced to eighty. (By a curious coincidence, the prison times, fines, and community service hours are all neatly divisible by three!)

If the plaintiff has the financial means, he or she will have secured the services of a barrister. Expats almost invariably hire a Senior Counsel, formerly known as Queen's Counsel. Those of modest means are represented by court-appointed lawyers, most of whom are newly graduated and inexperienced. Not infrequently, they make mistakes and have to stand, crimson-eared, as they are admonished like school children by the magistrate.

Counsel's job is to spin a narrative outlining the mitigating circumstances which led to his client's transgression. It precedes sentencing and follows a standard formula. Today, the first case involves a male expat with a Brooks Brothers suit and aquiline features. His head, normally held high, is lowered in suitable supplication while Counsel delivers the mitigation. His client's penitence is so extreme that it can scarcely be put into words. He is of unimpeachable character, as attested by the sheaf of character references piled high before the magistrate, is a leading member of the business community, and his charitable work is legendary. In fact, he falls not far short of sainthood. He had no intention of driving his Porsche at high speed through three red lights and into a bus while four times over the legal alcohol limit. It was all the fault of the waiter who, unbeknown to his client, constantly replenished his wine glass during a long charity dinner, which he was hosting to raise money for one of his many worthy causes. While his client is fully aware of the fact that the crime carries with it the possibility of a two-year prison term, he is throwing himself on the mercy of the court, and the magistrate's thoroughly well-deserved reputation for fairness. If he has managed to avoid the Hanging Judge, and his counsel has spun a compelling enough yarn, he will get off with a six thousand dollar fine (plus a thirty per cent discount).

*

While drawing on principles and procedures that had evolved in the United Kingdom, the Hong Kong legal system was never a mirror image of that back in Britain. Prior to the Handover, expats had been consistently privileged – in practice if not in terms of the letter of the law.

Bob, son of a senior British civil servant, was born in Hong Kong and recounted his experiences of growing up with a sense of entitlement and ownership when the place was still a colony. As teenagers, he and his friends knew exactly how to behave when it came to brushes with the law.

"I always knew I was English – British. It never occurred to me that I was living in a country other than where my parents were from until I went to boarding school. I just grew up in Hong Kong, where I was from, and didn't think twice about it. We owned the place back then, and thought we could do whatever we liked. We certainly got away with an awful lot. By the time we were fifteen, we were having beach parties at Repulse Bay and places like that, getting into under-age drinking and various other things. Some of my friends got into drugs, but I never did. They started off with weed, and then progressed to other harder drugs.

"As a teenager, pre-1997, you could get away with just about anything you wanted to. Two of my friends got caught shoplifting CDs from HMV. They did it quite blatantly, removing the security devices right there in the store. They got caught, and were taken to the police station, but the police let them off with a warning. The police would never arrest you. They might keep you sitting around for a couple of hours to drive home the fact that you'd done something unacceptable, but they wouldn't do anything, and we knew it. How well-behaved you were depended on how well you were brought up, not how much you feared authority.

"The Hong Kong police just wouldn't touch a foreign British kid because if they did, the chances are that the parent of the child is going to storm into the police station and kick up an enormous fuss. The father would almost certainly be a highly ranked member of the civil service or the head of some corporation or other.

"It was particularly a problem for police officers who didn't speak English very well. In those days, the Hong Kong police had red and blue ribbons behind their badge to indicate their language competence. If they had the wrong colour behind their badge, we'd know that they didn't speak English well enough and would get into all sorts of trouble if they did anything. So they did nothing – they just didn't go that route. The one thing that used to annoy me was when my friends didn't understand or didn't care about breaking the law, and didn't respect the police. It used to really bother me. Again, that's probably more upbringing than anything else. My father instilled in us the importance of upholding British values. Sure, I got into underage drinking, but I made sure I never got caught."

*

"The Hong Kong police force provides the front line troops for, and are the public face of, the government's legal system. It has been described as 'one of the best-trained, most highly motivated and dedicated police forces in the world.' International law enforcement bodies rank it among the most professional of its kind. It has also, to an almost unprecedented extent in Asia, won the trust and faith of the people it was created to serve." This glowing appraisal is hardly surprising, given that I lifted it directly from the official Hong Kong Police website. From time to time, however, this image is dented by the behaviour of the police during events such as the Occupy Central movement.

Letters to the editor in the *South China Morning Post* also reveal that this rosy picture is not universally held. A letter by a Dorothy Sin describes them as 'incompetent' (a term used more than once by Toby in relation to the treatment of his friend Patrick) following an incident in which two officers shot each other. As one of them had been shot multiple times, the suspicion arose that it had not been an accident. With a surname like Sin, drawing attention to police incompetence, and corruption, was possibly unwise. Her letter was quickly followed by several others, all defending the police, and suggesting that she might revise her opinion after a long vacation in the Mainland or the United States (although in either case, a long weekend would probably suffice).

*

Eve maintains that one thing is undeniable: Hong Kong is one of the safest places on earth. She argues that while this is not entirely down to the police, some of the credit must surely go to them. Most of the time they maintain public order quietly and unobtrusively, and they generally exercise restraint in dealing with unruly mobs. Admittedly, the generous use of pepper spray and batons during the Occupy Central protests was a little over-enthusiastic, particularly given the fact that the protesters were armed with nothing more lethal than umbrellas.

Eve admits that when she is in the United States, she finds the sheer size and physicality of the police officers menacing. She is sure this is not entirely accidental. Just passing a couple of cops in the street engenders feelings of guilt even though she's done nothing wrong. Officers on the beat in Hong Kong are about as menacing as fairy floss. On a maiden visit a few months before, a friend of hers from Los Angeles commented on how well turned-out the boy scouts were. "When I informed her that they were police officers, she laughed so long and loud that I thought she might break something. 'How is it possible for them to maintain law and order?' she asked. 'In Los Angeles, they'd be laughed off the street.'"

*

The truth is, the job for the police is made easier by the residents, who are generally well-behaved. This goes for expatriates and locals alike, and makes invidious any comparison between Hong Kong and more robust parts of the world. When a spate of domestic robberies occurred in my neighbourhood not so long ago, the word that came most readily to mind was "Mainlanders" who get blamed for most crimes these days. People in Hong Kong mind their own business. Public disturbances are so rare that when an elderly passenger on a bus lost his temper with a younger passenger and went on a five-minute tirade, it was filmed, put on YouTube and went viral.

Was Patrick's case, in which he was falsely accused and found guilty of sexual assault, an anomaly or part of a growing trend in Hong Kong's judicial system towards ineptitude and corruption? The conspiracy theorists latched onto cases such as this as evidence that the system was sliding towards the way that the legal system functions in the Mainland. I believe that the case and the way that Patrick was treated was an anomaly. The Mainland has its own form of efficiency. You are found guilty of a capital offence on Thursday, face death by firing squad on Friday, and have your organs harvested for transplants that afternoon. Will similar efficiencies be introduced into the Hong Kong justice system as we approach the end of the fifty-year moratorium negotiated between Britain and Beijing as the last vestiges of colonial rule are expunged? We will know eventually, and may not even have to wait fifty years if the growing practice of kidnapping and removing to the Mainland Hong Kong residents accused of disrespect becomes a common practice.

21.

WHITE BOYS

I look Chinese. I speak Cantonese and Mandarin. I live and work in Hong Kong. But I'm really a banana – yellow on the outside and white on the inside. I've had a few Chinese boyfriends, but I prefer white boys. (Janice)

It is not surprising that cultures in contact lead to relationships. For this chapter, I have extracted four stories from the interviews that place such relationships within their cultural context.

*

Susan has a dilemma. Her husband won't move out, and she doesn't know how to make him go. The house is stuffed with his possessions. She can't even get her car into the garage. She has raised the issue on several previous visits, but every time she arrived from Hong Kong, there he was, slumped in his ancient armchair in front of the television. It was a toss-up as to which of them would fall apart first, the armchair or her estranged husband. She'd fly down to Australia for a week or two every few months to visit her children and attend to her various financial affairs: an alien notion to her husband, who had neither finances nor affairs. On these relatively brief trips, it was possible, if not to avoid her husband completely, at least to keep contact to a minimum.

Having finally decided to move to Australia permanently, the issue became pressing. It was impossible to avoid someone when you were living permanently together under the one roof. There were several reasons for her decision to move. Her parents had passed away within a few months of each other, cutting the principal tie that bound her to Hong Kong. She had retired and was no longer required to show up in an office. Also, she wanted to spend more time with her children. When she left her husband, the children had blamed her for the collapse of the marriage. Her husband had encouraged the fiction that she alone was responsible, and on the surface this wasn't a difficult argument to sustain. It had taken her a long time to repair her relationship with the children, and now she wanted to make up for those lost years, when contact with them had been minimal. And, yes, there was the granddaughter.

After the split, he had moved back to Australia with the children. At the time it was reasonable for him to move into the house, which she had bought so that the children had a place they could call home. There had been a tacit agreement that once the children had left school and were independent he would move out. That time had passed long ago. Tina, now in her early thirties, was married with a ten-month-old baby, and Kevin was down in Sydney. And yet here he was – squatting jobless and useless as always in front of the television. Normally mild-mannered, if not downright timid, now she seethed inwardly. Damn it, she wanted him gone. She tried everything, but nothing worked. She couldn't even goad him into an argument, which was particularly galling. With his passive aggression, she suspected that he was taking his revenge on her for leaving him all those years ago. She had finally come crawling back, so he wasn't going anywhere. She knew exactly how his mind worked.

Why had she always been drawn to gweilos? She remembered the day on the beach at Repulse Bay all those years ago with a clarity that was almost scary. She and Linda had taken the bus from Central. Linda said that's where the white boys went to swim and lie in the sand. Linda was right. They put their towels embarrassingly close to the boy Linda had spotted from the shoreline. But the boy, when he noticed them, wasn't looking at Linda, he was looking at her. She remembered how alarmed she had been by the look in his eyes and by the sensation the look had stirred deep inside her, a nervous excitement. Later, Linda called that feeling 'women's hormones'. She was lucky, Linda said. Not all women had hormones. It was comforting to know that this feeling, this itch, had a name. It was also good to have a friend like Linda who knew all sorts of things back then. And Linda was generous, not minding at all when she went with the boy back to his place in Quarry Bay.

She couldn't remember the exact moment when she lost her virginity. It happened by degrees. She was sixteen, two years younger than the boy, and life was moving at a pace that bewildered her. The knowledge that she was possessed of an extraordinary beauty was slowly beginning to form. She got no satisfaction from this. It was more of a nuisance than anything, as it drew unwanted attention. The boy's father was from Manchester, his mother from Lisbon. It came as a surprise to both of them when his father announced that they were moving to America. "Come with us," the boy said, and cried when she pointed out the impracticality, no, impossibility of this notion.

When the recession hit, her parents took her out of school and put her to work in a bank. What money the family could spare was spent on the education of her brothers. Because her spoken English was good (it had improved rapidly with the help of the English/Portuguese boy) she was trained in customer service. Eliza, her best friend in the bank, also in customer service, was a returnee from Canada. Eliza had Western ways, which Susan found exciting. She also had Western boyfriends, which Susan found even more exciting. Through one of them, she met Hans, a young German teacher. When he invited her to his flat in Pokfulam for a meal, her hormones said yes. The relationship was developing nicely until the night Hans's flatmate decided to join in the fun by bursting naked into the bedroom and jumping into bed with them. Later, when she heard the expression 'two's company, but three's a crowd' she knew exactly what it meant.

Her next boyfriend was a serious young American. He was so serious that after dating her for three months he decided to marry her. He didn't ask her whether she wanted to marry him, possibly because he suspected that she might say no. Instead, he insisted on asking her father for her

hand in marriage. He actually used this quaint Western expression. It was
also foolish. If he had asked her, she'd have told him about his foolishness,
but he didn't. She had a pretty good idea that her father would take a
dim view of the proposal, and she was right. In fact, he exceeded her
expectations by punching the young man in the face. Her father was
a mild-tempered man, and his violent outburst surprised her almost as
much as it did her suitor. Exit the serious young American.

While she had vague regrets at seeing him go, she had other more
serious problems to deal with. The main one was that she had been
retrenched from the bank. She knew that if she really wanted one, she
could replace the serious young American without too much difficulty.
Jobs, however, were more difficult to come by. She applied for several
without much hope, and her pessimism was rewarded with rejection.
But this is Hong Kong, the can-do place where even the locals get lucky.
Her big break came when she responded to an advertisement for a flight
attendant traineeship with Cathay Pacific Airways and was accepted. At
the time, she thought that her excellent spoken English was a major factor
in getting the job. While it may have played a part, she soon realized that
Cathay Pacific saw her looks as her main asset. Within a year she had
been selected as the 'face' of the airline and became the centrepiece of a
major advertising campaign. The other girls who'd been shortlisted and
who now had to play second fiddle to her were wildly jealous, although
they did their best to hide it from her while spreading the rumour that
she only got the job because of her big breasts, her wide eyes, and her
winning smile. When Trevor, the director of the media company that had
been brought in to oversee the ad campaign in which she had the starring
role, referred to her as 'Sexy Susan', it became a term of derision among
the other girls. She took her revenge by marrying him. She had only ever
met three Trevors: all were Australian. She had wondered whether this
was a coincidence, or whether Trevor was a peculiarly Australian name.
In the short term, she found that it was not peculiar to Australia. In the
longer term it was a name she came to detest.

By the time she fell in love – truly fell in love – she was trapped in a marriage she realized in retrospect she hadn't really wanted in the first place. Back in those days, she didn't consciously realize she had views on her own destiny because she'd never been asked. Everyone, from her parents down, made assumptions about what she wanted based on their own desires. The object of her love was an unlikely Englishman. Overweight, balding, with halitosis and body odour – a frog to her princess – he gave her something more precious than a good-looking companion; he gave her kindness and consideration. Now, in her late middle age, she was puzzled by the notion that physical attraction was all about butts and six-packs. For years she was also puzzled by the term 'six-pack', which she thought had something to do with beer, until her son Kevin spelled it out to her.

She did the right thing, or so she thought, refusing to go to bed with the new man in her life until she had informed her husband. In retrospect, his reaction was hardly surprising, although at the time she thought it was somewhat extreme. He threw her out of the apartment, and refused her access to the children. For a while she led a nomadic existence, rotating around a circle of friends, before moving into a hotel near the airport, a tourist in her own home town. When she discovered that she was not the only recipient of kindness and consideration from the Englishman, she found herself no longer able to forgive his baldness and his smells. Resolutely single, she suffered in silence, looked after her ageing parents and put money aside for her own old age.

She sits in her bedroom mulling over the problem while the benign Australian sunshine plays against the curtains. The first time the thought comes to her she dismisses it. The second time she acts. Sexy Susan still, ageing to boot, but submissive no more. She never thought that she had it in her but, goaded beyond belief, she sells the house for far less than its market value. Then, with the opposing forces of salvation and guilt tearing her in two, she leaves the agent to deal with her husband and flees back to Hong Kong where she stays with an ancient aunt. There, caught between two cultures and continents, she contemplates what to do with the rest of her life.

*

Lisa is sitting in the lobby lounge of the Shangri-la hotel. I like Lisa, a former colleague. She's sharp, smart and acerbic: you'd like to know what she has to say about you when your back is turned. Her major shortcoming is her poor taste in clothes. Fortunately for her this is Hong Kong, so she gets away with it. In Tokyo, Singapore or even Seoul, she'd have been quietly derided. On this day, she has the pelt of some endangered species wrapped around her neck.

"What are you doing here?"

"I'm waiting for a friend. We're having lunch in the Lobster Bar."

"Good choice. Special occasion?"

"Very special. I finally got around to quitting my job."

"Again? What was wrong with this one?"

"It wasn't the job. It was the boss."

"What was wrong with the boss?"

"He's a Brit."

I'm surprised. Lisa is not particularly happily married to 'a boring Chinese guy' (her words). When we worked together, she had a couple of rather indiscreet relationships with expats in the office, so I assumed that she was well-disposed towards them regardless of race.

"I didn't know you disliked the British."

"Only some of them. This one was arrogant and incompetent. It's a bad combination. I was forever having to clean up his messes, and when he really screwed up, I was the one who got the blame. He's one of those Brits who think the Handover never happened and that they still own the place." Indignation and contempt mar her attractive features.

"So, your friend – male or female?"

"Oh, female."

"One of your school friends?" Hong Kong women form lifelong bonds with the girls they went through school with.

Lisa shakes her head. "Last summer, I went to Europe. I do that every couple of years just to – well, just to get away. One of the other members of the tour was also from Hong Kong, so we struck up a friendship and had dinner together most nights. She works in Central as a senior sales person with Chanel and she told me a lot about her personal life. She's unmarried, is thirty-nine years old, and has always had expats as boyfriends. She's very pretty – well, working for Chanel, she has to be. They're very particular about that. She'd just ended a ten-year relationship with an Italian guy and was taking the tour to get over it. Before the Italian, she had a British guy, and before that a German. I said to her, 'We have a lot in common. You're taking the tour to get over the ending of a ten-year relationship. I'm taking it to get over the fact that I'm stuck in a ten-year marriage I don't have the guts to get out of.' That made her laugh. We ordered more wine, got a little bit tipsy, and talked about men. I asked her why the ten-year relationship with the Italian ended, and she said that he was unfaithful to her, and I said (at this point, Lisa's voice takes on an indignant tone), 'How can you expect them to be faithful? They're expats. They're not the faithful type. They like adventure. They like to maintain romantic relationships, but once the love is gone, so are they. You can read it in the Hollywood magazines all the time.'"

Lisa has considerable energy on the subject, and I guess that her own experience is not a million miles away from her friend's. She says, "No matter how long they've been together, once they decide they don't love you any more, they go. The Chinese don't do that."

"There's this cynical idea that young Chinese women are just interested in Western men because they've got money and can provide them with a comfortable lifestyle."

Lisa dismisses this idea. "It isn't always about money. My friend didn't need the Italian's money – she had money of her own. Like a lot of women, she was looking for a romantic relationship, which you won't get from a Chinese man. But you have to take the unfaithful side of the Western man into consideration. I asked my friend, 'How could you expect your Italian boyfriend to be faithful to you? It isn't in their nature.' She said that while his affair was a major reason, it wasn't the only one. She was also doing very well in her job. She had money and status, so why should she put up with this unfaithful guy? So she left him. Now she wants a new partner, but is having difficulty finding one."

"Does she want another Western partner, or a Chinese – or doesn't it matter?"

"Oh, not Chinese. She's pretty, but once you see her you realize that she's an expat type of girl. She just has that type of face and that manner."

This has me intrigued. I ask Lisa what an expat type looks like. She doesn't answer my question directly, but says, "Oh, you can tell very easily. The first time I met her on that trip, I thought, 'Oh, I bet you have a Western boyfriend,' and I was right. She's never had a Chinese boyfriend. The Chinese find her too intimidating. Her facial features are too strong. When she got to know me on the European trip, she said that when she first met me she thought I was an insurance broker. She said there were two types of broker, and I was the honest type: she could tell that from my face. People would like to buy from me. That's one thing she learned from her job at Chanel – how to read people's faces. She doesn't have to work on the shop floor. She just deals with the millionaires and the billionaires. She sells them things and has lunch and dinner with them overseas. She has a very busy life. But she's lonely in the summer. She says she can't get anyone who can go with her on a trip in summer."

Then her expression changes. She smiles and waves at an unseen presence behind me. "Here's my friend," she says, "I have to go." Turning too late, all I see is her friend's retreating back, and am left to wonder at the mysteries of an expat type of face.

*

Eunice is an interesting contradiction in several respects. She professes a tremendous love of China and takes frequent train trips through the countryside on her own. She says that many Hong Kong people are afraid of going to China. They're afraid of the dirt and disease and the public toilets where you have to squat in a conga line to defecate, but Eunice isn't at all bothered by this. "My friends can't stand the toilets. I can stand them all."

On the other hand, she sees no value in mastering Putonghua beyond a rudimentary level. "There's not much point," she says. "You'll never be able to compete with the Mainland Chinese so why bother?" The one thing she dislikes is the political system. Like the majority of first-generation Hongkongers, she has a deep distrust of the communists, something which is drummed into their children by parents who gave up everything when they fled the Mainland.

When I point out her contradictory attitudes, she says, "At university, I came into contact with Western culture and studied literature, history and philosophy. I learned French and fell under the influence of French liberal ideas. I became a complete Francophile. Even today, I spend most of my summers in France. But I also understand the villagers in Hong Kong who live up in the New Territories. They're very nationalistic in supporting the Chinese government. In Hong Kong under Japanese rule, they helped the communists and nationalists against the Japanese. That's why they have a strong link. Those inhabitants of the villages, they all support the Chinese government. That's where my husband comes from, and on his side of the family, everyone supports the Mainland government. They also come from the villages around Tuen Mun. I understand that part because the link is so close. They were brought up to love China. They see it is as their country."

I make the point that many, many people came here after the communist takeover of the Mainland and she agrees. "Yes, they were afraid of the communists. I read books about some of them who fled to Hong Kong: *Falling Leaves*, and books like that. This was a refugee camp. People came from the Mainland on their way to somewhere else, but many of them settled here."

I return to her interest in Western ideas and culture. I know that she's married to a local Chinese and has two teenage children, and ask her if she had ever dated an expat. Her answer comes as a surprise.

"I've had Western male friends. I'm interested in their values and their history, so from that point of view I'm not a 'traditional' Chinese woman, but I never dated one until I had an affair with a Frenchman. I was married and my children were young."

"Really? You had an affair? You have pretty traditional views about marriage, so I don't understand why you had an affair. You must have been lonely."

"Maybe I was a little bit bored, but the real reason was love."

"You were in love with him?"

"Yes, I was. I still am."

"Do you ever see him now?"

"No, no. It was sparked off by love."

"How did you meet?"

"Oh, I'm not going to talk about that. I'll just keep it a secret. But, I respected him. He was younger than me. That doesn't matter. I respected him, and I did love him."

"Did he love you?"

"At first, I think he did. He told me that he did. Then later on, he told me that he didn't love me."

"So, how long were you together?"

"I think three or four years? Is that right? I can't remember exactly how long it lasted."

"How often would you meet?"

"Two or three times a month. We would have dinner. He was very romantic. Sometimes, I'd take an afternoon off work and meet him at his apartment, but it's finished now. I've left it behind me, and I don't think about it that much any more. I hope he's doing well. I respected his choice, even when I discovered that he had someone else. I couldn't really blame him, could I? I was married with young children."

"Would you have left your husband and kids for him if he'd asked you to?"

Eunice laughs at the question, and then pauses before answering. "Maybe. At that time my kids were really young, but even so, I probably would have done it even though divorce is very bad for the children. Anyway, he never asked me, so I wasn't faced with that choice."

Eunice's story, and her dilemma, were not uncommon. She repeats what I've heard from numerous local women – that the Hong Kong husband is the most boring on earth, and her husband was no exception. She craved romance, and in her view Western men were extremely romantic. "But they're also unfaithful," she says. "And so you have to take that into consideration." In the end, her head won out over her heart. Did she have regrets? "Yes," she says, "From time to time, I wonder how it might have ended if I'd taken that leap. But I never did, and now I never will. But I still visit France, and I still have my memories and dreams."

*

Gus and Jason met at a Sunday social tennis match. It was less a tennis club than a loose affiliation of friends who gathered at the tennis complex that was part of the Hong Kong Cricket Club at Wong Nai Chung Gap, just down from the exclusive Parkview residential enclave. The afternoons were organized by Ronnie, a member of the Cricket Club, who booked the courts and made sure there were six players available.

At fifty years of age, Gus was one of the older members of the group. The younger players were mostly fit, some fanatically so, fast around the court, and intensely competitive. This was anything but a hit-and-giggle affair. Gus had one serious advantage: at six feet six, he was by far the tallest member of the group. In fact, he was one of the tallest human beings in Hong Kong, possibly the whole of Asia. A couple of lunges each way, and he had the backcourt well covered. While the younger players tried to make every shot a winner by attempting to hit to the cover off the ball, Gus used guile: he was a master of the drop shot, and was able to catch his opponent off guard by changing the angle of his return – shaping up to hit the ball down the line, and then suddenly whipping it across court. In his younger days, Gus had been a college champion. He had managed to keep up his social tennis as he moved around the country, but in his six years in New York, prior to moving to Hong Kong, he had had little opportunity to play.

Gus and Ronnie had met at a party. They had chatted, and when Ronnie learned that tennis was one of Gus's interests, he was invited to join them on the following Sunday. In the months since his arrival in Hong Kong, Gus had been impressed at how easy it was to meet people in Hong Kong, although, because his ten-year relationship with Somchai had ended badly (don't they always?) and had prompted his move from New York to Hong Kong, he was cautious about jumping too precipitously into a new one. He had hoped that the Sunday social tennis group would provide an opportunity to learn more about the Hong Kong gay scene and its members, and in this he was proven correct. He'd exchanged phone numbers with several of the revolving-door tennis members, and had drinks with a couple of them. Good-looking was a given. They were pleasant, but somewhat naïve after the New York scene. But, and it was a big but, there was no real spark. Until Jason.

Even with his height advantage, it was no surprise to be beaten by a dangerously fit twenty-six-year-old, with a body tuned to Formula One levels of performance. However, he hadn't disgraced himself, and had actually come surprisingly close to taking a set off the much younger man, but choked on the break of serve and that was the end of that.

His plan had been to walk down the hill to Happy Valley, where he had a small but comfortable apartment. It was about a twenty-minute walk, and would allow him time to cool off. Although it was not yet full-blown summer, it was hot enough. Diffidently, he had asked Jason if he'd like to accompany him with the promise of a drink at the end of the walk. To his mild surprise, Jason had immediately accepted. They joined the other players, who had also finished their games, and chatted for a few minutes. John, a well-built man in his early thirties, said how much he enjoyed playing at this time of year when the air was soft and soapy. Gus was a little puzzled by this expression. He was unable to detect anything remotely soapy about the air – 'gritty' he thought was a better adjective – but the others seemed to agree, so he decided that it must be a local expression.

He and Jason walked down the hill to Happy Valley, presumably into less 'soapy' air, their racquet cases slung over their shoulders. Pausing at a set of traffic lights, he found his legs being viciously attacked by invisible insects. Jason was also being attacked and laughed at his attempts to swipe the insects away. "They're called 'cant-see-ems'," he said. "They sting like hell, but the sting will go away quite soon. And they won't attack you if you keep moving."

Gus still felt hot when they stopped at a juice bar in a side street not too far from his apartment block. The sweat had made his tennis shirt stick to his back, and beads reappeared on his forehead as soon as he dabbed them away. He hoped he didn't smell. It was difficult to smell your own sweat, which was why people with bad body odour were blissfully unaware of how nauseating they were to others. In his short time in Hong Kong, he had noticed that it was only the foreigners who smelled. The locals were sweatless and odourless even on the hottest days. He noticed, with a twinge of envy, that Jason had remained sweat-free through their three vigorous sets of tennis. Now, sitting on a stool, sipping his juice, the only strands of hair that were out of place were the ones that were artfully intended to be. He was as cool and together in his appearance as when they had first met.

He didn't mind at all that they chatted about trivia, just like people who have known each other for a long time. He also liked it that Jason seemed comfortable with the stretches of silence. If he had nothing to say he felt no compulsion to say it, and Gus was not the type to fill in the moments of dead air. He made no attempt to hide his delight when Jason suggested they pair up for a rematch the following Sunday, but then remembered that he had to fly out to Shanghai. His only satisfaction came with the look of disappointment on Jason's face.

Later, at home, standing under a cool shower, he had a vague sense of anticlimax. Not being one of those heroic seize-the-moment types, he had let the opportunity pass, and now had the luxury of regretting it at leisure. He cringed, remembering the moment of their parting, how he'd had to squat down awkwardly to accept Jason's parting hug, and then, remembering too late his sweat-soaked shirt, had tried to back away, in the process almost stumbling into the gutter. Oh, the embarrassment of it! Well, it just wasn't meant to be. Put it in the dead-letter box of his brain and move on.

By Wednesday, he has done some solid work on not thinking of Jason and the way he looked in his trim little tennis outfit, but then Jason undoes it all by calling him. Would he be free for dinner on Saturday evening? It takes approximately a nanosecond to reverse his decision to forget Jason. Yes, he would very much like to, is his response. He insists that Jason be his guest, and then spends the next two days selecting venues for meeting and greeting, for dining, and for a nightcap, assuming the meeting, greeting and dining go as hoped. All the while, an uncomfortable, and at this point, unanswerable question wiggles like a worm at the edge of his consciousness: What does Jason want?

Selecting venues for a first date was tricky. Having just met him, he had no idea of Jason's preferences. Gus's inborn preference for the very best had been fine-tuned from years of living in some of the best dining cities in America, but what were the tastes of a twenty-six-year-old Chinese boy who obviously took care of himself? He didn't want to start out at one of the gay bars because he wanted to have Jason to himself on this first evening. Petrus or Pierre would be overkill at this embryonic stage of the game: the fussiness of one and the pretentiousness of the other might send the wrong message. He finally decided on MO Bar for pre-dinner cocktails. It could be crowded and noisy, but the vibe was good – casual yet sophisticated – well, as sophisticated as you were likely to find in Hong Kong. And let's face it, where would you find somewhere that was not noisy, particularly on a Saturday night? He booked Island Tang for dinner. The décor hardly cried hip, but you couldn't complain about the food and it was practically next door to the MO Bar. Then, if the evening progressed the way that he hoped it would, they could finish up on the outdoor terrace at Armani Privé overlooking the Central business district.

Getting into the Armani Bar was often next to impossible, but the young Filipina bar manager had a gift for squeezing Gus and his companions in. This was partly due to his charm, but also, and principally, due to his gift for opening his wallet. When he arrived in Hong Kong, Gus discovered that locals were extremely stingy when it came to tipping. The tipping habits he brought with him from New York were quickly recognized, appreciated, remembered and rewarded.

As it happened, the evening turned out to be even better than he had expected. Although physically they were very different, he saw in Jason something of his younger self. He appreciated the fact that, while Jason's looks and charm might have led him to a sense of entitlement, he was quiet – but not too quiet. He confidently inhabited his own skin. He was unsophisticated when it came to food and wine. At twenty-six, Gus had been the same, so he knew this condition was curable.

In addition to his traffic-stopping looks, there was one personal quality that Gus valued above all else: when it came to relationships, Jason, like Gus, was a conservative. Prior to his arrival in Hong Kong, Gus had heard rumours that following the decriminalization of homosexuality, bed-hopping had become an epidemic. Gus himself had never subscribed to the quick-fuck fix. What he looked for were stable relationships. During the ten-year relationship that preceded his move to Hong Kong he had never – well, hardly ever – strayed.

So his first date with Jason ended, not in his bed in Happy Valley, but in Armani Privé. And he wasn't at all unhappy about this. In fact, they didn't even kiss until their fourth date. After that, the relationship progressed swiftly and satisfactorily. But in those first encounters, the question remained, unasked and unanswered. What did Jason want with a still presentable but obviously ageing gweilo when the town was running hot and cold with gorgeous young things of every conceivable nationality? What was Gus to read into this unexplained attraction?

Over time, he noticed that their relationship was anything but unique, and not even particularly unusual. It seems that we are blind to things we don't know. You hear a word that had previously been unknown to you, and suddenly it's on everybody's lips. A workmate acquires an electric car, and all at once, the roads are full of them. And so, as his relationship with Jason developed, he noticed Westerners of his own age, and even older, with younger Asian men. And you saw them not only in the usual bars and other gay hangouts, but in cinemas, shopping malls, concerts, exhibitions, regular bars and restaurants. Whether or not they held hands (still comparatively rare), it was clear that they were an item. You could tell it from the way they angled their bodies towards each other, the way their heads moved closer together when they spoke.

I caught up with Gus several weeks after our initial interview and asked him if he ever got his question answered. "I did," he said quietly, flashing his shy little sideway smile. "Jason is one of those people who are attracted to Western men. That's not to say that they don't hang out with or even date locals, but they find us exotic, which I thought was ironic. I don't know about you, but I find Asians exotic. I have no idea what's exotic about us, but I guess everything is in the eye of the beholder. So, not only was the attraction mutual, it had the same source."

"Ah, it's the 'white boy' phenomenon."

Gus looked puzzled. "I might be white, but it's a long time since I qualified as a boy."

"It's just a phrase one of my informants used. It explains a phenomenon I've observed among local women, as well," I said. "There's a subculture of Chinese women who prefer older, Western men."

"That was the other thing. The Eastern-Western attraction wasn't at all unusual to me. We have it in the States. In fact, as I told you, my long-term relationship there was with an Asian man. But you rarely see the age gap: that just wouldn't happen, not in my experience, at least. The explanation I got from another, older gweilo who was dating a younger Chinese guy was that older men are more sophisticated than younger ones, but more importantly, they have much more disposable income. The young Asian guy can be taken to expensive restaurants, weekend spa treatments, and long weekends in Phuket – flying business class, of course: no more flying in coach class crammed in between the toilets and a Mainland tour group."

22.

THE DEVIL'S LANGUAGE

I can pass myself off as a native speaker of French, I'm highly fluent in three other languages, and can get by in four more. I've always prided myself on being a 'good language learner', but Cantonese has largely defeated me. After years of exposure and study, formal and informal, I have nothing more than 'phrasebook facility'. It's the devil's language. (Raymond)

Although it can be divisive, language is the glue that holds many multiracial societies together. The majority language in Hong Kong is Cantonese, although a range of other Chinese dialects is spoken as a first language by around 11% of the population. These include Chiu Chow, Hakka, Fukienese, Putonghua, Shanghainese, and Sze Yap. On the streets, you will hear many other regional languages: Hindi, Assamese, Gujarati and other Indian languages, Urdu, Tamil, Arabic, Tagalog, Nepalese, Malay. The list goes on. And then there are the European languages, most notably English, of course, which as the language of the colonial masters was the language of the executive, the judiciary and the legislature. For most of Hong Kong's history it was never laid down as an official language: it just was. About 30% of the local population had some facility in the language, but only 2% of them, the educated elite, had a high degree of proficiency. It was not until 1974 that the Official Language Ordinance decreed English and Chinese to be the official languages of the colony. (Which dialect of Chinese the lawmakers had in mind was never specified, although it was assumed that Cantonese would be the *de facto* variety.) After the Handover, a biliterate and trilingual policy was adopted by the government.

I'm not sure that I'd describe myself as a natural language learner. I studied Latin at school as a form of insurance against future possible unemployment. (Having been raised Catholic, if all else failed, Latin might possibly have gained me entry into a seminary.) It stood me in good stead when, years later, I spent time in Rome and attempted to pick up Italian with minimal formal instruction. Needless to say, it was useless when I attempted, while working in Bangkok, to acquire Thai. It was just as useless when, on moving to Hong Kong, I attempted to learn Cantonese through self-study and torturing my local friends.

My experiences with Thai and Cantonese, both tonal languages that present considerable challenges to speakers of European languages, were quite different. Within a year, I was a reasonably comfortable, albeit basic, user of Thai. After many years, I am neither comfortable nor competent in my use of Cantonese.

With a couple of exceptions, all of my informants spoke at least one other language, and many of them spoke considerably more. Given my interest in language, and the centrality of the subject to life in another country, it was only natural that I should want to know about their ventures/misadventures into Cantonese. What follows is a selection of reflections from informants on their language backgrounds, and their experiences in tackling Cantonese.

*

Esther's first language is Hindi. She started to learn English when she went to pre-school nursery at the age of three. She acquired a number of other Indian languages as she was growing up: Assamese in Assam, where she lived until she was nine, and then Punjabi after the family moved to Delhi. When she got married, her husband's family spoke Gujarati, so she picked that up. Later, when she and her husband moved to London, she started learning French and developed a reasonable degree of proficiency in it, although these days it's pretty rusty as she hasn't used it in a long time.

Even though she describes herself as a pretty good language learner, she speaks almost no Cantonese. Initially she didn't make the effort because she never thought of Hong Kong as her home, and assumed she would only be here for three or four years, which was the limit she had set herself on first arriving. It was only after she returned to Hong Kong having lived in Canada, the United States and the United Kingdom, and she and her husband separated, that she realized Hong Kong was the best place for her, and began to entertain the possibility that she would be here for the long term – possibly the rest of her life. These days she discounts the notion of attempting to learn Cantonese. She's been here too long, she says, she gets by just fine in English, and so there's no motivation to try.

*

Originally from New Zealand, Ron is a very long-term resident of Hong Kong, having come here in the 1960s to take up a position as an academic at the University of Hong Kong, a position he held for almost fifty years. When interrogated on the issue of their linguistic facility, expats are either shamefully monolingual, or admit to possessing several languages. Ron is a member of the latter camp. His best foreign languages are Bahasa Malaysia and Bahasa Indonesia, which he maintains are effectively the same thing, although they have differences in spelling, pronunciation and vocabulary which can render them mutually unintelligible, just as varieties of English such as Scottish and Australian can be to their respective speakers.

Ron tells me that his French is a bit rusty and his German even rustier, but I've heard him speak both, and attribute the rust to his modesty. He gets by in Dutch, Spanish, Portuguese and Pashtu. However, when it comes to Cantonese, he has to admit defeat, and for that he blames his children as much as the devilish nature of the language.

"They all went to Anglo-Chinese schools, so they all have Cantonese. My attempts at speaking the language were so much derided by them that it was a severe psychological disincentive. You know, 'Oh, just listen to the old man' kind of thing. Many people will tell you that they had a go at learning Cantonese when they first arrived, but gave up, usually because their early attempts at speaking were greeted with such derision by locals."

He follows this by stating something blatantly obvious to anyone who has ever tried: the Chinese language is an especially difficult one to learn, and, in particular, the amount of time it takes to learn to read and write is massive. But he also tells me something I didn't know: that Mao Tse-tung wanted to go over to a Romanized form of Chinese, as the Vietnamese did years ago and have stuck with ever since. But historically other things intervened, and what was quite a major plank in Mao's political platform never got implemented. Uncharacteristically, Mao went for what was, in his opinion, second best – the simplification of the characters. These days, people who can only read the simplified version struggle mightily with the traditional form, which is still employed in Hong Kong, a fact that was used to political effect during the Occupy Central movement when student banners were written in traditional script. The symbolism of their message, if not the words, was clear to Beijing: "We are not like you. You cannot read our language. Don't tell us to use your language."

*

Peter has an endearing quality of answering a question with a question. "How many languages do I speak?" he echoes, scratching his head. "That's a hard question to answer." It begs the question of what it means to speak a language. In his household, it's his wife, a lawyer, and originally from Eastern Europe, who has the bragging rights when it comes to language: she admits to six, but in reality she has around eight. He's not sure that he can boast of any languages other than English, but then goes on to list a number of others, putting self-deprecating limits on each of them. Like most of his class and generation, he has schoolboy French, and could get by in Greek when he lived there. And, yes, he has quite a decent vocabulary in Arabic – knows all of the obscene words, but is not sure if that counts. He has a pretty good understanding of Romanian, the home language of his in-laws, but is not sure that his spoken Romanian is any better than that of a 'retarded monkey'.

Like virtually all other expats interrogated on the subject, he has a deep sense of shame when it comes to his Cantonese, which is virtually non-existent despite two attempts at studying it. He's always made an attempt to develop basic conversational skills in every country he's lived in, and embarked on studying Cantonese on first arriving in Hong Kong many years ago. His efforts faltered in the face of pressures from work, and then petered out altogether.

His second attempt occurred many years after the first. Driven by shame at having lived in Hong Kong for so many years without making inroads into the language, he and his wife signed up for a course at a language institute in Kowloon, and, despite the fact that they were both very busy people, stuck it out for the whole course.

"It was very traditional, in a way that shocked me: extremely drill-based and teacher-directed. Basically, 1950s-style teaching methods. And we didn't really get the chance to practise the phrases we'd so carefully written down. We did learn something, but not very much. We talked about signing up for a second course, to consolidate the little that we'd learned, but it never happened – we did other things with our time. So, yeah, that's the dismal story of my making no progress whatsoever in Cantonese. But still at the back of my mind, after all these years, I keep thinking I must try to do something, in spite of the discouragement."

*

Ken tells the following story:

"One of my colleagues was a sterling character called Jeff Spring. Brilliant chap. He was a musician, a playwright, and an outstanding English teacher. He was also gifted at language, fluent in the usual European ones such as French, German and Spanish, but also less usual ones such as Thai and so forth. Jeff signed up for a Cantonese course, and talked me into going along with him. So, one day, in the staff room of the college where we were lecturers in English language teaching, Jeff decided to try out his Cantonese on one of our Chinese colleagues. She let out this long exaggerated laugh, 'Haaaaa!' I remember it very clearly. Then she said, 'Wait a minute,' and called out to all of the Cantonese colleagues along the corridor to come in. When they were all assembled, she said to Jeff, 'Say it again,' which he did. They all absolutely killed themselves laughing. This incensed Jeff. As I say, he was brilliant at languages and had loads of them. He said, 'Fuck them. I'm not going to do that again.' I thought it odd that not only were they teachers, but they were training others to be English language teachers. Despite this, they had a wholly negative attitude to someone who was actually trying to make the effort to learn their language. It was profoundly discouraging, not only to Jeff, who'd been humiliated, but also to me. Elsewhere, it's totally different. You know what it's like in Italy, for instance. You go into a restaurant with a phrasebook in your hand, and you read it out and you make six mistakes in every sentence and they go 'Yeah! Yeah!' They get what you're trying to communicate, they make an effort to understand you, and they applaud your efforts. And I have to say that over the years my experiences have not changed here. You know, when you learn a few taxi phrases and try to use them, you'll get quite a negative response, or they'll repeat in English what you said, or they'll correct you."

*

It started on the second day of their arrival in Hong Kong. The shopkeeper replied in Cantonese to her request for a couple of simple items. She didn't have a clue what he was saying, so she repeated her request. Again, the reply came in Cantonese. She ended up leaving the shop empty-handed and confused.

When Stephen told her that the job offer had come through she was both excited and apprehensive. Their son Paul suffered from mild autism and she already knew that getting an outwardly undamaged kid into school in Hong Kong was a challenge. At the age of five, Paul could play

Chopin by ear. Would they be able to find a school where 'special needs' didn't equate to 'retarded'?

The second time it happened, she snapped. She knew the shop assistant spoke English because she heard him dealing with another foreigner. Impassive, he continued to reply to her requests in Cantonese. Exasperated, she finally burst out, "Speak to me in English. Why won't you speak to me in English?"

So he did. But it wasn't a message she wanted to hear. "Why don't you speak Cantonese?" he replied, in excellent English. "Who do you think you are? You should be ashamed of yourself." Ashamed of herself? What was he talking about? It slowly dawned on her that because she looked Chinese, she was expected to be Chinese. And as Chinese, she was expected to speak Chinese. A yawning gulf opened up between herself and her new home.

When relocating to Hong Kong, the first imperative is to obtain an identity card. Without a card, life is extremely challenging. Getting hospital treatment, accessing government services, getting a child into school, obtaining a driving licence are either difficult or impossible. So Stephen was staggered when his wife refused to accompany him and their son to the Department of Immigration to apply for an ID card. He knew better than to argue with her. When she made up her mind on something it stayed made up, and he knew that once a notion had lodged itself in her head it was impossible to dislodge. So, leaving her at home, he and his son presented themselves at the Department of Immigration knowing that the difficult process of relocating to a new country just got infinitely harder.

She was a fourth generation Australian, her ancestors having emigrated from southern China in the nineteenth century, many years before the introduction of the despicable White Australia Policy with its jingoistic slogans ('two Wongs don't make a white') had been introduced. Her grandfather's generation had spoken Chinese, but by her parents' generation, the family had become resolutely monolingual. There was nothing they could do about the colour of their skin, but in every other way, they were more Australian than the Caucasians who had been in the Antipodes for a mere generation or two. She came to realize that she was the archetypical banana – yellow on the outside, but white on the inside. As a child, a Big Mac, not fried rice, had been her dish of choice.

Their son was enrolled in one of the international primary schools. One day, the school called her as she was about to leave the apartment for the supermarket. There was something wrong with her son: he'd had some sort of a seizure, and needed to be taken to the hospital. In a panic, she called her husband. There was no point in her taking the son to the hospital, because the first thing she would be asked for was the ID card she had refused to obtain. Her husband was in a meeting and was unavailable. Leaving a message for him, she headed to school to be with her son. Her husband showed up shortly afterwards, and they headed to the hospital. They had to wait three hours in the accident and emergency department before a doctor was available to check their son and have him admitted for observation. Her husband lost half a day of work, something he could ill afford, all because of her overreaction to the perceived insults at not speaking Cantonese. It can't go on, he said. She should swallow her pride. Who cares what the locals think? But his words fell on deaf ears.

Every three months she had to make the round-trip to Macau in order to renew her visa. This caused further inconvenience. On one occasion, she was unable to get a same-day return ferry and had to stay overnight. Although they had a live-in helper, her husband had to cancel a business trip to Singapore in order to be on hand for their son in case of a medical or some other emergency. Tensions grew.

As the long summer break approached, she signalled her intention to return to Australia with their son to visit her parents and other friends. Her husband seemed relieved and the tension eased.

And then, as the long hot summer with its record run of seven typhoons in close succession wound down, she called to tell him that she wouldn't be coming back. She'd had enough.

*

Lara grew up in Malaysia where she was raised speaking English as her first language and a number of Chinese dialects as her second. Her parents are Fukienese by descent, and the family dialect is Hokkien which is what her paternal grandmother spoke. Her maternal grandmother was actually Cantonese, but she never spoke Cantonese to the children. In school they learned Bahasa and all of her lessons were in Bahasa except for English language and Chinese language classes, so for a while she was pretty fluent in Bahasa. She can still read it and get by in it if she needs to when in Malaysia. She also learned Putonghua as a child, and in those days in Malaysia in the seventies and eighties most of the Putonghua teachers were Taiwanese, so she learned the traditional script and acquired a Taiwanese rather than Mainland pronunciation. When she came to Hong Kong, she took Putonghua lessons for a few months, so her accent became closer to the Mainland norm, if it could be called that. She tried to use it when travelling for work but didn't get as much exposure as she would have liked. These days, her ear is much more attuned to Cantonese, because she hears it around all the time.

Although she's never taken formal lessons, she's been able to pick up a reasonable amount of Cantonese and can get by fulfilling all of her basic social and service needs such as reading a menu, and having a chat in a shop.

Lara says that as a language learner, she's not bad. She has an ear for languages, which she thinks is crucial. Recently, she spent two weeks in Germany, and in that time was able to communicate at a very basic level. She can read menus and environmental print in numerous languages. The downside is that sometimes her accent is just too accurate and people start to think she's a local, and speak at such a rate that she doesn't have a clue what they're saying, just because she's asked them "Where's the loo?" in a very good local accent. "It seems that the more accurate you are, the more confused the locals get," she says. Among my informants, hers is one of the rare success stories.

*

During her first year in Hong Kong, Michele hated the place. Her English was poor, and her Cantonese was non-existent. Within two weeks of arriving, she enrolled in a language institute on Nathan Road and started a very intensive course. It was two hours a day, three times a week; very different from those one-hour-a-week classes where you learn nothing. She made good progress, and after a few weeks was beginning to communicate, but then got sick and was hospitalized with a kidney problem. She missed three weeks and by the time she went back to class was too far behind the other students and had to drop out. She was determined to re-enroll for the next course, but then started working for a foreign trading company and had no time for study because she was working twelve hours a day, six days a week.

She continued to work on her Cantonese on her own, but is not at all proud of what she achieved. She can introduce herself, say her age, say that she's French and how long she's been in Hong Kong. She can give directions in a taxi, and negotiate the purchase of items in shops on Kowloonside when the assistant speaks no English, but that's the limit to her resourcefulness. She feels really guilty about her failure to master Cantonese beyond a rudimentary level and is apologetic about not speaking fluently despite having been here for thirty years.

"I don't want to be taken for one of these expats from white countries who have this sense of racial superiority. In Europe, poor, coloured immigrants come to the country, and the locals say, 'These bloody people are worth nothing. They are like animals. They come here and eat our bread. They come here and take our jobs. They take our seats on the bus. We *demand* that they learn our language and speak it. They *must* do it. They owe it to us.' Actually, the immigrants speak at least two languages, and more often than not they speak three or four. They're human beings, they're *good* human beings. And then the white people come to Hong Kong, and say, 'Oh, no, I'm not going to learn their language. They can speak to me in my language.'"

*

"Some of my friends would do endless courses in Cantonese but I only ever saw them using it superficially. Take Keith, for example. I only see him use it at a phatic level, you know, the French call it *badinage*, banter with the bar staff and people like that. So he would come into the bar and he would produce all of their 'waahs' and 'aiyahs' and it would all be in joshing and jest. But I've never seen him use it in a serious way to run a conversation. The end result of all that study was that yes, he could read some signs and so on but in terms of speech, it all amounted to simply that kind of joshing. Well, most people around you are able to josh in English, so there's hardly a motivation to learn. Even though I took several courses over the years, I always felt that Cantonese was a bridge too far."

*

Putting aside any false claims to modesty, Leo has to admit that he's a good language learner, and the evidence bears him out. He has a good ear and is an excellent mimic: he's fluent in Danish, French, German and Romanian, and gets by in several other languages including Italian, Spanish and Portuguese. But when it comes to Cantonese, he has to say *siu, siu* at best. Why *siu, siu*? His response is more an excuse than a reason. Initially, he thought he would only be in Hong Kong for two years, which was the extent of his contract. But then the contract limped into a third year following which a second contract was offered.

By that time, he realized that he could get by with English, but that was true of any other country in which he had lived. He admits that Cantonese and Mandarin Chinese are difficult languages, but any language is difficult if you don't speak it. In the end, to be truthful, he has to admit that he never really made the effort.

"So, why is that? It's a reasonable question, but a difficult one to answer. I don't know, I honestly don't know. It's not that I look down on the Chinese or anything like that, or that I think their culture is inferior. Certainly not. Absolutely not. I suppose if I were to search for a reason, it might just be that it reflects something that Kipling once observed: 'East and West – never the twain shall meet' and all that. And I think there is an element of truth here. Maybe it's a subliminal or subconscious reaction, I don't know.

"One or two of the colleagues I worked with were fluent speakers of Cantonese. David Bunton, for example, was exceptional, although I was to learn later that he had come from a family of missionaries, and spent a lot of his childhood on the Mainland and so on. There were other long-term expats who spoke some Cantonese but not a great deal. Then there were others of Chinese descent who don't speak it either. Patricia Lam would be an example. By her own admission she was a non-speaker of Cantonese. So, what is it that has driven some expats to try at mastering the language but not me, and other expats like me who never bothered? Certainly a sense of identity with the place would be a factor. Do I identify with Asia, with the Chinese? Ultimately, no I don't. My identity is very much rooted in Europe. And that's something I've come to recognize increasingly in the time that I've been here. A former tutor said to me that you need to be out of your country and, indeed, away from your continent in order to get a sense of who you are and to appreciate the various values which have been inculcated in you. It's that sense of standing back that I often talk about. I *love* being in Europe, and this hit me the last time I was in Berlin, which is a bit of a crossroads within Europe for obvious reasons. This is, as the Germans would say, my *heimat*, my belonging, my place of being. Whether it's Berlin or somewhere else is another question. So, I don't have that sense of belonging here, but I do remember having a sense of pride when I got my permanent residency. I was very happy about that because it indicated that the locals, at some level, were prepared to accept me."

*

One reason that Nigel would never see himself as anything other than an expat is that his Cantonese never got beyond an elementary level. He did a full year course in Cantonese three times. It was the same course, done at seven-year intervals. He's quasi-fluent in French, was able to go to France, work there and learn the language, so considers that he can't be completely hopeless as a language learner. It's a matter of being motivated to become fluent. When he lived in Kuwait, he struggled to learn Arabic, undertaking long courses, as he did with Cantonese, but as with Cantonese he never succeeded.

*

Towards the end of my conversation with Margaret, an elegant English woman in her seventies who has lived in Hong Kong for many years, I ask her if she had ever tried to learn Cantonese. She gives me a look of abject horror and replies, "Good God no! Why on earth would I do that?"

*

What sense can be made of these vignettes of the linguistic failure of expats in the face of 'the devil's language'? For years, I've been beating myself up over my inability to conquer Cantonese. Why was I able to master an equally if not more difficult language like Thai to the point where I could get my need for goods and services met and socialize to some degree, and do it in less than a year? It was some consolation to discover that I was in good company. With few exceptions, my informants reported embarking with enthusiasm on the learning of Cantonese but being largely defeated by it, despite having mastered a range of other languages. The road to mastery of the devil's language, like the road to hell, is paved with good intentions.

The perceived difficulty of the language was not the principal, or even a major, factor in defeat. As Leo said, "All languages are difficult when you don't speak them." Five factors thread their way through expat misadventures with Cantonese. The first of these was the emotional toll that the endeavour took on the learners. The fancy phrase for this is 'negative effect'. The second factor, which is related to the first, was the indifference of the locals to the efforts of foreigners to learn their language. Factor three was the lack of communicative need, the fourth was time, or lack of it, and the fifth and final factor was an inability to identify with the local culture.

In the early stages, using a new language in public is an exercise in ritual humiliation. I cringe at the memory of early, overly optimistic attempts to use the language. Like the time the shopkeeper who, in response to my request for a newspaper, asked me in immaculate English what language I imagined I was trying to speak. "Why don't you try Cantonese?" he asked. I knew exactly how Jeff Spring, that 'sterling chap and brilliant linguist', felt when he was mocked for rehearsing his Cantonese in the workplace. Apart from abandoning the language altogether, there is only one cure for this condition, and that's to grow a thicker skin.

If you want a pat on the head from the locals for attempting to use their language, then forget it. By and large they simply don't care. They want to get on with business as efficiently and effectively as possible. They are world leaders in this, and they prefer to do it in English. They're well aware that their English isn't perfect (although many are unaware of just how less than perfect it is), but they also know that in general their English will trump your Cantonese any day of the week.

It takes two to tango, and if they don't want to dance to your tune then you just have to put up with it. In Bangkok, my initial pathetic efforts to communicate in Thai were met with approving nods that at times even approached admiration. Sure, I was frequently laughed at – like the time I got the tone wrong and instead of asking for iced water, requested shinbone water. But the laughter was always good-natured and the constant head-patting highly motivating. Effective communication requires co-operation and goodwill on the part of both parties, and my Thai interlocutors were nothing if not co-operative. Well, they had to be. Thirty-five years ago, English was largely non-existent in Thailand, so if a taxi driver or a shopkeeper wanted my custom, and my money, they had to work with me as we negotiated in my less than perfect Thai.

This brings me on to the third factor: communicative need, or the lack of it. In most of the habitats where expats hang out, competence in Cantonese is unnecessary. As a number of informants noted, "I soon realized that I could get by just fine without Cantonese." There are, of course, parts of Hong Kong where lack of competence isn't fine at all, but these can be avoided.

The time factor is not insignificant. In this technology-driven, globalized world, everyone is busy, but in Hong Kong, life roars along on steroids. The salaries might be eye-watering, but so are the hours. You thought you were busy working a sixty-hour week? Try eighty or ninety. Stefan, a refugee from the economic basket case formerly known as France, said to me, "Sure the money is great, but for that they own you." And the first things that go when temporal push comes to communicative shove are non-essential activities such as cooking lessons, meditation, yoga and, of course, Cantonese.

You're newly arrived: 'fresh off the boat' in colonial lingo. You pick up phrases which you sprinkle into your conversation with friends who are passing through on their way to somewhere else. "My *pung yau* (friend) would like a *baedzou* (beer)," you say to the barman at your local pub, and then, after the second beer, "Order another round, I just have to go to the *sai sou gan* – sorry, that's the bathroom." "Your Cantonese is impressive," your friends will say. Encouraged by the flattery, you master a dozen utterances with near-perfect intonation and impress visiting family members from the Midlands or the Midwest. In a restaurant, you rattle off orders for dim sum so fluently that the relatives are mightily impressed and the waiter replies in kind. You don't understand a word, and, embarrassed, switch back to English. "He must be from the Mainland," you mutter to your relatives.

The most successful group of non-locals at mastering Cantonese for functional purposes are so low on the social scale they're not even considered expats. I'm referring to the army of domestic helpers. Most helpers can get by in three or four languages, including Cantonese, but are commonly considered to be ill-educated, if not downright stupid, by their monolingual masters. They acquire Cantonese because it's useful, particularly for those who have a local Chinese employer, which is ironical, because many local employers want their helpers to speak English in the home to provide exposure in the language to their children.

To forestall the notion that I'm not allowing truth to get in the way of a good story, let me say that of course there are expats who achieve high levels of proficiency in Cantonese. While they are very much to be admired, they are also very much in the minority. Those who marry into the local community and find themselves living in the New Territories have waived any right to the litany of excuses I've documented in the chapter. But take the case of Gaye, a highly privileged expat, married to a judge and living what you might imagine is the stereotypical expat life on the Island. She became highly proficient in Cantonese through force of will. "It didn't hurt that I'm an extreme extrovert," she says, as though I hadn't noticed. "I refused to let any local, whether it be a taxi driver, a waiter or anyone else, speak to me in English. One of the first phrases I memorized was: 'Please don't talk to me in English.' A lot of them wanted to, because they wanted to practise their English. Not on my dime, they didn't." Gregory is another interesting example. Living with his long-time Chinese boyfriend on Kowloonside, he immersed himself in the local gay community, asked for no concessions to his English background, got none, and was fluent in remarkably short order.

23.

THROUGH OTHER EYES

'Othering' is the way members of one social group distance themselves from, or assert themselves over, another by construing the latter as being fundamentally different (the 'Other').   (Edward Said)

The complexities of social relationships, both personal and racial, are bewilderingly entangled and ever-changing. Many inhabitants, locals, expatriates and those who fit neither category, stick to their own, effectively inhabiting parallel universes. However, contact at some level is inevitable, from sharing a ride on the MTR to sharing a bed. Regardless of the level of contact, locals have views on Mainlanders, expats and others, expats have views on locals, Mainlanders and others. The views are by no means uniform, as this chapter illustrates. Here is a montage of views expressed by locals on Mainlanders and expats, and those expressed by expats on locals.

Locals on Mainlanders

It wasn't too long after the Handover that cracks began to appear in the seamless fabric of greater modern China. Resentment built at the influx of Mainlanders who turned up with their bad haircuts, their unhygienic habits and, worst of all, flaunting the fact that they had more cash than the average local. Pregnant women staggered across the border, filling hospital beds and producing their offspring who would subsequently have the possibility of permanent abode in Hong Kong. Locals scratched their heads and asked why, if the Mainland was such a wonderful place, the inhabitants with the cash to do so want to get out.

On Sunday, March 2, 2015, a riot broke out at Yuen Long, near the border between the Special Administrative Region and the Mainland. This was the third clash in a month, following those in Tuen Mun and Sai Kung between locals and Mainland traders who came across the border to buy up goods to take back to China to sell. Police used pepper spray to break up the clash between the traders and the locals. They had previously warned village strongmen who aligned with the Mainlanders not to use triad thugs to confront the protesters. Thirty-three people were arrested for possession of weapons and assaulting police. Locals were outraged at the parallel traders who, they claimed, crowded out shopping centres and ransacked shops to take goods back across the border where they were sold at a significant profit.

In Tung Chung, the factory outlet shops are crammed with Mainlanders with outsized roll-away luggage trolleys. They buy up anything that presents itself: handbags, running shoes, powdered milk, pharmaceutical goods and, of course, designer clothes. The latter are made in China, shipped to and bought in Hong Kong, and subsequently re-imported to the Mainland. Apparently, the fact that items are purchased on the other side of the border is proof-positive that they are genuine, high-quality fakes.

While resentment runs deep, not all locals are resentful. Those who benefit appreciate the Mainland money that keeps the local economy buoyant, but in general, as time passes, resentment is growing among locals who can't compete with Mainland money for apartments, hospital beds and other necessities.

*

Fiona, an office administrator in her thirties, is a frequent traveller to the Mainland. Her boyfriend, a Hong Kong local, has relocated to Shanghai where he works in the financial services sector. On those weekends when he doesn't return to Hong Kong, she flies to Shanghai. Our conversation turns to cross-border relations.

"The other week, there was a riot on the border between locals and Mainlanders. Why is there such a negative attitude towards Mainlanders?"

"Hong Kong people think that Mainlanders are pillaging Hong Kong. The newly-rich come here with their money and snap up residential properties. This has driven prices sky-high and has led to serious housing shortages. Young people can no longer afford to buy property here. The high cost of property is definitely blamed on Mainlanders. They come here in such numbers and so often that the streets are constantly crowded. Pregnant women come here to have their children because they want their children to have the right of abode in Hong Kong. They take up all the hospital beds, so that locals can't get a bed when they need one. And you must have noticed the increasing number of drugstores in Hong Kong. They exist to serve the Mainlanders: shelves and shelves of powdered milk. They buy it here because the powdered milk in China is fake and contaminated. There are stories all the time of babies getting sick and dying because of the contaminated milk. They also come here to buy luxury goods like gold watches and other jewellery. So, in Central, Kowloon and Causeway Bay, all the shops are either drugstores or luxury goods stores."

"You seem pretty worked up about Mainlanders. What's your own personal opinion?"

"They don't get in my way, so I don't have any feelings about them one way or the other. I'm just telling you what locals in general think. There's a great deal of resentment."

"Would you go so far as to call this attitude on the part of locals racist?"

"Well, I guess you could."

"What about other subgroups? Is it only Mainlanders who are the subjects of racism?"

"Only Mainlanders."

"What about domestic helpers? We hear a lot about Chinese discrimination against them."

"Not really. Not that I've heard of."

"You've never heard about locals physically abusing their helpers?"

"No."

"What about people who are racially physically different in appearance, like black people?"

"No, I don't think Hong Kong people have any prejudice against black people. First of all, they're not too common in Hong Kong, so I don't think they're a concern to Hong Kong people."

*

Chloe and May are Cathay flight attendants. In general, flight attendants make interesting interviewees. They are obviously well-travelled, they have extensive contact with a wide variety of expatriates and other foreigners, and most have comprehensible levels of English. Chloe and May were interviewed jointly, but for the purposes of representing their views, I have kept their comments separate.

Chloe is the more senior of the two, being an in-flight service manager, while May is a senior purser. Chloe is married to a Taiwanese businessman, and commutes between Kaohsiung and Hong Kong. I begin our conversation by making the point that in the run-up to 1997, there was a rapid growth in self-censorship on the part of the media. I also felt that there was a reasonable amount of goodwill towards the Mainland, but now, almost twenty years later, the goodwill has largely evaporated, replaced by antipathy and resentment. This was particularly apparent during the Occupy Central movement.

Chloe agrees. When she was young, China was closed. Very few Mainlanders could get out, and so, like a lot of other Hong Kong locals, the family would go to the Mainland to visit their relatives and to take them things that were either difficult or impossible to obtain there. She recalls one trip that she took with her mother. The relatives had asked for the latest type of television, so they took televisions and several large bags crammed with lots of other goods that the relatives had requested. At the border, the customs officials had opened the bags to inspect what they were bringing in, and it was impossible to close the bags again. With economic liberalization, the relatives grew rich, much richer than Chloe and her immediate family, but they had no appreciation for what the Hong Kong family had done for them in the past when life was such a struggle. These days, they come to Hong Kong to speculate on properties, and drive the prices up. Chloe would like to get a place of her own, but even a modest flat is beyond her means. While she doesn't think her relatives should make any kind of reparation, she resents the total lack of gratitude for what was done for them. There was no acknowledgment whatsoever of what Chloe's side of the family did.

She and her friends who have had similar experiences share stories and simmer in resentment. The previous week, the aunt and cousins of one friend turned up from the Mainland and got into a big fight in a shop in Kowloon over milk powder. Chloe's assessment is that their Mainland relatives are 'uncivilized', a term she feels no compulsion to define.

When I suggest that 'uncivilized' is a pretty strong term, she retorts, "But it's true. And there's a lot of cheating and robbery and violence going on in China. It's not safe there any more, and so Mainlanders want to flee their own country. They're flooding in here and making it so crowded. There are very big cultural conflicts between the Hong Kong people and the Mainlanders. And it isn't just Hongkongers who think this. I've read interviews with Westerners who went to China to work, and they say they get cheated all the time, and that the Chinese there just can't be trusted."

Another of her Hong Kong friends, an architect, has worked in Beijing and Shanghai for over ten years. When he first went to the Mainland, he thought, "OK, give them time, the country is just opening up." These days, however, he said that when he goes out for lunch, he doesn't know if he's going to get food poisoning.

"Now," says Chloe, "I don't think there's any hope of them becoming civilized. Everyone just wants to get as many material possessions as they can and then leave the country. So who will be there to contribute? Only the old people will be left. It's very sad."

May's views are similar to Chloe's. In the past, she had compassion for Mainlanders, but now her feelings have turned sour. Her attitude has been particularly coloured by the sister-in-law who came from the Mainland and married her brother. "Lucky for her," she says. "He was a very good catch."

Unlike the family into which she had married, her sister-in-law was very much on the pro-Beijing side during the Occupy Central movement. May agrees with Chloe's assertion that Mainlanders come to Hong Kong to take advantage of everything it has to offer. They show no respect for Hongkongers, or even for each other. All they want to do is get all of their cash out of China, so they bring it to Hong Kong and exploit the economy for their own gain. Hongkongers are being put in a very disadvantaged position, and becoming second-class citizens in their own country. And then there's the way they behave as non-civilized tourists as well.

I'm curious about the use of the term 'uncivilized' by May as well as Chloe.

"I'm sorry," she says, not looking at all sorry, "but it's true. I really look down on them, I'm afraid to say. It all comes from the Cultural Revolution in the 1960s. It destroyed the Chinese value system. In Hong Kong, we still have Chinese values. My sister-in-law, she doesn't appreciate what we have given her and what we have done for her. She takes everything, and gives nothing back. That's the difference between her and our family."

"Do you see any solutions?" I ask.

"Not in the short term. I think that the whole country will have to be demolished and rebuilt on a fairer system. That would be the only hope. As I said, the Cultural Revolution completely wiped out the Chinese value system, like being polite, respecting the elderly, valuing the family. In fact, you could say that it wiped out human nature."

"So, like Chloe, you have a pretty bleak view."

"I'm afraid so. I just read a book by someone who was in prison at the beginning of the communist revolution, and everyone had hope. They looked forward to building a fairer society. We had the Communists and Chairman Mao, and everything. But the Cultural Revolution just wiped out the history, the pride and the confidence and the goodness of the Chinese people. And they just abandoned their rich cultural history for nothing. No religion, no values, nothing to look up to: nothing except money and power."

*

Ken recently retired to Australia after a life in academia in Hong Kong, China and Australia. He is a difficult person to characterize. He was born in and raised in Guangdong, moved to Hong Kong when he was nine, and then emigrated with his mother and siblings to Australia to join his father, who had worked there since before Ken was born. When I ask him which box to put him in – Mainlander, Hongkonger or expat – he laughs and replies, "I guess I'm all three. I belong everywhere and nowhere, I fit in everywhere and nowhere, so I guess I can give you a unique perspective. I had three long periods in Hong Kong: when I moved from Zhongshan and became a school kid, when I came back from Australia to do graduate study, and then, years later, when I returned as an academic. And then I also spent long periods as an adult, studying and teaching in the Mainland."

I use this comment as an opportunity to ask him how, in his view, Hongkongers view Mainlanders. He laughs at the question and says because I know he's an academic, I must also know I'm not going to get a straight answer. However, I do get one, and one which is consistent with my own observations, as well as with comments from other informants. "In the first place," says Ken, "Hong Kong is a place of constant change, and views on the Mainland and Mainlanders are constantly changing. Secondly, Hong Kong is deeply divided on issues and attitudes towards Mainlanders. Not only are people split between each other on the pro- versus anti-Mainland issue, but they're also split within themselves. In terms of identity, there are many schizophrenics among the population. And so, as I say, there are no straight answers."

Some years prior to the Handover, Ken interrupted his doctoral studies in Australia and returned to Hong Kong to do a master's degree. He did so in order to gain access to documents held by the university library that were central to his doctoral research into Confucian thought and Communist rule. He also did some undergraduate tutoring and was surprised at how fervently pro-Chinese the students were. They were sick of the British, and couldn't wait to be united with the Mainland. One day, on entering the tutorial room, he found the students talking passionately about reunification. Ken has a gentle, almost meek, disposition, and he shocked the class by telling them that they were not Chinese. When they disputed this, he asked, "All right, then, how many of you have been to China? Let me see a show of hands."

Not one student raised a hand, so he said, "None of you have ever been. I knew it. You have all these romantic ideas, but you're completely different from the Chinese." Even though none of the students had ever been to the Mainland, they were extremely offended. They began shouting at him. "We *are* Chinese. What are you talking about?"

"I was born and raised in China, and I've been back many times," he replied. "That's how I know what I'm talking about. You've never been, so what are *you* talking about?"

But now, twenty years after the Handover, Ken says that attitudes have changed. Now, students are increasingly saying: "We're Hongkongers. We're different; we're not like those Northerners."

"It was the students who were the foot soldiers in the Occupy Central movement," says Ken. "They were the ones who faced down the police."

I ask him what the Occupy Central movement tells him about Hongkongers' views of the Mainland, and he replies, "Well, I'd moved back to Australia by the time it happened, so my views come from Facebook, the media and what my friends say. There's no doubt that it deeply divided the community. Again, it isn't that straightforward, because not all those who were opposed to the protest were necessarily pro-Beijing. It certainly split my Hong Kong friends quite deeply. After this incident, some who were quite friendly with each other, including me, were saying, 'Do I really want to continue being friendly with such-and-such a person, whose views are so different from mine?' In my case, I'm not anti-China, but I think the Hong Kong people should be able to say they want universal suffrage."

Locals on Expats

The temptation in asking a question is to take the answer you receive at face value. Is the individual under interrogation telling you what they really believe, or what they think you want to know? If you're relentless enough, interviewees will generally confess to anything. When asked what locals thought of expats, most informants reported that the majority had little, if any, contact with expats, but that those who did, accepted and appreciated expats as part of the tapestry of Hong Kong. That said, there was clear resentment at the colonial past and privilege, and annoyance at persistent bad behaviour on the part of some expats. Three examples of bad behaviour are presented below.

*

At a certain point in my conversation with Yvette, a store manager, I ask whether she's seen much evidence of racism in Hong Kong. She pauses and replies that if, by racism, I mean unpleasant or negative attitudes towards other people, then she'd have to say that the only racism she's experienced is by gweilos. When I express surprise at her response, she replies, "Yes, lots of gweilos have bad manners and use bad language. Not all of them – but enough. You can see it all the time. They act like they still own Hong Kong."

"For example?" I ask.

"For example, I live on Hong Kong Island and work in Kowloon. I take an express bus from Pokfulam through the Central Tunnel to Hung Hom, where I catch a train to where I work. Yesterday, I was sitting on the bus chatting to a friend. A gweilo was sitting opposite me. As we approached the tunnel, he called out to the driver that he wanted to get off because he wanted to go to Wan Chai. The driver just shook his head and indicated that he couldn't stop until he got through the tunnel, which would take the gweilo in the opposite direction to where he wanted to go. The gweilo started shouting and using four-letter words. I tried to calm him down, and told him that the driver couldn't stop because it was an express bus. However, that didn't stop him cursing. He kept shouting and cursing and saying that he had a job interview and that now he was going to miss the interview and that meant he wouldn't get the job. I was ready to have an argument with him. I said, 'Well, next time you should make sure that you get a regular bus, not an express bus. You have no one to blame but yourself.' He looked quite shocked that a nice Chinese lady would speak to him like that. My bus friend was also a bit shocked. She said, 'Just don't get involved.' I don't know if this is racism or not, but to me it just showed this guy has contempt for our way of life."

*

When I ask Anna what Hongkongers think of expatriates, she tells a similar story.

"What do Hongkongers think of expats? What do you want to know?"

"What's the general impression? Are they seen as arrogant, privileged, just here to exploit the financial benefits and the lifestyle?"

"Well, first of all, most Hongkongers, like people living in the New Territories, don't have any contact with expats. They'll see them on the MTR occasionally, but that's about all."

"How about people like you, who have a lot of contact?"

"Oh, for people like me, gweilos are just part of the scene. There are just a few who give the rest a bad name."

"Can you give me an example?"

"Let's see. OK, so when I've had a stressful time at work, I like to have a foot massage – a little bit of pampering after a long day. I go to a place on Caine Road, not too far from where I live. They have two branches on opposite sides of the road. The branch that I go to has a girl who speaks reasonable English. She's a pretty girl with long hair. Because she speaks good English, the gweilos like to go to her. Anyway, one evening she's not in the branch I usually go to, she's in the branch across the street working on another customer. While I'm having my foot massage, the phone rings. I gather that it's a gweilo asking if the masseuse who speaks English is there. The receptionist, who doesn't really speak English says 'Yes, yes.' I imagine she thinks the customer just wants a massage. A short time later, this gweilo comes into the shop. He's a big guy with red hair. He looks around for the English-speaking girl with the long hair, and when he sees that she isn't there, he starts cursing like crazy at the receptionist, saying she's wasted his time, that he has come for a massage, and the girl he asked for isn't available. The receptionist doesn't have a clue what he's talking about, so I try to help out, translating for both sides and trying to calm the gweilo down. At one point I say, 'Just take it easy. All of the masseurs here are good. Any one of them can give you the treatment that you want.'

"That makes him even more furious. He turns on me and shouts, 'What the fuck do you know? I want the girl with the long hair who speaks English. I asked if she was here, and they said that she was. They shouldn't have said that. Now I'm here and I don't have the person I want.'

"'What do you want?' I ask him. 'One of the other girls can help.'

"The gweilo says, 'Fuck! Fuck! Fuck!', stamps his foot like a spoiled kid and leaves the shop. I've experienced this kind of behaviour from gweilos before, but I was shocked. The other customers, the masseurs, the receptionist, everyone was shocked. The woman in charge of that branch came over and spoke to me. She said that she felt bad for me – but she didn't give me a discount!"

*

Eliza is an insurance clerk who works for a British medical insurance company with an office in Wan Chai. Her co-workers are both expats and locals, and the atmosphere is generally harmonious, although sometimes tensions arise. She recounts a recent incident that left her feeling particularly uncomfortable.

"Some of us meet for lunch in one of the noodle shops in the neighbourhood. One day I was having lunch with Pete, one of my expat colleagues. I do yoga, and I know that Pete does too, so on this day we talked about yoga practices as we were having lunch – a Pure Yoga pose conversation. As we were eating and talking, we were joined by Dan, another expat colleague. Dan is a bit of a slob, a bit overweight, and certainly had no interest in yoga. Anyway, Pete and I continued our conversation and got to talking about heat yoga. I asked him if he'd tried heat yoga. I haven't because I don't like getting all hot and sweaty. Pete said that he loves heat yoga, that with the heat, you can get into the poses that you can't do normally and that I ought to try it. But then, he's tall and very flexible to start with. I said that there must be something in it because there are certain poses I can't do except when I'm in a hot bathtub and then they're easy, so there must be something in heat. There's one exercise in particular where I have to fold myself and touch my thighs on my chest. I find that one really difficult, but in the bath, it's easy. Pete mentioned that in the English Premier football league, in the changing rooms, there are hot water tubs for the players to relax their muscles in the half-time break.

"Dan was listening to the conversation, and interrupted, saying, 'Eliza, are you trying to turn the conversation into a pornographic one – talking about all of these naked poses in the bathtub?' Pete looked a bit surprised, but Dan has made this kind of comment before. You can be talking about anything, and he'll make something sexual about it. I told him to stop, that we'd better stop the conversation right there.

"So this is another thing I don't like about expats. They're not all like it, but lots of them are always wanting to turn the conversation around to sex, and making all sorts of comments. I don't like it. Some of my friends work for expat companies, and they say the same thing – there's all this innuendo, and sometimes it even goes further than that. It's really a form of sexual harassment in the workplace. I think that for people like Dan it's all about power. It's all about, 'I'm European. Without us you'd be nothing. We can say and do as we like, and you'd better not forget it.' I might be wrong, but that's how I interpret his attitude."

*

Lisa, another local informant, thinks that, generally speaking, Westerners in Hong Kong are a respected group. They're usually businessmen, or in some kind of professional occupation, they're law abiding, well educated, and make a good living. They're generally seen as a plus for society in terms of bringing their skills and knowledge to Hong Kong, and contributing to the growth of the economy. Unless they work with expatriates, most locals might not really know what they do, and they won't be particularly interested. They're seen as an outside group who keep to themselves, but the general perception is a positive one. She doesn't think it's possible to lump together and make generalizations about all foreigners who live in Hong Kong. You have to think of particular groups. The Filipinas and other domestic helpers, and the Mainland group are different, and local people have different perceptions of them.

Expats on Locals

Jalil is a surgeon, and a highly skilled one, according to his peers. Not surprisingly, he is treated with great respect by his patients, and this deference is reflected in the rosy view he has of locals.

"One of the things about this society, which is also one of the reasons why it's so wonderful, is that we expats – let's call us that – are accepted. This society does not accept the road workers who come from Pakistan, or somewhere. It does not accept Filipina maids. You can be a Filipina maid here for forty years, but you'll never be accepted, and you'll never be given the right of abode. The minute your work contract has expired you'll be given a couple of weeks to get out. And if you don't go, then you'll be arrested, thrown into prison, and then deported. That may or may not be racism, but what's undeniably racist is the way they're treated

– or mistreated. Now and then one of these cases makes its way into the media. Do you remember the maid who scorched her employers dress when she was ironing it? The employer forced the maid to place her hands on the ironing board, and she then ironed them. 'That's how you iron,' she said. But we're seen as coming here as experts and specialists, and therefore we're accepted and respected. And definitely medical specialists are very accepted here. Where's the development coming from? Where are the discoveries coming from? Us. And so they're very happy to have us here. Personally, I've never, never experienced any negative situations or racist attitudes on the part of patients or anyone else for that matter."

*

Jalil's sanguine view of racism amongst locals is not shared by all. When I ask Terri, a teacher, whether racism exists in Hong Kong she asks whether I'm referring to locals or expats.

"I was thinking about locals."

"Well, they're quite blatantly prejudiced. The way they act, particularly towards black people – it's pretty dreadful. Every single black person I know, whether they're refugees or not, every one of them has told me, at least once, that they've got into a lift, and there'd be Chinese people there, and someone will put their hand over their nose as if there's a bad smell. Every single black person I know has had that experience. I think that would be pretty hurtful, don't you? But then, you can hardly blame them. Racism was instilled in the culture by the British, who were an incredibly racist lot."

*

Jeff, an architect, focuses on the issue of democracy, which has become a hot topic. When I ask him why this is so, he replies, "Because of the Mainlanders. It seems like the C.Y. Leung government is leaning more towards the Mainlanders, and bowing to the wishes of the Mainland. A few years ago, the government opened the door for all the Mainlanders to come in, and that also opened the way for issues such as democracy to become part of the public debate and led to all this social unrest."

"So, you see that as a bad thing?"

"Well, there are positives and negatives. On the positive side, because they've opened the place up for Mainlanders, the Hong Kong economy is booming. But most Hong Kong people can only see the negative impact, for example, how Mainlanders are taking hospital beds and crowding out the place – all that sort of stuff."

"There's a difference between those who come to Hong Kong legitimately to work, and those who are just sneaking in to have their kids."

"Oh, no, they don't have to sneak in any more. They can just come in very easily. The Mainlanders I'm referring to are the tourists. But the tourists are affecting the Hong Kong people a lot. And you see it on the news – the Mainlanders who come here have no manners. And they're dirty, they spit, they're not clean."

"You don't believe that."

"Of course not, I'm ventriloquizing: although some of them test my tolerance from time to time."

"Like?"

"Like the ill-mannered types who bully their way through the traffic in their big, black Mercedes – pushing in here and pushing in there. I was in a taxi one night, and one of these guys ran into the back of us. Then he got out and offered the taxi driver some money – not nearly enough to cover the cost of the damage. I told the driver to call the police, and the Mainlander told me to keep out of it in a most threatening way. The driver was clearly scared, and drove off. It was quite unpleasant. This is another type of behaviour that's giving Mainlanders a bad name. Some of my local friends say that they've just exchanged one colonial master for another."

*

Esther came originally from India to work as a flight attendant, then married and settled permanently in Hong Kong. When asked how Hong Kong has changed in the years since she has been living here, she replies that Hong Kong hasn't changed much, although she does feel that people are much more polite and considerate. She puts this down to events that had a major impact on society: she mentions the Handover, SARS and the global financial crisis.

"When I go out they're much more willing to help foreigners and those they perceive as foreigners. There's less discrimination. I notice this especially with my mum when she comes to Hong Kong to visit and we go shopping. In the early days, we would go to the night market, and she would start bargaining and they would just dismiss her. And they would do that to anyone who looked Indian."

"How about you?"

"I was never discriminated against. My Indian friends would tell me that on the MTR they were discriminated against, that at work they were discriminated against. But it never happened to me."

"But you experienced it when you went out with your mum."

"In the early days, I did. But after the economic crisis, things changed: the shop assistants were very nice to her. They would show her things, and even when we went to the wet market or wherever, they would recognize her and almost treat her like family. 'Oh, this lady comes to us every time,' and would show her the freshest stuff. So, I think in that sense things have changed."

*

In general, expatriates are respected as making important contributions to society and to the economy. However, this respect does not extend to foreigners such as domestic helpers, nor does it apply to what I would call the 'invisible expats', those Westerners who work in the service industry as waiters or tradespeople, and who struggle to make ends meet in one of the most costly cities on earth. Nor does it extend to Mainlanders who are arriving in increasing numbers in Hong Kong, either as tourists or workers.

The spectre of racism raises its head in some of the extracts, as it does in some of the preceding chapters. When cultures cohabit as intimately as they do in Hong Kong, it seems that in these days of hyper-critical correctness, racism, real or imagined, will be sensed lurking in even the most innocent of utterances.

IV.

WHAT IS THIS THING CALLED AN EXPATRIATE?

Expats are a hangover from the colonial era. White, Western, and inculcated with a sense of entitlement, they should be extinct in this post-colonial age we live in, but they refuse to die out.
(Rebecca – white, Western, and a hangover from the colonial era)

When I set out on this admittedly haphazard exploration into the place of expatriates within the social fabric of life in Hong Kong, I used *The Expat Project* as a convenient working title. I never intended that it would be the title of the book, and it isn't. There are too many books in the marketplace entitled *Project This* or *Project That*. The book starts out as *The X Project,* or *Project Y* as a working title, but by the time the author gets to finish writing, they're stuck with it. Either they can't imagine it being called anything else, or they're too creatively spent to come up with an alternative. The fact is that titles are tough. Confronted with having to come up with a title, I trawled through the various metaphors my informants had used to capture what Hong Kong meant to them: the graveyard of relationships, the gweilo ghetto, the city of masks, the transit stop, and so on, but each was selective, and failed to capture the diversity of views and lived experiences of its inhabitants. *Other Voices, Other Eyes* seemed vague enough to encompass the diversity in what my informants saw and what they said about what they saw.

I knew that coming up with a title would cause me sleepless nights, which it did. However, a problem unanticipated at the beginning of the project, which loomed over it as it grew, was defining the subject of my enquiry. What *was* this thing called an expat?

I'd planned to begin the book with a preface that included a definition of the expatriate. However, as conversations with informants accumulated, the breezy little preface that was going to kick-start the book had to be put aside. Most of my informants had little trouble saying what an expatriate wasn't, but were coy about saying what it was. In fact, about the only thing they agreed on was that the dictionary definition – 'an expat is a person who is living in a country other than the one in which they were born' – was clearly inadequate. What did 'living in' mean? The term would include asylum seekers, refugees, immigrants and even domestic helpers, but my informants, foreigners and locals alike, generally agreed that these groups were not part of the expatriate community. As for Mainlanders – you must be kidding!

This chapter contains vignettes from informants who thought they had an answer to the question of what it is to be an expatriate. After presenting the vignettes, I will see what sense can be made of them.

*

Ron has lived in Hong Kong since 1965 – long enough for the rough edges of his New Zealand accent to be largely sanded off. We're having tea in the Senior Common Room at the University of Hong Kong. In another university, it would have been called the Faculty Club, but the University of Hong Kong has its idiosyncrasies, and the Senior Common Room is one of them. When the question is put to him, he worries at his beard, and says that technically speaking he isn't an expat. Technically? Where's the technicality in expatness? Is it because he has lived in the place for just on fifty years? He shakes his head. No, the fact that he's lived in Hong Kong since the days when water and electricity were rationed for several hours every day had nothing to do with his status. He's entitled to vote, and therefore 'technically speaking' (he repeats the phrase), he isn't an expat. This is a new one on me. I, too, am entitled to vote, and have been for years. One day, I received a letter out of the blue informing me of my right, which, when the spirit moves me, I exercise. However, it never occurred to me that with the entitlement came an exemption from the status of an expatriate. It also raised a question, and one I put to Ron: if we were no longer expats, what were we? We certainly weren't locals. Ron agreed that we couldn't claim local status – for one thing, our Cantonese just wasn't up to scratch – but he was at a loss as to the question of our identity. He could state with confidence what we weren't but not what we were. Typically, the question was settled in the negative.

*

Monique is one informant who has no doubt about the nature of expatriates and the expat life. The word *expatriate*, pronounced in the French way with an epiglottal end, sounds more enticing than the English word. She can recount stories of her childhood in Tangier so vividly that they might have happened last week. She knows about expatriate life all right. Both her parents were born in Algeria, she in Morocco, so she is a second-generation expatriate. As a child, the term hummed constantly in her ears. This was a time when the *tricolore* flew proudly (although not as globally as the Union Jack) in different parts of the world, and many thousands of French nationals went abroad, where they found the work that eluded them at home. But then the *tricolore* came down the flagpole, and they were told to pack up and go home. Home? Where was that?

She draws a distinction between people who were born abroad, and those who were sent by French companies and organizations to work in the colonies and bring glory and money to France. Uprooted from what they saw as their homeland, and transplanted to Normandy, she and her brother were bewildered by the utter foreignness of France. Also bewildering was the brand of French that was spoken, and the fact that she and her schoolmates were divided by a common language. "Why do they call us *pied noir?*" she cries to her mother. "Our feet are not black." She knows from the look on the faces of the other children that it is not a good thing to be a *pied noir*. She and the legions of decolonized humanity, repatriated to France from Morocco, Algeria, Tunisia, New Caledonia, the Black African countries and Southeast Asia, had lost their identity: or rather they had a new, unwelcome identity imposed upon them. *Pied noir*. But where was the sense in the derogatory label just because they were born and had lived outside of France, some for generations? She recalls her mother's indignation at being treated as a second-class citizen. "They should treat us like heroes," her mother said. "We made France great, while they stayed at home." She was determined that Monique would excel in all things, from books to ballet, and beat her when the child failed to meet her expectations.

She knew about expatriates, all right, but she never considered herself one, not in Morocco, and only for a short time in Hong Kong. An expatriate is someone who is sent abroad for a limited period and whose salaries and conditions are the responsibility of the company that has sent them. In Morocco, she may not have been a native, though she was native-born. She was French only because of the passport she carried. In her heart, she belonged to Morocco, the country of her birth. Its sights and sounds and smells were familiar to her. All her friends were there. She was a reluctant returnee, not wanting to be transplanted to France, but had no choice. Only employees working for very rich companies with substantial financial interests were able to stay, and the rest had to return to France, where they weren't wanted. The best job her father could secure was to drive a train.

Monique arrived in Hong Kong under her own steam. She came to have a fling with someone she met who worked there for a multinational company. It wasn't bad, as flings go, and as flings go, it went. For a time she taught at the French International School and it was only during this time that, by any stretch of the imagination, could she call herself an expat because her salary was paid by the French government. That didn't last long either. Things not lasting was a feature of her landscape. The only thing that endured was her tenure in Hong Kong where, for thirty years, she worked at not being an expatriate. Without a car, without a fancy apartment, she lived out her days in a tiny flat, and got by on the proceeds of a small bequest from a relative in France and by giving private lessons to the dwindling number of people who had any interest in learning French. In recent years, she has had to compete with a 'third wave' of French nationals who flowed into Hong Kong seeking refuge from a crumbling French economy, cultural stagnation and an incompetent political administration. This younger generation arrived with all manner of qualifications from schools, colleges and universities, pieces of paper that were worthless in a country without work. Like her, these young people aren't stereotypical expatriates. They live, as she does, on the edge, and like her, as far as she can tell, they don't seem to mind at all.

*

As far as Pat, a teacher from the UK, is concerned, the attempt to define the expatriate is an exercise in futility. Hong Kong expatriates can be placed on a continuum from the vagrant backpacker to the career businessperson and, in any case, stereotypes evaporate once one gets to know a particular individual: only ignorance could lump them all together. She would rather address the question of how local people see her, because identity is determined as much by how others define you as how you define yourself. She hopes she is perceived as someone who is respectful of their traditions, interested in their culture and, in terms of her work as a teacher, someone who is making a positive contribution to society. "Over the past century, millions of expats have flowed in and out of Hong Kong. I'd like to believe that I'm among those who made it a better place, if only one student at a time."

*

Alastair is a big man but well-proportioned, so you don't realize how imposing he is until he towers over you. Like many overgrown individuals, he hunches his shoulders and stoops a little to bring himself within earshot of mere mortals. His hair brushes his collar at the back, and flops onto his brow at the front, and a faint burr in his voice reminds you that he was once a Scot. Like many informants, he has led the expatriate life, growing up in Singapore, Malaysia and Egypt before completing school and university in the United Kingdom. He worked in France, Mongolia and China before taking up a university position in Hong Kong in the 1980s and has lived and worked here ever since.

"Will you stay in Hong Kong once you retire?"

An emphatic shake of the head. "No, once I finish working, I'll leave. That's me. *That's* an expat. "

"Why is that? Why do you have no interest in retiring here?"

"Well, essentially I'm here to work. When I'm done working, I'm out of here. I'm here to work and to live as a working person, but not to stop working, retire and somehow try to assimilate and generally become part of the social matrix as a non-contributing member of society. There are a lot of people who do stay on here. You know some of them. I know some of them. They can't afford to go back, and they can't afford to live the high life here. They live in a village house in Mui Wo, and they're going to be here forever.

"In essence, expats occupy an alien space: they've got a completely different language, a completely different culture, and in all probability they're ethnically very different. The notion of a South African or an American living in Britain and calling themselves an expat may be fair enough, but it lacks some of the resonances of the same person living in Hong Kong or Seoul."

*

For several years, the date was a vague prospect on the horizon, far enough off to be largely ignored, but unlike the horizon, it crept inexorably closer. Then it sped up, and Norman, sometimes accompanied by his wife Marjorie, had to endure the round of social events – drinks, dinners, and worse, that were the inevitable accompaniment to retirement. At these events, he turned up the corners of his lips which he hoped gave him a look of amused regret, but in reality made him look slightly inebriated: he had to make small talk with people he had never liked, and listen to genial speeches about someone he barely recognized. He loathed every minute of it and despised himself for going along with the charade. When he was offered the usual clichés about going on to life's next adventure and being a lucky chap, his lips curled into a sneer that was close to genuine. He was evasive about the future, because there was none.

"Are you going back, or staying on?" he would be asked, as though there were a choice. The reality was that Norman and Marjorie were not so much expatriates as economic and social exiles. They had been away from England for so long that on the occasional visits home to visit Marjorie's demented sister, they barely recognized it as the place from which they had departed all those years ago. When the sister died, the last connection to home was gone. Without making a deliberate decision to do so, they had stayed away too long. In Hong Kong this wasn't difficult to do: "Time passes quickly here," he was told on first arriving. He had laughed at the time, but he now knew what the old hands had meant. Over time, he and Marjorie lost contact or cut themselves off: former friends died or simply disappeared.

They had never lived extravagantly, but one unwise investment saw his pension shrink to the point of no return. So, they found themselves in a position where it was socially and economically impossible to return to their country of origin.

And it wasn't peculiar to Hong Kong. Many Britons had stayed on in India and elsewhere after decolonization, either by choice or because, like Norman and Marjorie, they had no choice. A novel he'd read years before came to mind, a touching Paul Scott story called *Staying On*. It was subsequently turned into a film with Celia Johnson and Trevor Howard playing the central characters. At the time he had rather patronizingly pitied the married couple who had stayed on in India because they couldn't afford to go back, but also felt sorry for the fate that had befallen them. And now here they were, he and Marjorie, in exactly the same boat.

*

Joe, whose insights are otherwise unremarkable, has an eccentric perspective on the issue of expatriates. Like others, he finds it easier to talk about what they're not, and launches into a monologue on what he calls 'reverse migration': descendants of British emigrants to former British colonies such as Australia and Canada who chose to move to Britain for a range of reasons: work, study, love, the cultural experience. A Brit himself, he tells the story of a great-uncle who emigrated to Canada in the 1930s. Many years later his granddaughter, Joe's cousin, moved to England to do graduate study, met and married an Englishman, and never returned to Canada. "She is definitely not an expat, she's a reverse immigrant," he says emphatically, as if proving something. "These days, many of you Australians are from non-Anglo backgrounds. Someone from a Greek or Vietnamese background would have to go back to Athens or Ho Chi Minh City for the question to have the same relevance."

Relevance? I let it pass and change the subject. However, the anecdote about his cousin returning to England on what appears to be a permanent basis reminds me of Josie, a young Anglo-Australian woman I met in London. A chartered accountant, she was in England for the professional experience afforded by the multinational company she worked for in Sydney. When I asked her whether she considered herself an expatriate, the answer was an emphatic yes. If, like Joe's cousin, she were to fall in love with a local, get married and settle down, she'd probably cease to see herself as an expatriate, but in her current circumstance she definitely was one. The crowd she hung out with consisted almost exclusively of expatriates with a particular profile: like her, they were young, single, high net-worth professionals whose relocation was definitely temporary, and they flocked to London in their thousands. When I met her she was about to return to Australia, even though her contract had another year to run. England had not lived up to her expectations. "The longer I live here, the less I understand them," she says. "This is a foreign country. The only thing we have in common is a language – and even then I'm not so sure."

*

On the disintegration of his marriage, Frank did what thousands of others in similar circumstances have done – he ran away. Rather than solving his problems at home, he shifted them to another continent. From Europe, he drifted through the Middle East and several Asian countries before finding himself in Hong Kong. And here, like many other global wanderers who come for love or intrigue or no apparent reason, he got stuck. Also like other displaced persons, he became an odd-job man, scratching a living out of part-time bartending and working as a handyman. It was a massive comedown for someone who had occupied a senior management position as an automotive engineer, but at least he wasn't reduced to teaching English in some backstreet cram school in Quarry Bay. As he pulls pints and pours pinot grigios for the bankers and professors and other moneyed regulars, the bile rises in his throat. He suffers indirectly because of them and the myth they perpetuate that all gweilos are wealthy Peak-dwellers. He's never even been to the Peak, let alone lived there. There's an automatic assumption that he's wealthy, not because he's Frank, but because he's a Westerner. Not even his current girlfriend, a grasping Indonesian domestic helper and, he suspects, part-time prostitute, believes him when he says that he can't afford to buy her the latest iPhone. Whatever happened to the other phones, and handbags and computers and tablets? She claims to have lost them, but how can you lose five iPhones and three notebook computers in less than a year? 'Lost' on the crowded streets of Causeway Bay for a few dollars, most likely. If he had money, does she really think he'd be living in a squalid room enduring the foul smells from the restaurant downstairs? "It's time to move on," he thinks to himself as he plunges glasses into cold water. But he knows he never will.

*

"Well, it's all about identity," says Rory. "And identity is as much about how others see you as how you see yourself. So you have to ask the locals. There is a certain amount of resentment among local Cantonese towards expats, however they're defined, because they're educated in English, have better English, and therefore get the better jobs. This animosity is longstanding, and it goes beyond the aversion towards the stereotypical Western male living on the Peak or in Tai Tam, belonging to exclusive clubs, drinking too much, being loud and aggressive, having a sense of entitlement, breaking the rules and thinking he can get away with it. No, it goes much deeper than that. Have you heard the expression 'the hundred years of shame'? No? I hadn't either, until fairly recently, but I'm hearing it increasingly now, particularly with this rumpus between Beijing and Hong Kong. The Mainland government and its cronies in Hong Kong have spread the view that the current agitation is fomented by 'foreign interests' – in other words, the United States – to encourage the development of Western-style democracy. They think that locals need to be reminded of the hundred years of shame between 1840 and 1949 when Hong Kong was invaded, exploited and made subservient to their colonial overlords. On Hong Kong Island, they were crowded into tenements along the harbour foreshore, while the expats sat in their luxury houses on the Peak. Locals were forbidden from venturing up the slopes beyond a certain point, and were severely punished if they did.

"Of course, Mainland China had its own hundred years of shame, being corrupted and humiliated by foreign governments and overseas trading interests. But remember that modern Hong Kong is very much a post-1949 creation. The majority of Hong Kong Chinese fled here after the revolution to escape communist oppression: so there are all sorts of tensions and contradictions. Beijing is telling locals, 'Get your perspective right, you're part of China now.' The leadership in Beijing is looking back beyond the Maoist, working-class, anti-education revolution, and they're now returning to their historical roots and are re-establishing pride in that history. So, there are various levels of resentment of the expat in both contexts: both Hong Kong and Beijing have their special reasons to resent the expat. And on top of that, there is a resentment on the part of at least half of the population of Hong Kong against Beijing. The attitude is very much, 'Don't tell us what to do.'

"Anyway, back to the tricky business of defining the expat. A number of factors come into play here – the context, the style of living, self- and mutual identity construction between expats and locals and so on. Context is paramount. I'd say that the 'ghetto' effect is important as well: how, where and why foreigners cluster together socially. Look beyond Hong Kong to Europe, for example. In parts of the Dordogne, you see expat communities, expat clusters. In places like Majorca, they won't see themselves as expats, and they won't really care what they're called. There are so many wealthy northern Europeans living in places like Majorca that for them it's just a cosmopolitan place. And then look at places like Monaco. Who's going to talk about being an expat in Monaco?

"Ultimately, for me, the idea of an expat has a number of necessary conditions. Firstly that the context has to be exotic. As an expat, one is from a first-world background moving into a third, or possibly second-world context. You need to be from a more affluent background living in a largely less affluent context – although the place will have a wealthy middle class. It could be a cosmopolitan place like Hong Kong, but the bulk of the population will not be enjoying the conditions that you're enjoying. There are, of course the exceptions, the expats who are down-at-heel, who have found themselves stuck here and can't live out the expat dream."

*

I return to some of my local informants for their insights. Lisa is a former colleague who spent two years abroad as a graduate student. She describes how, armed with her electric rice cooker ("The first thing you need to pack," she'd been advised), she arrived at the University of Birmingham and befriended a Taiwanese girl at the hall of residence. She never considered herself an expatriate. She was a student, and the vast majority of the people she interacted with were members of the academic community: teachers and other mainly overseas students. Expatriates were people who lived in a foreign culture and interacted professionally and socially with people from that culture.

Pressed for more specifics on what the archetypical expat would look like, she pursues the criterion of not just working in a place but also interacting socially within the local community. "You don't just interact within your work circles, but have a fuller social life within the host community." With this statement, she challenges the belief of other informants, locals as well as expats such as Rory, that creating and inhabiting enclaves or ghettos is a defining characteristic.

Lisa agrees with the conventional view that domestic helpers, construction workers, asylum seekers and so on are not expats. She quickly and emphatically rejects the notion that Mainlanders in Hong Kong, could ever be considered expatriates or locals. An executive from Shanghai working in the financial sector alongside managers from Seattle and Sydney would never be considered an expatriate. Why? Because he is a Mainlander. But then so is her father, who arrived in Hong Kong as a young man in the 1960s. She admits that he is a Mainlander, but, like most of his generation, he is also a local.

Faced with yet another contradiction, Lisa retreats to conventionality.

Expatriates are Westerners, and their incomes are generally higher than the locals. Their lifestyle is different: they frequent pubs and bars, where they gather together with other expatriates. While they do interact with locals professionally, and to some extent, personally, they have their own circles. There isn't a single expatriate type: there are those who genuinely like the local culture, make some attempt to learn the language and are here for the longer term, and those who have come mainly, if not exclusively for financial reasons. Some want to acculturate, some want to accumulate, and some want to do both.

"Generally speaking, expatriates are respected within the community. They're seen as educated and have a superior standard of living to the average Chinese. They're seen as a plus for the society in terms of bringing in skills and knowledge that might not exist here, and contributing to economic growth. In a sense, they're part of the local scene, but they're also separate. Locals may not be particularly interested in what they do, and they might not really know what they do, unless they work with expatriates. If not, they see them as an outside group and that seems to be the general perception of expats."

*

Although he admits that it probably reflects his own personal history, for Dave the word that sums up the expat is 'risk-taker'. Giving up a secure life in England and leaving his family behind, he came to Hong Kong to work in a small firm of financial advisors. Despite their differences, he and his colleagues have one thing in common; they have no-one to rely on but themselves. At the end of the month, no salary magically appears in their bank accounts. Their income depends on their ability to sell financial plans. If they fail, there is no safety net, but if they succeed, the rewards are considerable.

There's the stereotype, of course. It's always a male who comes to mind. He has money. He's confident, a bit arrogant, drinks too much, behaves badly when he wants to and gets away with it. If you asked a local, they'd probably describe the expat as a money-motivated, white Caucasian banker. There are plenty of those, but at heart, an expat is someone who is chasing a dream. It may be money or some other material thing, or it may be to lead a certain lifestyle.

He recalls the English couple he met the previous night. They were long-term expatriates who had raised a couple of children here. One of the boys had felt sufficiently comfortable to give up his British passport, and take out Hong Kong citizenship, which enabled him to qualify for the Hong Kong rugby team. He must have been born here to qualify for a local passport – but it was an interesting story, one expatriate generation on. The last thing Dave would want to give up was his British passport, but if you were born and raised here, and lived here most of your life, you were bound to see things differently.

He would never be seen as a local, and wouldn't want to be, but after about five years, despite the frequent visits home to see his wife and children, he began to regard himself as an insider, someone who knew the ropes. He joined a local football team, and over the objections of his wife, instead of coming back from the UK on a Saturday night for work on Monday, would arrive a few days early to get over jet lag and to play his Sunday soccer. He enjoyed that phase of his life, a phase in which he felt that he really belonged because he was meeting people other than those connected with his work. And they had a common cause – the Sunday soccer game.

So, from seeing himself as an outsider, he gradually began to see himself as an insider. This was not the same thing as a local, of course, but it made you feel good – smug almost – when a new arrival, 'fresh off the boat', was impressed by the fact that you'd been here six or seven years. You knew about the system and how it worked. How do I go about getting an ID card? What do I do about paying tax? What are the best schools to get my kids into? All that knowledge you'd accumulated – you could pass it on.

*

"Expatness is defined by a whole host of factors, isn't it?" asks Andrea, rhetorically. "An obvious one is the kind of community you find yourself moving in at work and socially. Another is where you live. I live on Hong Kong Island, and sometimes when I go to deepest, darkest Kowloon and the New Territories, I think, 'Well, I really know very little about these places even though I've been here for a long time.' I've made a genuine effort to understand the society and to participate in it. And if you look at my bookshelves, you'll see there are many, many books on Hong Kong history, Hong Kong culture, archaeology, all sorts of aspects of the society, which I find fascinating. I suppose for those of us who've been living and working for a long time in different countries, we acquire 'multiple expat identity disorder' which adds so many other dimensions to the concept. It's not just like Brits buying a holiday home in Spain and deciding to settle there. As an expat, I've had so many different experiences throughout my life. The main difference for me between my other expat experiences and my experience in Hong Kong is the length of time I've been in this place."

*

At the beginning of the chapter, I said that I would let my informants speak for themselves, and then see what sense could be made of what they had to say. Having completed the first part of the assignment, I'm now confronted by the second. The first thing that comes to mind is the movie title *It's Complicated*. Making sense always is. Sense, like meaning, doesn't lie around waiting to be discovered, it has to be made.

If the stereotypical expatriate exists, he (portraits of the stereotypical expatriate are invariably male) keeps a very low profile. It may be that I move in the wrong circles, but the plain truth is that I failed to find him. There was nothing scientific in the selection of the expatriates who have spoken here. However, they do allow observations, if not generalizations. Wherever they come from, for whatever reason, and regardless of what we call them, the individuals who choose to make Hong Kong their home add richness and diversity to the social fabric. Without them, Hong Kong would be poorer, not just materially, but culturally as well.

*

In concluding this chapter, I will make some observations on a number of themes that emerge from the vignettes. These include wealth, time in the host country, cultural contact between expatriates and locals, the influence of Hong Kong's colonial heritage, and issues of identity.

While wealth is part of the stereotype, it does not define the expatriate. Few of my informants were excessively wealthy, although, of course, 'excess wealth' is a relative matter. Once upon a time, Tokyo, London or New York sprang to mind when the question of the most expensive city on earth was mooted. These days, it's a toss-up between Hong Kong and Singapore, although London is never too far behind. So it's almost impossible to survive in Hong Kong on what would be considered a reasonable salary in provincial western cities such as Atlanta, Adelaide or Auckland. To survive in Hong Kong would require considerably more than the average income in these cities, and to live well would require wealth which their citizens would probably consider excessive. Expatriates such as Monique and Frank (and they are not alone) do it though. Monique survives with equanimity and acceptance, Frank struggles along with a chip on his shoulder. What do they have in common with the bankers on the Peak? Very little, apart from the burden of their expatriate label.

Time is another confounding criterion. For some informants, the expatriate is a creature whose occupation of foreign soil is strictly temporary: they enter, forage and, having no intention of establishing a permanent home, retreat. On the other hand, for some, longevity in one's adopted home is an important criterion. For yet others, time is irrelevant. One informant, born in Hong Kong of British parents, has spent his whole life here apart from a few years in England at school and university. He would never consider himself as anything other than an expatriate, speaks a couple of languages but not Cantonese, and has a wide circle of friends. Several of his circle are, like him, offspring of the colonial class, some are local, and some, such as a Hong Kong-born Pakistani friend, occupy an identity twilight zone – neither expatriate nor local. When Lisa suggests that I might consider myself a local on the basis of my long-term residence, I reject the notion: my command of the language is rudimentary, I don't look local, and would never be seen as one by locals. Although I have numerous Chinese friends, I can hardly say that I'm integrated into the local community.

While length of residence is not a defining characteristic, all of these informants, with the exception of Frank, have been in Hong Kong for more than twenty years. Most have lived here considerably longer than that. Ron has been here for more than fifty years, while Norman and Marjorie have resided here for almost forty.

Those locals who have professional and social contact with expatriates acknowledge and appreciate the contribution they make to society. The vast majority of locals have no contact with expatriates apart from the occasional sighting on a bus or the MTR. However, due to the colonial heritage of Hong Kong, expatriates are part of the bloodstream of the place. You don't get stared at in the street as you might on the Mainland, although, even here, things are changing. As Ron says, fifty years ago when he made forays to Guangzhou he was followed down the street. These days you can pass virtually unnoticed in increasingly cosmopolitan Mainland cities.

There is little consensus about whether contact with locals is a defining characteristic of the expat. For Lisa, the one local whose views I have included in this chapter, professional and personal contact with locals sets expatriates apart from other foreigners. For a number of informants, however, the 'ghetto' mentality is a defining characteristic. The metaphor of ghettoization emerged in several interviews, not just in the vignettes that make up this chapter. One doesn't have to reside physically in one of the numerous 'gweilo ghettos' dotted around Hong Kong Island. The ghetto mentality is created and maintained by those who build their social life around other like-minded individuals, joining the same clubs and associations and attending the same events. According to one informant, this clustering together with its implications of inclusion/exclusion, can lead to resentment on the part of locals.

Many expatriates such as Pat make a deliberate effort to establish and maintain contact with locals, have a stab at learning their language and appreciate their culture. Informants who want to integrate with locals appear in a number of chapters throughout the book, and, although they are not in the majority, they have to be seen as part of the fabric of expatriate life. Some of them even go so far as to minimize, if not eschew, contact with fellow expatriates.

A 'new wave' of arrivals in Hong Kong is also reshaping the profile of the expatriate. These young people in their 20s and 30s do not have highly-paid positions to come to. They arrive often with no job at all.

Some are impelled to escape the claustrophobia and lack of opportunity in Europe. Others are driven by the same motives that prompted their parents to become a part of the 1970s backpacker generation: adventure, love or simply wanderlust – a desire to see the world, warts and all. According to one informant, "The younger generation of expats has a sense of excitement. They travel not so much for making money but out of a desire for adventure." Hong Kong is attractive because of its unusual combination of intrigue and security. As one young informant put it, it's a place where you can go out at night and not end up in a punch-up.

The cultural interpenetration of the younger generation is also partly due to the fact that their Chinese counterparts are becoming more Westernized. You see them intermingling on the street, in bars and cafes, at sporting events, at tango clubs in ways that would have been unimaginable to their parents' generation. Not surprisingly, relationships form, marriages ensue, and children appear. It has always been this way, although the frequency with which interracial marriages are occurring is increasingly evident.

The ghetto mentality can be seen, at least in part, as a hangover from the colonial era when, for much of Hong Kong's history, there was a strict social divide between the rulers and the ruled. Although, at the time of writing, it is just on twenty years since the British handed over the colony to China, the legacy of their lengthy tenure is still strongly felt, and there is still a sense of ownership and entitlement on the part of many long-term British expatriates. I would not go as far as some have done to argue that colonialism and expatriatism go hand in hand, or that a colonial past is a necessary condition for the evolution of an expatriate subculture, although I can see what prompted Rebecca to argue that the expat is a hangover from the colonial era. I have no idea whether French expatriates in North Africa or Vietnam have the same attitude to these former colonies as do the British in Hong Kong. I do know, however, that my experience of living in Hong Kong has been a very different one from my life as an expatriate in other countries.

Ultimately, expatness is all about identity, yet another hydra-headed concept entangling self-perception with the perceptions of others. "It doesn't matter if I don't consider myself an expat. If I'm constructed by the local community as an expat, then I'm a bloody expat," said Don. Another informant made a similar point. "The locals don't embrace you, or invite you to be part of their community – and there's no reason why they should. You're never going to get invited into their home, and that's one way of making you aware that if you want to build up a social circle that includes locals, it's going to be pretty superficial. It won't include their family. You're very rarely going to be admitted to that level of familiarity. There might be one or two people who will do that, but by and large they won't. I can count on one hand the number of times I've been invited to the home of a local here, and that's in over thirty years." Along with this other-construction comes a raft of assumptions. Frank, the battler, is assumed to be wealthy because he is an expatriate, even though financially he struggles to keep his head above water. Their Chinese acquaintances were surprised when, on retiring, Norman and Marjorie retreated to a village house in Mui Wo rather than a villa in Spain.

The original intention behind this book was to provide a portrait of expatriate life in Hong Kong by documenting the stories and experiences of expatriates. A logical first step was to stalk and capture my quarry. However, I quickly realized that this creature called an expat was very slippery. Each informant had a different idea of what constitutes an expatriate, and each had different criteria for determining the status of someone living abroad.

A precise definition of the expatriate has eluded me as I suspected it might when I embarked on this chapter, but I'm glad that I gave it a shot. In retrospect, I realize that I set out with the wrong tool – a microscope – when I should have used a multi-faceted prism. Expatness, it seems, can be whatever you want it to be.

A LAST WORD: GLOBAL FLOW

Either that wallpaper goes, or I go. (Oscar Wilde's dying words)

The last word, or last few words, capture something that should have dawned on me years before I embarked on a thing I called The Expat Project. As I said at the beginning of the previous chapter, the expatriate is as difficult to define as many other commonly used constructs. In these days, in terms of numbers, the global flow of people is greater than at any other time in history: greater than the post-World War II diasporas, we are told. The transnational flow of people who leave their birthplace, either by choice or from force of circumstance, will be one of the defining characteristics of this generation.

People leave their place of birth for many reasons. In these pages I have introduced people who were not born here but who ended up in Hong Kong for a wide range of reasons, some of which overlapped. They came because:

- they were relocated by their company for a short to medium term;
- they were on a stopover to somewhere else, fell in love and never got any further;
- they landed here escaping persecution and almost certain death in their place of birth;
- people would pay them to do jobs they weren't prepared to do for themselves: cook for them, look after their children, wash and iron their clothing, and clean their toilets;

- they were on the run and found in Hong Kong a tolerant if uncaring place where they would be left alone;
- they could reinvent themselves and even prosper, indifferent to being labelled FILTH (Failed in London, Try Hong Kong).

The great majority of peoples who are part of this human swirl engulfing our world are experiencing the pain of separation, which is often glossed over, if not ignored entirely, in economic tomes on the 'global flow of labour'. However, if one sits down and talks to people who are living in a place other than that of their birth, it will come up in some shape or form. It lurks in the story of the young Filipina domestic helper whose second son was badly injured in a rural province and died before she could get back to him; in the story of the British businessman whose mother developed Alzheimer's disease and has no one to care for her in rural East Anglia; the Canadian teenager who misses her cousins in Toronto; the asylum seeker whose younger brother is facing beheading back home; the Irish academic who was incarcerated for rape after being falsely accused.

Every family with one or more members who are part of this transmigration will experience, to a greater or lesser degree, the pain of separation. Call them expatriates, refugees, migrants or even world travellers, whether they have gone for the short term or forever, someone elsewhere in the world will feel their loss.

The global flow has created competing tensions. On the one hand, those seeking refuge from persecution and turmoil at home have been blamed by the xenophobic and those fearful of change for causing conflict and chaos, when in fact what they want is the reverse. On the other hand, those who freely choose, for whatever reason, to live in a country other than their place of birth, are creating an invisible chain that I would like to think has the potential to reduce global conflict. In an earlier chapter, I quoted Pablo Casals who argued that, while the love of one's country is a splendid thing, love should not stop at the border. Pulling up the drawbridge, or building a wall around territory over which one's claims are dubious to say the least, will neither stem the global flow nor quell conflict and chaos.

WOULD YOU LIKE TO KNOW MORE?

My home office has a shelf groaning with books on Hong Kong. Here are some of my favourites.

Booth, M. (2004) *Gweilo*. London: Bantam Books.
An engaging memoir of an English boy's childhood in colonial Hong Kong.

Chabot, N. & M. Perini (2014) *Street Life Hong Kong: Outdoor workers in their own words*. Hong Kong: Blacksmith Books.
This is a unique portrait, in photographs and words, of Hong Kong as seen by its outdoor workers.

Ho, P. & Tsang, A. (2012) *Sex and Desire in Hong Kong*. Hong Kong: Hong Kong University Press.
Despite the lurid title, this is a scholarly and yet candid examination of sex and desire in Hong Kong.

Mann, P. (2016) *Sheriff of Wan Chai: How an Englishman helped govern Hong Kong in its last decade as a British colony*.
An entertaining portrait of Hong Kong in the years leading up to the handover by one of its 'top cops'.

Ng, J. (2010) *Hong Kong State of Mind*. Hong Kong: Blacksmith Books.
37 vignettes of 'a city that doesn't blink'.

Ng, J. (2014) *No City for Slow Men: Hong Kong's quirks and quandaries laid bare*. Hong Kong: Blacksmith Books.
The second of Jason Ng's engaging portraits of life in contemporary Hong Kong.

Yang, Y. (2010) *Whispers and Moans*. Hong Kong: Blacksmith Books.
This book is based on extensive interviews with people in the 'bewildering range' of sex businesses in Hong Kong.

About the Author

David Nunan has been an expatriate for much of his professional life. For the last 25 years he has lived and worked in Hong Kong, where he is Professor Emeritus of Applied Linguistics at the University of Hong Kong. He has published over 30 books on linguistics, culture and education as well as many textbooks on English language teaching. His textbook series *Go For It* is a number one best-seller, with sales exceeding 4 billion copies. His non-academic books include a memoir and a travel book based on his experiences as an author and speaker in Latin America.

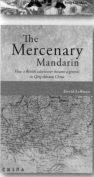

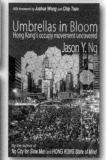

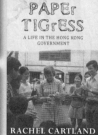